DOMESDAY BOOK

Warwickshire

History from the Sources

DOMESDAY BOOK

A Survey of the Counties of England

LIBER DE WINTONIA

Compiled by direction of

KING WILLIAM I

Winchester
1086

DOMESDAY BOOK

text and translation edited by

JOHN MORRIS

23

Warwickshire

edited from a draft translation prepared by

Judy Plaister

PHILLIMORE
Chichester
1976

1976

Published by

PHILLIMORE & CO. LTD.,
London and Chichester

Head Office: Shopwyke Hall,
Chichester, Sussex, England

© John Morris, 1976

ISBN 0 85033 141 2 (case)
ISBN 0 85033 142 0 (limp)

Printed in Great Britain by
Titus Wilson & Son Ltd.,
Kendal

WARWICKSHIRE

Introduction

The Domesday Survey of Warwickshire

Notes

Index of Persons

Index of Places

Map

Systems of Reference

Technical Terms

History from the Sources
General Editor: John Morris

The series aims to publish history
written directly from the sources
for all interested readers, both
specialists and others. The first
priority is to publish important
texts which should be widely
available, but are not.

DOMESDAY BOOK

The contents, with the folio on which each county begins, are:

Domesday Book is termed *Liber de Wintonia* (The Book of Winchester) in column 332c

INTRODUCTION

The Domesday Survey

In 1066 Duke William of Normandy conquered England. He was crowned King, and most of the lands of the English nobility were soon granted to his followers. Domesday Book was compiled 20 years later. The Saxon Chronicle records that in 1085

> at Gloucester at midwinter ... the King had deep speech with his counsellors ... and sent men all over England to each shire ... to find out ... what or how much each landholder held ... in land and livestock, and what it was worth ... The returns were brought to him.[1]

William was thorough. One of his Counsellors reports that he also sent a second set of Commissioners 'to shires they did not know, where they were themselves unknown, to check their predecessors' survey, and report culprits to the King.'[2]

The information was collected at Winchester, corrected, abridged, chiefly by omission of livestock and the 1066 population, and fair-copied by one writer into a single volume. Norfolk, Suffolk and Essex were copied, by several writers, into a second volume, unabridged, which states that 'the Survey was made in 1086'. The surveys of Durham and Northumberland, and of several towns, including London, were not transcribed, and most of Cumberland and Westmorland, not yet in England, was not surveyed. The whole undertaking was completed at speed, in less than 12 months, though the fair-copying of the main volume may have taken a little longer. Both volumes are now preserved at the Public Record Office. Some versions of regional returns also survive. One of them, from Ely Abbey,[3] copies out the Commissioners' brief. They were to ask

> The name of the place. Who held it, before 1066, and now?
> How many *hides*?[4] How many ploughs, both those in lordship and the men's?
> How many villagers, cottagers and slaves, how many free men and Freemen?[5]
> How much woodland, meadow and pasture? How many mills and fishponds?
> How much has been added or taken away? What the total value was and is?
> How much each free man or Freeman had or has? All threefold, before 1066,
> when King William gave it, and now; and if more can be had than at present?

The Ely volume also describes the procedure. The Commissioners took evidence on oath 'from the Sheriff; from all the barons and their Frenchmen; and from the whole Hundred, the priests, the reeves and six villagers from each village'. It also names four Frenchmen and four Englishmen from each Hundred, who were sworn to verify the detail.

The King wanted to know what he had, and who held it. The Commissioners therefore listed lands in dispute, for Domesday Book was not only a tax-assessment. To the King's grandson, Bishop Henry of Winchester, its purpose was that every 'man should know his right and not usurp another's'; and because it was the final authoritative register of rightful possession 'the natives called it Domesday Book, by analogy

---

[1] Before he left England for the last time, late in 1086. [2] Robert Losinga, Bishop of Hereford 1079-1095 (see *E.H.R.* 22, 1907, 74). [3] *Inquisitio Eliensis*, first paragraph. [4] A land unit, reckoned as 120 acres. [5] *Quot Sochemani.*

from the Day of Judgement'; that was why it was carefully arranged by Counties, and by landholders within Counties, 'numbered consecutively ... for easy reference'.[6]

Domesday Book describes Old English society under new management, in minute statistical detail. Foreign lords had taken over, but little else had yet changed. The chief landholders and those who held from them are named, and the rest of the population was counted. Most of them lived in villages, whose houses might be clustered together, or dispersed among their fields. Villages were grouped in administrative districts called Hundreds, which formed regions within Shires, or Counties, which survive today with minor boundary changes; the recent deformation of some ancient county identities is here disregarded, as are various short-lived modern changes. The local assemblies, though overshadowed by lords great and small, gave men a voice, which the Commissioners heeded. Very many holdings were described by the Norman term *manerium* (manor), greatly varied in size and structure, from tiny farmsteads to vast holdings; and many lords exercised their own jurisdiction and other rights, termed *soca*, whose meaning still eludes exact definition.

The Survey was unmatched in Europe for many centuries, the product of a sophisticated and experienced English administration, fully exploited by the Conqueror's commanding energy. But its unique assemblage of facts and figures has been hard to study, because the text has not been easily available, and abounds in technicalities. Investigation has therefore been chiefly confined to specialists; many questions cannot be tackled adequately without a cheap text and uniform translation available to a wider range of students, including local historians.

Previous Editions

The text has been printed once, in 1783, in an edition by Abraham Farley, probably of 1250 copies, at Government expense, said to have been £38,000; its preparation took 16 years. It was set in a specially designed type, here reproduced photographically, which was destroyed by fire in 1808. In 1811 and 1816 the Records Commissioners added an introduction, indices, and associated texts, edited by Sir Henry Ellis; and in 1861-1863 the Ordnance Survey issued zincograph facsimiles of the whole. Texts of individual counties have appeared since 1673, separate translations in the Victoria County Histories and elsewhere.

This Edition

Farley's text is used, because of its excellence, and because any worthy alternative would prove astronomically expensive. His text has been checked against the facsimile, and discrepancies observed have been verified against the manuscript, by the kindness of Miss Daphne Gifford of the Public Record Office. Farley's few errors are indicated in the notes.

[6] *Dialogus de Scaccario* 1,16.

The editor is responsible for the translation and lay-out. It aims at what the compiler would have written if his language had been modern English; though no translation can be exact, for even a simple word like 'free' nowadays means freedom from different restrictions. Bishop Henry emphasized that his grandfather preferred 'ordinary words'; the nearest ordinary modern English is therefore chosen whenever possible. Words that are now obsolete, or have changed their meaning, are avoided, but measurements have to be transliterated, since their extent is often unknown or arguable, and varied regionally. The terse inventory form of the original has been retained, as have the ambiguities of the Latin.

Modern English commands two main devices unknown to 11th century Latin, standardised punctuation and paragraphs; in the Latin, *ibi* ('there are') often does duty for a modern full stop, *et* ('and') for a comma or semi-colon. The entries normally answer the Commissioners' questions, arranged in five main groups, (i) the place and its holder, its hides, ploughs and lordship; (ii) people; (iii) resources; (iv) value; and (v) additional notes. The groups are usually given as separate paragraphs.

King William numbered chapters 'for easy reference', and sections within chapters are commonly marked, usually by initial capitals, often edged in red. They are here numbered. Maps, indices and an explanation of technical terms are also given. Later, it is hoped to publish analytical and explanatory volumes, and associated texts.

The editor is deeply indebted to the advice of many scholars, too numerous to name, and especially to the Public Record Office, and to the publisher's patience. The draft translations are the work of a team; they have been co-ordinated and corrected by the editor, and each has been checked by several people. It is therefore hoped that mistakes may be fewer than in versions published by single fallible individuals. But it would be Utopian to hope that the translation is altogether free from error; the editor would like to be informed of mistakes observed.

The map is the work of Tony King.

The preparation of this volume has been greatly assisted by a generous grant from the Leverhulme Trust Fund.

Conventions

*	refers to a note to the Latin text.		
[ ]	enclose words omitted in the MS.	( )	enclose editorial explanations.

IN BVRGO De *WARWIC* habet rex in dñio ſuo

.c.xiii. domus.7 barones regis hñt. cxii . de quibʒ

omibʒ rex habet geldũ ſuum.

Eps de Wireceſtre hĩ . ix . maſuras . Eps de Ceſtre . vii.

Abb de Couentreu . xxxvi. 7 iiii . ſunt uaſtæ ꝓpt ſitũ caſtelli.

Eps conſtantienſis . i . domũ hĩ . Comes de Mellend . xii . maſur.

Albicus habuit . iiii . quæ ptiñ ad trã quã tenuit.

Hugo de grentemaiſnil . iiii. 7 monachi hñt . i . de eo.

Heinricus de fereres . hĩ . ii . Harold . ii . Robtus . vi.

Rogeri . ii . Ricard uenator . i . Radulf de Limeſi . ix.

Abb malmeſberie . i . Wills bonuaſlet . i . Wills . fili

corbucion . ii . Goisfrid de Magneuille . i . Goisfrid de Wirce . i.

Gislebt de gant . ii . Gislebt budi . i . Nicolaus baliſtar . i.

Stefan ſtirman . i . Turchil . iiii . Harold . ii . Osbn . f . Ricard . i.

Criſtina . i . Luith Monialis . ii.

Hæ maſuræ ptiñ ad tras q̃s ipſi barones teñ extra burgũ.

7 ibi apꝑciatæ ſunt.

Præt has ſuꝑdictas maſuras . ſunt in ipſo burgo . xix.

burgſes . qui hñt . xix . maſuras cũ ſaca 7 ſoca . 7 omnibʒ

conſuetudinibʒ . 7 ita habeb T.R.E.

Tēpore Regis . E . uicecomitat de Waruuic cũ burgo

7 cũ regalibʒ Manerijs . reddeb . lxv . lib . 7 xxx . vi.

ſextaria mellis . aut . xxiiii . lib 7 viii . ſolid . ꝑ omibʒ quæ

ad mel ptinebant.

Modo inter firmã regaliũ Manerioʒ 7 placita comitat

reddit ꝑ annũ . cxlv . lib ad pondus. 7 xxiii . lib pro

conſuetudine canũ . 7 xx . ſolid ꝑ ſũmario. 7 x . lib ꝑ accipitre.

7 c . ſolid reginæ ꝓ gersũma.

Pter h̃ reddĩ xxiiii . ſextar mell cũ majori menſura.

7 de Burgo . vi . ſextar mell . Sextar ſcilicet ꝓ . xv . denar.

De his hĩ comes de mellend . vi . ſext . 7 v . ſolid.

WARWICKSHIRE

B In the Borough of WARWICK

1 the King has 113 houses in his lordship, and the King's barons
have 112, from all of which the King has his tax.

2 The Bishop of Worcester has 9 dwellings; the Bishop of Chester 7; the
Abbot of Coventry 36; and 4 are waste, because of the castle site.
The Bishop of Coutances has 1 house; the Count of Meulan 12 dwellings.
Earl Aubrey had 4, which belong to the land which he held; Hugh of
Grandmesnil 4, and the monks of Pillerton have 1 from him. Henry of
Ferrers has 2, Harold 2, Robert of Stafford 6, Roger of Ivry 2, Richard
Hunter 1, Ralph of Limesy 9, the Abbot of Malmesbury 1, William
Bonvallet 1, William son of Corbucion 2, Geoffrey de Mandeville 1,
Geoffrey of La Guerche 1, Gilbert of Ghent 2, Gilbert [of] Bouille 1,
Nicholas the Gunner 1, Stephen the Steersman 1, Thorkell 4, Harold 2,
Osbern son of Richard 1, Christina 1, the nun Leofeva 2.
    These dwellings belong to the lands which these barons hold outside
the Borough and are there assessed.

3 Besides the said dwellings, there are 19 burgesses in this Borough who
have 19 dwellings, with full jurisdiction and all customary dues, and
had them thus before 1066.

4 Before 1066 the Sheriffdom of Warwick, with the Borough and with the
royal manors, paid £65 and 36 sesters of honey, or £24 8s for all that
belonged to the honey. Now the revenue of the royal manors and
the pleas of the County between them pay £145 a year by
weight, £23 for dog-custom, 20s for a packhorse, £10 for a hawk
and 100s for gifts to the Queen.

5 Besides this, it pays 24 sesters of honey, with the larger measure,
and from the Borough 6 sesters of honey, that is, a sester at 15 pence.
Of these, the Count of Meulan has 6 sesters and 5s.

Confuetudo Waruuic fuit . ut eunte rege p̄ terrā in expē
ditionē:́ decē burgenfes de Waruuic ꝓ om̄ib꜀ alijs irent.
Qui monitus non ibat:́ c . folid regi em̄dabat.
Si ū p̄ mare c̄tra hoftes fuos ibat rex:́ uel . iiii . batfueins
uel . iiii . lib̄ denario꜀ ei mittebant.

Hic Annotant Tenentes terras In Warwicscire.

<table>
<tr><td>.I. Rex Willelmus.</td><td>.XX. Rogerius de Juri.</td></tr>
<tr><td>.II. Ēp̄s de Ceftre.</td><td>.XXI. Robertus de Oilgi.</td></tr>
<tr><td>.III. Ēp̄s de Wireceftre.</td><td>.XXII. Robertus de Statford.</td></tr>
<tr><td>.IIII Ēp̄s Baiocenfis.</td><td>.XXIII. Robertus difpenfator.</td></tr>
<tr><td>.V. Ēp̄s Cōnftantienfis.</td><td>.XXIIII Robertus de Veci.</td></tr>
<tr><td>.VI. Abbatia de Couentreu.</td><td>.XXV. Radulfus de Mortemer.</td></tr>
<tr><td>.VII. Abbatia de Abendon.</td><td>.XXVI Radulfus de Limefi.</td></tr>
<tr><td>.VIII Abbatia de Bertone.</td><td>.XXVII Willelm⁹ fili⁹ Anfculfi.</td></tr>
<tr><td>.IX. Abbatia de Malmesbie.</td><td>.XXVII Wills filius Corbucion.</td></tr>
<tr><td>.X. Abbatia de Wincelcūbe.</td><td>.XXIX Wills buenuafleth.</td></tr>
<tr><td>.XI. Abbatia de Euefham.</td><td>.XXX. Goisfrid de Māneuile.</td></tr>
<tr><td>.XII Comes Rogerius.</td><td>.XXXI. Goisfridus de Wirce.</td></tr>
<tr><td>.XIII Comes Hugo.</td><td>.XXXII Giflebertus de Gand.</td></tr>
<tr><td>.XII Comes Albericus.</td><td>.XXXIII Giflebtus filius Turold.</td></tr>
<tr><td>.XV. Comitiffa Godeua.</td><td>.XXXIIII Gerinus.</td></tr>
<tr><td>.XVI Comes de Mellent.</td><td>.XXXV. Vrfo de Abetot.</td></tr>
<tr><td>.XVII Turchil de Waruuic.</td><td>.XXXVI. Stefanus.</td></tr>
<tr><td>.XVII Hugo de Grentemaifnil.</td><td>.XXXVII Ofbern⁹ filius Ricardi.</td></tr>
<tr><td>.XIX. Henricus de Ferieres.</td><td>.XXXVIII Herald⁹ filius Radulfi.</td></tr>
<tr><td></td><td>.XXXIX Hafcoit mufard.</td></tr>
<tr><td></td><td>.XL. Nicolaus balistarius.</td></tr>
<tr><td></td><td>.XLI. Nigellus de Albengi.</td></tr>
</table>

.XLII. Criftina. .XLIII. Leueua 7 Eddid. .XLIIII. Ricard⁹ 7 alij taini 7 feruient regis.

.XLV. Adeliz uxor Hugonis.

6 The custom of Warwick was that when the King went on an expedition by land 10 burgesses of Warwick went for all the others; whoever was notified but did not go paid a fine of 100s to the King. But if the King went against his enemies by sea, they sent him either 4 boatmen or £4 of pence.

LIST OF LANDHOLDERS IN WARWICKSHIRE

1 King William
2 The Bishop of Chester
3 The Bishop of Worcester
4 The Bishop of Bayeux
5 The Bishop of Coutances
6 Coventry Abbey
7 Abingdon Abbey
8 Burton Abbey
9 Malmesbury Abbey
10 Winchcombe Abbey
11 Evesham Abbey
12 Earl Roger
13 Earl Hugh
14 Earl Aubrey
15 Countess Godiva
16 The Count of Meulan
17 Thorkell of Warwick
18 Hugh of Grandmesnil
19 Henry of Ferrers
20 Roger of Ivry
21 Robert d'Oilly
22 Robert of Stafford
23 Robert the Bursar

24 Robert of Vessy
25 Ralph of Mortimer
26 Ralph of Limesy
27 William son of Ansculf
28 William son of Corbucion
29 William Bonvallet
30 Geoffrey de Mandeville
31 Geoffrey of La Guerche
32 Gilbert of Ghent
33 Gilbert son of Thorold
34 Gerin
35 Urso of Abetot
36 Stephen
37 Osbern son of Richard
38 Harold son of Earl Ralph
39 Hascoit Musard
40 Nicholas the Gunner
41 Nigel of Aubigny
42 Christina
43 Leofeva and Edith
44 Richard and others of the King's Thanes and Servants
45 Adelaide wife of Hugh [of Grandmesnil]

TERRA REGIS. *IN FEXHOLE HVND.*

Rex ten̄ *BRAILES*. Eduin tenuit. Ibi ſunt. XL.VI. hidæ.

Tra.ē. LX. car̄. In dn̄io ſunt. VI. 7 XII. ſerui. 7 III. ancillæ.

7 c. uiłłi 7 XXX. borđ. cū. XLVI. car̄. Ibi moliñ de. X. ſoł.

7 c. ac̄ p̄ti. Silua. III. leuu lḡ. 7 II. leuu lat.

T.R.E. reddeb̄. XVII. lib̄ 7 X. ſoł. Modo ualet. LV. lib̄

7 XX. ſūmas ſalis.

Rex ten̄ *QVINTONE* 7 *WALEBORNE*. Rex. E. tenuit.

Ibi ſunt. III. hidæ. Tra.ē   In dn̄io ſunt. VI. car̄.

7 III. ſerui 7 II. ancillæ. 7 c. uiłłi VII. min. 7 XVIII. borđ

cū. XXXII. car̄.

Ibi. CXXX. ac̄ p̄ti. Silua dimiđ leuu 7 II. q̃z̃ lḡ. 7 IIII. q̃rent

lat. Hoc. ē int M̄ 7 Bereuuicħ.

Rex ten̄ *BEDEFORD*. Rex. E. tenuit. Ibi ſunt. V. hidæ.

Tra.ē   In dn̄io ſunt. V. car̄. 7 VIII. ſerui 7 V. ancillæ.

7 XXVIII. uiłłi 7 XIII. borđ cū. XVI. car̄.

Ibi. IIII. molini de. XL.III. ſoliđ 7 IIII. den. 7 CL. ac̄ p̄ti.

Silua. IIII. leuu lḡ. 7 una leuu lat.

Rex ten̄ *STANLEI*. Rex. E. tenuit. Ibi ſunt. VI. hidæ.

Tra.ē   In dn̄io ſunt. V. car̄. 7 I. ſeru 7 I. ancilla.

7 LXVIII. uiłłi 7 IIII. borđ cū. II. p̄bris hn̄t. XXX. car̄.

Ibi. II. molini de. XXX.V. ſoliđ. 7 IIII. den. 7 XX. ac̄ p̄ti.

Silua. IIII. leuu lḡ. 7 II. leuu lat. Paſt ad. II. mił porc.

Rex ten̄ *COLESHELLE*. Rex. E. tenuit.

Ibi ſunt. III. hidæ. Tra.ē

Ibi XXX. uiłłi cū p̄bro 7 XIII. borđ hn̄t. XVI. car̄.

Ibi moliñ de XL. denar. 7 in Tameuuorde. X. burḡſes huic M̄

p̄tin. Silua. III. leuu lḡ. 7 II. leuu 7 dimiđ lat.

1 HIDE = 120 ACRES

LAND OF THE KING

238 b

The King holds
  in FEXHOLE Hundred
1 BRAILES. Earl Edwin held it. 46 hides. Land for 60 ploughs. In
   lordship 6; 12 male and 3 female slaves;
       100 villagers and 30 smallholders with 46 ploughs.
       A mill at 10s; meadow, 100 acres; woodland 3 leagues long and
         2 leagues wide.
   Before 1066 it paid £17 10s; value now £55 and 20 packloads of salt.

2 KINETON and WELLESBOURNE. King Edward held them. 3 hides. Land for....
   In lordship 6 ploughs; 3 male and 2 female slaves;
       100 villagers less 7 and 18 smallholders with 32 ploughs.
       Meadow, 130 acres; woodland ½ league and 2 furlongs long and
         4 furlongs wide. This is the manor and the outlier together.

   [in FERNCOMBE Hundred]
3 BIDFORD (-on-Avon). King Edward held it. 5 hides. Land for....
   In lordship 5 ploughs; 8 male and 5 female slaves;
       28 villagers and 13 smallholders with 16 ploughs.
       4 mills at 43s 4d; meadow, 150 acres; woodland 4 leagues
         long and 1 league wide.

   [in STONELEIGH Hundred]
4 STONELEIGH. King Edward held it. 6 hides. Land for ....
   In lordship 5 ploughs; 1 male and 1 female slave.
       68 villagers and 4 smallholders with 2 priests have 30 ploughs.
       2 mills at 35s 4d; meadow, 20 acres; woodland 4 leagues
         long and 2 leagues wide; pasture for 2000 pigs.

   [in COLESHILL Hundred]
5 COLESHILL. King Edward held it. 3 hides. Land for ....
       30 villagers with a priest and 13 smallholders have 16 ploughs.
       1 mill at 40d; 10 burgesses in Tamworth belong to this
         manor; woodland 3 leagues long and 2½ leagues wide.

Rex ten̄ *COTES*. Eduin tenuit. Ibi ē. ɪ. hida.

Tra̅. ē. xx. car̄. In dn̄io. ē una. 7 ɪɪɪɪ. ſerui. 7 x. uilti 7 vɪ. borđ

cū. ɪɪɪ. car̄. Ibi. ɪɪ. molini de. c. ſoliđ. 7 q̄t xx. ac̄ p̄ti.

Silua. ɪɪɪ. q̄rent lḡ. 7 tn̄tđ lat̄. De p̄tis 7 paſcuis. ɪɪɪɪ. liɓ.

Extra burḡu. c. borđ cū hortulis ſuis redđt. ʟ. ſoliđ.

H̄ tra cū burgo de Waruuic 7 tcio denario placitoʒ ſiræ.

redđeɓ T.R.E. xvɪɪ. liɓ. Qᵈdo Roɓt recep̄ ad firmā.

ualɓ. xxx. liɓ. Modo tn̄tđ cū om̄ibʒ quæ ibi p̄tin.

Rex ten̄ *SVTONE*. Eduin tenuit. Ibi ſunt. vɪɪɪ. hidæ. 7 ɪ. virg træ.

Tra̅. ē. xxɪɪ. car̄. In dn̄io. ē. ɪ. car̄. 7 ɪɪ. ſerui. 7 xx. uilti 7 ɪɪɪɪ.

borđ cū. vɪɪ. car̄. Ibi. x. ac̄ p̄ti. Silua. ɪɪ. leuu lḡ. 7 ɪ. lat̄.

Cū onerat̄ ual̄. xxx. ſoliđ. Totū M̄ Valuit 7 ual̄. ɪɪɪɪ. liɓ.

In *OPTONE* ten̄ Alɓt cleric̄. ɪɪɪ. hiđ de rege in elemos.

Ibi ſunt. ɪ̈ɪ. pɓri cū. ɪɪ. car̄. 7 x. int uittos 7 borđ cū. ɪɪɪɪ. car̄.

Silua dimiđ leuu lḡ. 7 ɪɪɪ. q̄rent lat̄.

In *CHINEWRDE* ten̄ Ricarđ foreſt. ɪɪɪ. virg træ de rege.

Ibi ſunt. x. uilti 7 vɪɪ. borđ cū. ɪɪɪ. car̄. Silua dim̄ leu lḡ.

7 ɪɪɪɪ. q̄ʒ lat̄. H̄ duo m̄ebra jac̄ ad *STANLEI* M̄ regis.

238 c

.ɪɪ. TERRA EP̄I DE CESTRE.   *IN HONESBERIE H̄D.*

Eᵖs De CESTRE tenet de rege. ɪɪɪ. hiđ in *FERNEBERGE*.

Stori tenuit T.R.E. 7 liɓ hō fuit. Tra̅. ē. xɪɪɪɪ. car̄. In dn̄io. ē

una. 7 ɪɪ. ſerui. 7 xvɪɪɪ. uilti 7 ɪ. borđ eū. ɪx. car̄. Ibi. ʟx. ac̄ p̄ti.

T.R.E. ualɓ. c. ſol̄. Cū recep̄. ʟx. ſol. Modo. c. ſoliđ.   ʃ HVND.

Iſđ eᵖs ten̄ in *CALDECOTE*. ɪɪ. hiđ. Tra̅. ē. vɪ. car̄. *IN COLESHELLE*

In dn̄io. ē una. 7 ɪɪ. ſerui. 7 vɪɪ. uilti cū pɓro hn̄t. v. car̄.

[in TREMLOW Hundred]

6 COTEN. Earl Edwin held it. 1 hide. Land for 20 ploughs.
In lordship 1; 4 slaves;
10 villagers and 6 smallholders with 3 ploughs.
2 mills at 100s; meadow, 80 acres; woodland 3 furlongs
long and as wide; from meadows and pastures £4;
outside (Warwick) Borough 100 smallholders with
their gardens pay 50s.
This land, with the Borough of Warwick and the third penny of the
pleas of the Shire, paid £17 before 1066; when Robert acquired it for the
revenue, value £30; now as much, with all that belongs there.

[in COLESHILL Hundred]

7 SUTTON (COLDFIELD). Earl Edwin held it. 8 hides and 1 virgate of land.
Land for 22 ploughs. In lordship 1 plough; 2 slaves;
20 villagers and 4 smallholders with 7 ploughs.
Meadow, 10 acres; woodland 2 leagues long and 1 wide;
when exploited, value 30s.
The value of the whole manor was and is £4.

[in FERNCOMBE Hundred]

8 in UPTON Albert the Clerk holds 3 hides from the King in alms.
2 priests with 2 ploughs; 10 villagers and smallholders
with 4 ploughs between them.
Woodland ½ league long and 3 furlongs wide.

[in STONELEIGH Hundred]

9 in KENILWORTH Richard the Forester holds 3 virgates of land from the King.
10 villagers and 7 smallholders with 3 ploughs.
Woodland ½ league long and 4 furlongs wide.
These two members lie in (the lands of) the King's manor of Stoneleigh.

2   **LAND OF THE BISHOP OF CHESTER**   238 c

In HUNSBURY Hundred

1 The Bishop of Chester holds 3 hides in FARNBOROUGH from
the King. Stori held it before 1066; he was a free man.
Land for 14 ploughs. In lordship 1; 2 slaves;
18 villagers and 1 smallholder with 9 ploughs.
Meadow, 60 acres.
Value before 1066, 100s; when acquired 60s; now 100s.

In COLESHILL Hundred

2 The Bishop also holds 2 hides in CALDECOTE. Land for 6
ploughs. In lordship 1; 2 slaves.
7 villagers with a priest have 5 ploughs.

Ibi molin̄ de . ii . ſolid . 7 xii . ăc p̃ti . Silua . iii . leūu l̄g . 7 tntđ
lat . T.R.E. ualb̄ . xl . ſolid . 7 poſt 7 modo . lx . ſolid .

Hanc trā Tonna tenuit . ſed cū tra quó uoluit ire n̄ potuit .

Iſđ ep̄s ten̄ . vii . hiđ in *TASCHEBROC*. *IN K̄EMELAV HD̄*.
Tra . ē . xii . car̄ . In dn̄io ſunt . ii . car̄ . 7 ix . ſerui . 7 xi . uiłłi
cū p̄bro 7 vii . borđ hn̄t . ix . car̄ .

Ibi . ii . molini de . xii . ſolid 7 viii . denar̄ . 7 xii . ăc p̃ti .
T.R.E. ualb̄ . iii . lib̄ . Modo . vii . lib̄ . 7 tntđ qdo recepit .
h̄ tra . ē de æccła S̄ CEDDE.

.III. TERRA EP̄I DE WIRECESTRE. *IN PATELAV HVND̄.*

Ep̄s de WIRECESTRE ten̄ *HANTONE* . Ibi ſunt . xii . hidæ .
Tra . ē . xxii . car̄ . In dn̄io ſunt . ii . 7 iiii . ſerui . 7 xxii . uiłłi
7 ix . borđ . cū p̄bro hn̄tes xxiiii . car̄ . Ibi molin̄ de . vi . ſoł
7 viii . den̄ . 7 xv . q̃rent p̃ti in l̄g . 7 una q̃₹ in lat̄ .
In Waruic . iii . dom̄ de . xvi . denar̄ . Silua . i . leūu l̄g .
7 alia lat̄ .

T.R.E. ualb̄ . iiii . lib̄ . 7 poſt tntđ . Modo ualet . xx . lib̄ .
Iſđ ep̄s ten̄ 7 tenuit *STRADFORDE* . Ibi . xiiii . hidæ 7 dimiđ .
Tra . ē . xxxi . car̄ . In dn̄io ſunt . iii . car̄ . 7 xxi . uiłł cū p̄bro
7 vii . borđ hn̄t xxviii . car̄ . Ibi molin̄ de x . ſoł . 7 mille
anguiłł . 7 p̃tū . v . q̃₹ l̄g . 7 ii . q̃₹ lat̄ .

T.R.E. 7 poſt . ualuit . c . ſolid . Modo . xxv . lib̄ .
Iſđ ep̄s ten̄ *ALVESTONE* . Ibi ſunt . xv . hidæ . Tra . ē . xxiiii .
car̄ . In dn̄io ſunt . ii . 7 xxviii . uiłłi 7 xv . borđ 7 i . ancilla .

A mill at 2s; meadow, 12 acres; woodland 3 leagues long
and as wide.
Value before 1066, 40s; later and now 60s.
Tonni held this land, but he could not go where he would
with the land.

In TREMLOW Hundred
3 The Bishop also holds 7 hides in (BISHOP'S) TACHBROOK.
Land for 12 ploughs. In lordship 2 ploughs; 9 slaves.
11 villagers with a priest and 7 smallholders have 9 ploughs.
2 mills at 12s 8d; meadow, 12 acres.
Value before 1066 £3; now £7; as much when acquired.
This land is St. Chad's church's (Lichfield).

3   LAND OF THE BISHOP OF WORCESTER

In PATHLOW Hundred
1 The Bishop of Worcester holds HAMPTON (LUCY). 12 hides.
Land for 22 ploughs. In lordship 2; 4 slaves;
22 villagers and 9 smallholders with a priest who
have 24 ploughs.
A mill at 6s 8d; meadow, 15 furlongs in length and 1
furlong in width; in Warwick 3 houses at 16d;
woodland 1 league long and another wide.
Value before 1066 £4; later as much; now £20.

2 The Bishop also holds and held STRATFORD. 14½ hides.
Land for 31 ploughs. In lordship 3 ploughs.
21 villagers with a priest and 7 smallholders have 28 ploughs.
A mill at 10s and 1000 eels; meadow, 5 furlongs long and
2 furlongs wide.
Value before 1066 and later 100s; now £25.

The Bishop also holds
3 ALVESTON. 15 hides. Land for 24 ploughs. In lordship 2;
28 villagers, 15 smallholders and 1 female slave.

Hi hnt . xxII . caɍ . Ibi . IIII . molini de . xL . foliđ . 7 xII . ſticħ

anguiłł . 7 mille . In Waruuic . IIII . dom de . xvI . denaɍ.

p̊tū . vI . q̊ɀ lḡ . 7 una q̊ɀ laɍ.

T.R.E. 7 poſt . ualꝥ . vIII . liꝥ . Modo . xv . liꝥ.

☞ Iſđ eꝑs ten in *LOCHESHĀ* . I . hiđ . Traɍ . ē . III . caɍ.

In dñio . ē una . 7 IIII . uiłłi cū . I . caɍ.

T.R.E. 7 poſt . ualꝥ . xx . foliđ . Modo . xxv . foliđ.

Iſđ eꝑs ten *SPELESBERIE* . 7 Vrſo de eo . Ibi ſuɴ͑ . x . hidæ.

Traɍ . ē . xvI . caɍ . In dñio ſunt . IIII . caɍ . 7 v . ſerui.

7 xxv . uiłłi 7 xII . borđ cū . xII . caɍ . Ibi moliñ đe . L . den.

7 xxx.II. a̅c p̊ti . 7 paſcua . xxx.vI . a̅c . Silua . I . leůu

7 una q̊ɀ lḡ . 7 vII . q̊ɀ laɍ . Valuit 7 ualet . x . liꝥ.

In Mere ton hđ. Iſđ eꝑs ten in *FLECHENHO* . II . hiđ 7 dimiđ v̅ træ . 7 Leuuin

de eo . Traɍ . ē . II . caɍ . Ibi ſunt . II . uiłłi 7 I . borđ . cū . I.

caɍ . Ibi . vI . a̅c p̊ti.

T.R.E. 7 poſt . ualꝥ . x . foliđ . Modo . xx . foliđ.

☞ Bricſtuin T.R.E. tenuit In *ALVESTONE* . vII . hiđ 7 dimiđ . De hac tra habuit

Eldred archieꝑs ſoca 7 ſaca . 7 tol 7 teim . 7 cerſet . 7 oms alias forsfacturas p̅ter

★ illas . IIII . quas rex h̅ꞇ p totū regnū . Hoc teſtant filij ej Leuuin . Edmar

7 alij . IIII . ſed neſciunt de quo an đe æccła an de Comite Leuric cui ſeruiebat

hanc trā tenuit . Dñt tam qđ ipſi tenuer ̅ eā de . L . comite . 7 q̊ uolebant

cū tra poteraɴ͑ ſe uertere . Reliq̊s aut . vII . hiđ 7 dimiđ tenuit Britnod 7 Aluui T.R.E.

Sed comitat̅ neſcit de q̊ tenuerint . Wlſtan aut̅ eꝑs dicit ſe hanc trā deplacitaſſe

corā regina Mathilde in p̅ſentia . IIII . uicecomitatuū . 7 inde h̅ꞇ breues regis . W . 7 teſti

moniū comitat̅ Waruuic.

They have 22 ploughs.
3 mills at 40s and 1012 sticks of eels; in Warwick 4 houses
at 16d; meadow 6 furlongs long and 1 furlong wide.
Value before 1066 and later £8; now £15.

_/._ *(4 is entered, with transposition marks, after 3,7).*

5 in LOXLEY, 1 hide. Land for 3 ploughs. In lordship 1;
4 villagers with 1 plough.
Value before 1066 and later 20s; now 25s.

[in OXFORDSHIRE]
6 SPELSBURY. Urso holds from him. 10 hides. Land for 16
ploughs. In lordship 4 ploughs; 5 slaves;
25 villagers and 12 smallholders with 12 ploughs.
A mill at 50d; meadow, 32 acres; pasture-land, 36 acres;
woodland 1 league and 1 furlong long and 7 furlongs wide.
The value was and is £10.

in MARTON Hundred
7 in FLECKNOE 2 hides and ½ virgate of land. Leofwin holds from him.
Land for 2 ploughs.
2 villagers and 1 smallholder with 1 plough.
Meadow, 6 acres.
Value before 1066 and later 10s; now 20s.

4 _/._ *Added in small letters at the foot of col. 238 c. Directed by transposition*
marks to its proper place above.
Before 1066 Brictwin held 7½ hides in ALVESTON. Archbishop Aldred
had the full jurisdiction of this land, and market rights and church-tax,
and all other forfeitures except those four which the King has throughout
his whole Kingdom.

His sons Leofwin, Edmer and four others testify thereto, but they do
not know from whom he held this land, whether from the church or from
Earl Leofric, whom he served. They state however that they held it
themselves from Earl Leofric, and could turn where they would with the land.

Brictnoth and Alfwy held the remaining 7½ hides before 1066, but the
County does not know from whom they held. Bishop Wulfstan however states
that he established his claim to this land before Queen Matilda in the presence of
the four Sheriffdoms, and he has King William's writ for it, and also the witness
of the County of Warwick.

.IIII. TERRA EṔI BAIOCENSIS.

EṔS Baiocenſis teñ de rege *ARVE* .7 Stefaṅ de eo.

Leuuiṅ tenuit 7 liƀ hō fuit. Ibi . VII . hidæ 7 dimiđ . Tra̅ . e̅ . VII .

car . In dñio ſunt . II̅ . 7 VIII . uiƚƚi 7 x . borđ cū . IIII . car .

Ibi moliñ de . VI . ſoliđ 7 VIII . den . 7 xxx . ac̅ p̅ti . Silua . I . leuu lg̅ .

7 II . q̅rent lat . T.R.E. ualƀ . LX . ſoƚ . 7 poſt . XL . ſoƚ . Modo . IIII . liƀ .

Iſđ eṕs teñ in *EDRICESTONE* . IIII . hiđ . *IN K̅EMELAV HVND̅ .*

7 Corbin de eo . Sberne tenuit 7 liƀ hō fuit . Tra̅ . e̅ . VII . car .

In dñio ſunt . II̅ . 7 IIII . uiƚƚi cū p̅bro 7 IIII . borđ 7 IIII . ſeruis

hñt . III . car . Ibi moliñ de . x . ſoliđ 7 x . ſticħ anguiƚƚ .

Ibi . III . ac̅ p̅ti . T.R.E. 7 modo . uaƚ . IIII . liƀ . cū recep̅ .́ IIII . liƀ .

Iſđ eṕs teñ in *BEOSHELLE* dimiđ hidā *IN FERNECV̅BE HVND̅ .*

7 Wadard de eo . 7 Gerold ſub eo . Eduin tenuit . 7 liƀ hō fuit.

Tra̅ . e̅ . I . car . Ibi ſunt . VII . uiƚƚi 7 IIII . borđ cū . III . car̅ . Ibi . IIII .

ac̅ p̅ti . 7 II . q̅rent ſiluæ . Valuit . V . ſoliđ . Modo . xx . ſoliđ .

Iſđ eṕs teñ in *VLWARE* . I . hiđ 7 dimiđ . 7 Wadard de eo . 7 Gerold

ſub eo . Aluric tenuit 7 liƀ hō fuit . Tra̅ . e̅ . I . car . Ibi ſunt . III .

uiƚƚi cū dimiđ car . 7 ibi . VI . ac̅ p̅ti . Vaƚuit . x . ſoƚ . Modo . xx . ſoƚ .

Iſđ eṕs teñ in *BEDEFORD* . II . v̄ træ 7 dimiđ . 7 Roƀt de eo .

Ernulf 7 Ernegrin tenuer̅ 7 liƀi hōes fuer̅ . Tra̅ . e̅

Ibi . e̅ uṅ liƀ hō 7 I . ſeru . 7 I . borđ . cū . I . car̅ . 7 XIIII . ac̅ p̅ti . Silua

II . q̅rent lg̅ . 7 una lat . Valuit . XII . den . Modo . x . ſoliđ .

Iſđ eṕs teñ in *BROME* . IIII . hiđ 7 dimiđ . 7 Stefaṅ de eo .

Quinq̨ liƀi hōes tenuer̅ . T.R.E. Tra̅ . e̅ . IIII . car̅ . In dñio ſuꜩ . II .

7 IIII . uiƚƚi 7 x . borđ cū . II . car̅ . Ibi . XIIII . ac̅ p̅ti .

T.R.E. ualƀ . XL . ſoliđ . 7 poſt . xxx . ſoƚ . Modo . LX . ſoliđ .

[In FERNCOMBE Hundred]
1 The Bishop of Bayeux holds ARROW from the King, and Stephen
   from him. Leofwin held it; he was a free man. 7½ hides.
   Land for 7 ploughs. In lordship 2;
       8 villagers and 10 smallholders with 4 ploughs.
       A mill at 6s 8d; meadow, 30 acres; woodland 1 league
          long and 2 furlongs wide.
   Value before 1066, 60s; later 40s; now £4.

The Bishop also holds
   in TREMLOW Hundred
2 in ATHERSTONE (-on-Stour) 4 hides. Corbin holds from him. Esbern held it;
   he was a free man. Land for 7 ploughs. In lordship 2 .
       4 villagers with a priest, 4 smallholders and 4 slaves have 3 ploughs.
       1 mill at 10s and 10 sticks of eels; meadow, 3 acres.
   Value before 1066 and now £4; when acquired £4.

   in FERNCOMBE Hundred
3 in BEAUSALE ½ hide. Wadard holds from him and Gerald
   under him. Edwin the Sheriff held it; he was a free man.
   Land for 1 plough.
       7 villagers and 4 smallholders with 3 ploughs.
       Meadow, 4 acres; woodland 2 furlongs.
   The value was 5s; now 20s.

   [in BARCHESTON Hundred]
4 in WOLFORD 1½ hides. Wadard holds from him and Gerald
   under him. Aelfric held it; he was a free man. Land for 1 plough.
       3 villagers with ½ plough.
       Meadow, 6 acres.
   The value was 10s; now 20s.

   [in FERNCOMBE Hundred]
5 in BIDFORD (-on-Avon) 2½ virgates of land. Robert d'Oilly holds from him.
   Arnulf and Arngrim held it; they were free men. Land for....
       1 free man, 1 slave and 1 smallholder with 1 plough.
       Meadow, 14 acres; woodland 2 furlongs long and 1 wide.
   The value was 12d; now 10s.

6 in BROOM 4½ hides. Stephen holds from him. 5 free men held it
   before 1066. Land for 4 ploughs. In lordship 2;
       4 villagers and 10 smallholders with 2 ploughs.
       Meadow, 14 acres.
   Value before 1066, 40s; later 30s; now 60s.

.V. Terra Ep̄i Constantiensis.

Ep̄s Conſtantienſis ten dimid hiđ in *FILVNGELEI*.7 Leuuiⁿ
de eo.Tra̅.e̅.ii.car̄.In dn̅io.e̅ una.cu̅.ii.ſeruis.7 v.uiłłi cu̅.ii.borđ
hn̅t.i.car̄.Ibi.ii.ac̄ p̄ti.Silua.ii.q̨ꝗ lḡ.7 una q̨ꝗ lat̄.
Valuit.x.ſoliđ.Modo.xxx.ſoliđ.Aluuiⁿ liƀe tenuit.

.VI. Terra Æcclæ De Coventrev. *In Coleshelle Hvnđ*.

Abbatia de Coventrev.tenⁿ in *FILVNGER* dimiđ hiđ.
Tra̅.e̅.ii.car̄.Ibi ſunt.viii.uiłłi 7 vi.borđ cu̅.ii.car̄.Ibi ſiluæ
q̄rta pars leuue.cu̅ onerat̄ val̄.x.ſoł.

* T.R.E.ualƀ   x.ſoliđ.Modo.xxx.ſoliđ. *In Meretone*
* Ipſa æccl̄a . . . . . . *RANEBERGE*.Ibi ſunt.viii.   *HVNĐ*.
* hidæ 7 una v . . . . Tra̅.e̅.xvii.car̄.In dn̅io ſunt.ii.7 xxvii.
uiłłi 7 xi.borđ 7 iiii.ſerui.cu̅.xiiii.car̄.Ibi moliⁿ de xvi.deⁿ.
7 xxxii.ac̄ p̄ti.T.R.E.ualƀ.vi.liƀ.7 poſt.c.ſoł.Modo.viii.liƀ.
Ipſa æccl̄a ten *SVRLAND*.Ibi ſunt.vi.hidæ.Tra̅.e̅.xii.car̄.
In dn̅io ſunt.ii.7 iiii.ſerui.7 xxvi.uiłłi 7 ix.borđ cu̅.viii.car̄.
Ibi.xl.ac̄ p̄ti.T.R.E.ualƀ.vii.liƀ.7 poſt.iiii.liƀ.Modo.vi.liƀ.
Ipſa æccl̄a ten *DERBINGERIE*.Ibi ſunt.ii.hidæ.Tra̅.e̅.iiii.car̄.
In dn̅io ſunt.ii.7 iii.ſerui.7 iiii.uiłłi 7 vi.borđ cu̅.i.car̄.
Ibi.vi.ac̄ p̄ti.T.R.E.ualƀ.xl.ſoł.7 poſt.xx.ſoł.Modo.xxx.v.ſoł.
Ipſa æccl̄a ten *BILVEIE*.Ibi ſunt.iii.hidæ. *In Stanleie Hvnđ*.
Tra̅.e̅.viii.car̄.In dn̅io.e̅ una car̄.7 iiii.ſerui.7 x.uiłłi 7 vi.
borđ.cu̅.v.car̄.Ibi.viii.ac̄ p̄ti.Silua dimiđ leuu lḡ.7 una
q̄rent lat̄.T.R.E.7 modo ual̄.lx.ſoliđ.
Hanc tr̄a tenuit Aldgid uxor Grifin.Hanc emit ab.O.filio Ricardi

5   LAND OF THE BISHOP OF COUTANCES

[In COLESHILL Hundred]
1   The Bishop of Coutances holds ½ hide in FILLONGLEY. Leofwin holds
from him. Land for 2 ploughs. In lordship 1, with 2 slaves.
    5 villagers with 2 smallholders have 1 plough.
    Meadow, 2 acres; woodland 2 furlongs long and 1 furlong wide.
The value was 10s; now 30s.
    Alwin held it freely.

6   LAND OF COVENTRY CHURCH

In COLESHILL Hundred
1   Coventry Abbey holds ½ hide in FILLONGLEY. Land for 2 ploughs.
    8 villagers and 6 smallholders with 2 ploughs.
    Woodland, the fourth part of a league; when exploited, value 10s.
Value before 1066, ..0s; now 30s.

The Church itself holds
  in MARTON Hundred
2   GRANDBOROUGH. 8 hides and 1 virgate [of land].
Land for 17 ploughs. In lordship 2;
    27 villagers, 11 smallholders and 4 slaves with 14 ploughs.
    A mill at 16d; meadow, 32 acres.
Value before 1066 £6; later 100s; now £8.

3   *SURLAND.*   6 hides. Land for 12 ploughs. In lordship 2; 4 slaves;
    26 villagers and 9 smallholders with 8 ploughs.
    Meadow, 40 acres.
Value before 1066 £7; later £4; now £6.

4   BIRDINGBURY. 2 hides. Land for 4 ploughs. In lordship 2; 3 slaves;
    4 villagers and 6 smallholders with 1 plough.
    Meadow, 6 acres.
Value before 1066 40s; later 20s; now 35s.

  in STONELEIGH Hundred
5   BINLEY. 3 hides. Land for 8 ploughs. In lordship 1 plough; 4 slaves;
    10 villagers and 6 smallholders with 5 ploughs.
    Meadow, 8 acres; woodland ½ league long and 1 furlong wide.
Value before 1066 and now 60s.
    Aldith wife of Gruffydd held this land.
The Abbot bought it from Osbern son of Richard.

Ipſa æccła teñ in CONDONE.III.virg̓ træ.Tra.e̅.II.car̓.

Ibi ſunt.IIII.uiłłi 7 VI.borđ cu̅.II.car̓.7 I.ſeruo.Silua.III.q̓᷼

7 XXX.p̓tic̓ łg̅.7 III.q̓rent lat̓.Valuit 7 uał.XX.ſoliđ.

Ipſa æccła teñ in COBINTONE.II.hiđ.Tra.e̅.IIII.̓car̓.In dn̅io

e̅ dimiđ car̓.7 II.ſerui.7 V.uiłłi 7 I.borđ cu̅.I.car̓.Ibi.VIII.ãc

p̓ti.Valuit.XX.ſoliđ.modo.XXX.ſoliđ.

Ipſa æccła teñ in SVCHA̅.IIII.hiđ.Tra.e̅.XII.car̓.In dn̅io ſunt

II.car̓ 7 VII.ſerui.7 XX.uiłłi 7 VIII.borđ cu̅.VIII.car̓.Ibi.II.mo

lini de.IIII.ſoliđ.7 X.ãc p̓ti.Silua.I.leuu łg̅.7 dim leuu lat̓.

ħ ſilua.e̅ in manu regis.T.R.E.7 modo.vał.c.ſoł.Cu̅ recep̅:́LX.ſoł.

Huic æcctæ deđ Aluuiñ uicecom̅ CLIPTONE conceſſu regis.E.

7 filioʒ ſuoʒ ꝓ anima ſua.7 teſtimonio comitatus.

Comes ałbicus hanc injuſte inuaſit.7 æcctæ abſtulit.

Ipſa æccła teñ in SOWA.III.hiđ 7 dim.Tra.e̅.V.car̓.

In dn̅io.e̅ una.7 IIII.ſerui.7 X.uiłłi cu̅.V.car̓.Ibi moliñ de.

.II.ſoliđ.Silua dimiđ leuu łg̅.7 IIII.q̓rent lat̓.

T.R.E.uałb.XL.ſoliđ.Modo.LX.ſoliđ.

Ipſa æccła teñ in VLCHETONE.IIII.hiđ.Tra.e̅.VIII.car̓.

In dn̅io ſunt.II.7 VII.ſerui.7 XII.uiłłi 7 II.borđ cu̅.VI.car̓.

Ibi.I.ãc p̓ti.T.R.E.uałb.IIII.lib̅.7 poſt.XL.ſoł.Modo:́c.ſoliđ.

Ipſa æccła teñ ICETONE.Ibi.V.hidæ.Tra.e̅.XVI.car̓.

In dn̅io ſunt.II.7 VI.ſerui.7 XXX.uiłłi 7 VII.borđ cu̅.XIII.car̓.

Ibi.L.ãc p̓ti.T.R.E.uałb.X.lib̅.7 poſt.III.lib̅.Modo.XII.lib̅.

6   in COUNDON 3 virgates of land. Land for 2 ploughs.
      4 villagers and 6 smallholders with 2 ploughs and 1 slave.
      Woodland 3 furlongs and 30 perches long and 3 furlongs wide.
  The value was and is 20s.

7   in CUBBINGTON 2 hides. Land for 4 ploughs. In lordship ½ plough;
  2 slaves;
      5 villagers and 1 smallholder with 1 plough.
      Meadow, 8 acres.
  The value was 20s; now 30s.

      [in MARTON Hundred]
8   in SOUTHAM 4 hides. Land for 12 ploughs. In lordship 2 ploughs; 7 slaves;
      20 villagers and 8 smallholders with 8 ploughs.
      2 mills at 4s; meadow, 10 acres; woodland 1 league long and ½ league
        wide; this woodland is in the King's hands.
  Value before 1066 and now 100s; when acquired 60s.

9   Alwin the Sheriff gave CLIFTON (-upon-Dunsmore) to this church with
  the assent of King Edward, and of his own sons, for his soul's sake,
  and by the witness of the County. Earl Aubrey wrongfully annexed
  it and took it from the church.

  The Church itself holds   239 a
      [in STONELEIGH Hundred]
10 in (WALSGRAVE-ON-) SOWE 3½ hides. Land for 5 ploughs.
  In lordship 1; 4 slaves;
      10 villagers with 5 ploughs.
      A mill at 2s; woodland ½ league long and 4 furlongs wide.
  Value before 1066, 40s; now 60s.

11 in UFTON 4 hides. Land for 8 ploughs. In lordship 2; 7 slaves;
      12 villagers and 2 smallholders with 6 ploughs.
      Meadow, 1 acre.
  Value before 1066 £4; later 40s; now 100s.

12 (BISHOP'S) ITCHINGTON. 5 hides. Land for 16 ploughs. In
  lordship 2; 6 slaves;
      30 villagers and 7 smallholders with 13 ploughs.
      Meadow, 50 acres.
  Value before 1066 £10; later £3; now £12.

Ipſa æccła ten in *EDBVRBERIE*.I.hiđ 7 unā v̄ træ.

Tra.ē.I.car̄.Vaſta.ē p̄ exercitū regis.Ibi.II.ac̄ p̄ti.

Valuit.x.ſoliđ.Modo.II.ſoliđ. *IN HONESBERIE HĐ.*

Ipſa æccła ten *HERDEWICHE*.Ibi ſunt.xv.hidæ.Tra.ē.xvI.

car̄.In dn̄io ſunt.II.7 IIII.ſerui.7 xLIIII.uiłłi 7 II.borđ cū.xIII.

car̄.Ibi.xL.ac̄ p̄ti.T.R.E.ualℬ.Ix.liℬ.7 poſt.IIII.liℬ.m̂.x.liℬ.

Ipſa æccła ten *HVNITONE*.Ibi ſunt.v.hidæ. *IN FEXHOLE HĐ.*

Tra.ē.xvI.car̄.In dn̄io ſunt.III.car̄.7 xxxvI.uiłłi 7 xIII.

borđ 7 IIII.ſerui.cū.x.car̄.Ibi.IIII.molini de.LIIII.ſoliđ

7 IIII.denar̄.7 xL.ac̄ p̄ti.

T.R.E.ualℬ.x.liℬ.7 poſt.vII.liℬ.Modo.x.liℬ.

Ipſa æccła ten *CEDELESHVNTE*. *IN TREMELAV HVND.*

Ibi ſunt.v.hidæ.Tra.ē.xvI.car̄.In dn̄io ſunt.II.7 vI.ſerui.

7 xvIII.uiłłi 7 xII.borđ cū.vIII.car̄.Ibi.xII.ac̄ p̄ti.

T.R.E.ualℬ.vI.liℬ.7 poſt.III.liℬ.modo.vII.liℬ.

Ipſa æccła ten in *CESTRETONE*.I.hiđ 7 dimiđ.Tra.ē.IIII.car̄.

In dn̄io ſunt.II.7 III.ſerui.7 v.uiłłi 7 Ix.borđ cū.II.car̄.

Ibi.x.ac̄ p̄ti.T.R.E.ualℬ.xL.ſoł.7 poſt.xx.ſoł.modo.L.ſoł.

Ipſa æccła ten *WASMERTONE*.Ibi ſunt.v.hidæ.Tra.ē.xI.

car̄.In dn̄io.ē una 7 II.ſerui.7 xvIII.uiłłi 7 I.borđ cū.vII.

car̄.Ibi molin de.xx.ſoł.7 IIII.ſūm ſał.7 mille anguiłł.

Ibi.xxx.ac̄ p̄ti.Silua dimiđ leuū lḡ.7 II.q̄rent lat̄.

T.R.E.ualℬ.IIII.liℬ.7 poſt.L.ſoliđ.Modo.Lxx.ſoliđ.

Ipſa æccła ten *NEWEHA*.Ibi ſunt.v.hidæ. *IN FERNECVBE HĐ.*

Tra.ē.xIIII.car̄.In dn̄io ſunt.II.7 IIII.ſerui.7 xv.uiłłi

7 v.borđ cū.vIII.car̄.Valuit 7 uał.vI.liℬ. *IN HONESBERIE HĐ.*

Ipſa æccła ten in *RADWEI*.III.hiđ.7 Ermenfrid de abℬe.

Tra.ē.vI.car̄.In dn̄io.ē una.7 IIII.ſerui.7 xIII.uiłłi

7 vI.borđ hn̄t.v.car̄ 7 dimiđ.Ibi.xvI.ac̄ p̄ti.

Valuit.xx.ſoliđ.Modo.L.ſoliđ.

13   in HARBURY 1 hide and 1 virgate of land. Land for 1 plough.
It was wasted by the King's army.
    Meadow, 2 acres.
The value was 10s; now 2s.

  in HUNSBURY Hundred

14   (PRIORS) HARDWICK. 15 hides. Land for 16 ploughs. In lordship 2; 4 slaves;
    43 villagers and 2 smallholders with 13 ploughs.
    Meadow, 40 acres.
Value before 1066 £9; later £4; now £10.

  in FEXHOLE Hundred

15   HONINGTON. 5 hides. Land for 16 ploughs. In lordship 3 ploughs;
    36 villagers, 13 smallholders and 4 slaves with 10 ploughs.
    4 mills at 54s 4d; meadow, 40 acres.
Value before 1066 £10; later £7; now £10.

  in TREMLOW Hundred

16   CHADSHUNT. 5 hides. Land for 16 ploughs. In lordship 2; 6 slaves;
    18 villagers and 12 smallholders with 8 ploughs.
    Meadow, 12 acres.
Value before 1066 £6; later £3; now £7.

17   in CHESTERTON 1½ hides. Land for 4 ploughs. In lordship 2; 3 slaves;
    5 villagers and 9 smallholders with 2 ploughs.
    Meadow, 10 acres.
Value before 1066, 40s; later 20s; now 50s.

18   WASPERTON. 5 hides. Land for 11 ploughs. In lordship 1; 2 slaves;
    18 villagers and 1 smallholder with 7 ploughs.
    A mill at 20s, 4 packloads of salt and 1000 eels; meadow, 30 acres;
      woodland ½ league long and 2 furlongs wide.
Value before 1066 £4; later 50s; now 70s.

  in FERNCOMBE Hundred

19   NEWNHAM. 5 hides. Land for 14 ploughs. In lordship 2; 4 slaves;
    15 villagers and 5 smallholders with 8 ploughs.
The value was and is £6.

  in HUNSBURY Hundred

20   in RADWAY 3 hides. Ermenfrid holds from the Abbot.
  Land for 6 ploughs. In lordship 1; 4 slaves.
    13 villagers and 6 smallholders have 5½ ploughs.
    Meadow, 16 acres.
The value was 20s; now 50s.

★ VII. TERRA ÆCCLÆ DE ABENDONE *IN MERETONE HVND*.

ABBATIA de ABENDONE hт̃ in *HILLE* . II . hiđ . q̃s emit de feudo
Turchilli . 7 Wariñ teñ de abƀe . Tra . ē . III . cař . Nc̃ in dñio . II . cař .
7 v . uitti cũ . VII . borđ hñt . I . cař . Ibi . XII . ãc p̃ti . Valuit . XXX . foliđ .
Modo . XL . foliđ .

★ .VIII. TERRA ECCLÆ DE BERTONE. *IN COLESHELLE HD̆*.

ABBATIA de BERTONE teñ in *ALDVLVESTREV* . ᵃˢ II . hiđ .
7 dimiđ . Tra . ē . IIII . cař . In dñio . ē una . 7 VI . uitti 7 IIII . borđ .
cũ . II . cař . T.R.E . ualƀ . XL . fol . 7 poſt . X . fol . Modo . XXX . foliđ .
Hanc тr̃a deđ Leuric eiđ æcclæ .

★ .IX. TERRA ÆCCLÆ DE MALMESBERIE.

ABBATIA DE MALMESBERIE teñ in *NIWEBOLD* . III . hiđ . Tra
VI . cař . Nc̃ in dñio . II . cař . 7 IIII . ferui . 7 VIII . uitti cũ . III . borđ
hñt . III . cař . Ibi moliñ de . VIII . foliđ . 7 XVI . ãc p̃ti .
Valuit . XXX . foliđ . Modo . L . foliđ . Vluuiñ monach tenuit . 7 ipfe
deđ æcclæ qdo faĉtus . ē monachus .

★ .X. TERRA ÆCCLÆ DE WINCELCVMBE.

ABBATIA de WINCELCVMBE teñ . VI . hiđ in *ALNE* . Tra . VI . cař .
In dñio . ē una cař . 7 III . ferui . 7 XI . uitti cũ . IIII . borđ hñt . V . cař .
Ibi moliñ de . V . foliđ . Silua . dim leu lg̃ . 7 IIII . q̃ᵹ lat .
Valuit . III . liƀ . Modo . IIII . liƀ .

7   # LAND OF ABINGDON CHURCH

In MARTON Hundred
1   Abingdon Abbey has 2 hides in HILL, which the Abbot bought
from Thorkell's Holding. Warin holds from the Abbot. Land
for 3 ploughs. Now in lordship 2 ploughs.
     5 villagers with 7 smallholders have 1 plough.
     Meadow, 12 acres.
The value was 30s; now 40s.

8   # LAND OF BURTON CHURCH

In COLESHILL Hundred
1   Burton Abbey holds 2½ hides in AUSTREY. Land for 4 ploughs.
In lordship 1;
     6 villagers and 4 smallholders with 2 ploughs.
Value before 1066, 40s; later 10s; now 30s.
     Earl Leofric gave this land to this church.

9   # LAND OF MALMESBURY CHURCH

[In STONELEIGH Hundred]
1   Malmesbury Abbey holds 3 hides in NEWBOLD (COMYN).
Land for 6 ploughs. Now in lordship 2 ploughs; 4 slaves.
     8 villagers with 3 smallholders have 3 ploughs.
     A mill at 8s; meadow, 16 acres.
The value was 30s; now 50s.
     The monk Wulfwin held it; he gave it to the church himself
when he was made a monk.

10   # LAND OF WINCHCOMBE CHURCH

[In FERNCOMBE Hundred]
1   Winchcombe Abbey holds 6 hides in (GREAT) ALNE. Land
for 6 ploughs. In lordship 1 plough; 3 slaves.
     11 villagers with 4 smallholders have 5 ploughs.
     A mill at 5s; woodland ½ league long and 4 furlongs wide.
The value was £3; now £4.

.XI. TERRA ÆCCLÆ DE EVESHAM. *IN FERNECŨBE HD̄.*

ABBATIA de EVESHAM teñ in *WITELAVESFORD*
v . hidas . Tra . ē . vi . car̄ . In dñio ſunt . ii̅ . 7 iii . ſerui . 7 ii .
ancillæ . 7 iiii . uilli 7 vi . borđ cū . ii . car̄ . Ibi moliñ de . x .
ſol 7 xx . ſtich anguill . Ibi . xxiiii . ac̄ p̄ti . Silua . i . q̄rent
lḡ . 7 dimiđ lat̄ . T.R.E . ualb̄ . xl . ſol . 7 poſt . xxx . Modo . l . ſol .
Hanc trã tenuit Wigot . T.R.E .

Ipſa æccła teñ in *SANDBVRNE* . iii . hiđ . Tra . ē . iiii . car̄ .
In dñio . ē una . 7 ii . ſerui . 7 ii . uilli 7 iiii . borđ . cū . iii . car̄ .
Silua . i . leuu lḡ . 7 dimiđ leuu lat̄ .
Valuit . xx . ſoliđ . Modo . xxx . ſoliđ .

Ipſa æccła teñ in *SALFORD* . ii . hiđ . Tra . ē . vi . car̄ . In
dñio . ē una . 7 ii . ſerui . 7 ix . uilli 7 v . borđ cū . vii . car̄ .
Ibi moliñ de . x . ſoliđ . 7 xx . ſtich anguill . 7 p̄tū . vi .
q̄rent 7 dim lḡ . 7 i . q̄rent 7 dim lat̄ .
Valuit . xl . ſoliđ . Modo . lx . ſoliđ .

Ipſa æccła teñ in *CHENEVERTONE* . iii . hiđ . 7 Rannulf
de abb̄e . Tra . ē . v . car̄ . In dñio . ē una . 7 iii . ſerui . 7 iii . uilli
7 ii . borđ cū . i . car̄ . Ibi moliñ de . iii . ſoliđ . p̄tū . i . q̄rent
lḡ . 7 xii . p̄tic lat̄ . Valuit . xl . ſol . 7 poſt . v . ſol . M̄ . xx . ſol .
Ipſa eccła teñ in *WILELEI* . iii . hiđ . Tra . ē . iiii . car̄ . Ibi ſuɴ̄ .

★ .XII. TERRA ROGERIJ COMITIS. *IN STANLEI HVND̄.*

COMES ROGERIVS teñ de rege *LAMINTONE* . Ibi ſunt . ii . hidæ
Tra . ē . viii . car̄ . In dñio ſunt . ii . 7 iii . ſerui . 7 v . uilli cū p̄bro
7 iii . borđ hñt . iiii . car̄ . Ibi . ii . molini de xxiiii . ſol . 7 xxvi . ac̄ p̄ti .
Valuit . l . ſol . 7 poſt . xxv . ſol . Modo . iiii . lib̄ . Oluuin tenuit lib̄e . T.R.E .

In FERNCOMBE Hundred
1 Evesham Abbey holds 5 hides in WIXFORD. Land for 6 ploughs.
In lordship 2; 3 male and 2 female slaves;
    4 villagers and 6 smallholders with 2 ploughs.
    A mill at 10s and 20 sticks of eels; meadow, 24 acres;
        woodland 1 furlong long and ½ wide.
Value before 1066, 40s; later 30s; now 50s.
Wigot held this land before 1066.

The Church itself holds
2 in SAMBOURNE 3 hides. Land for 4 ploughs. In lordship 1; 2 slaves;
    2 villagers and 4 smallholders with 3 ploughs.
    Woodland 1 league long and ½ league wide.
The value was 20s; now 30s.

3 in (ABBOT'S) SALFORD 2 hides. Land for 6 ploughs. In lordship 1; 2 slaves;
    9 villagers and 5 smallholders with 7 ploughs.
    A mill at 10s and 20 sticks of eels; meadow, 6½ furlongs
        long and 1½ furlongs wide.
The value was 40s; now 60s.

4 in KINWARTON 3 hides. Ranulf holds from the Abbot. Land
for 5 ploughs. In lordship 1; 3 slaves;
    3 villagers and 2 smallholders with 1 plough.
    A mill at 3s; meadow, 1 furlong long and 12 perches wide.
The value was 40s; later 5s; now 20s.

5 in WEETHLEY 3 hides. Land for 4 ploughs. They are there.

12   LAND OF EARL ROGER

In STONELEIGH Hundred
1 Earl Roger holds LEAMINGTON(PRIORS) from the King. 2 hides.
Land for 8 ploughs. In lordship 2; 3 slaves.
    5 villagers with a priest and 3 smallholders have 4 ploughs.
    2 mills at 24s; meadow, 26 acres.
The value was 50s; later 25s; now £4.
Wulfwin held it freely before 1066.

Idē cōm teñ in *FRANCHETONE*.IIII.hid una v́ miñ.Tṛạ.ẹ̄.vi.caṛ
In dñio ſunt.III.caṛ.7 VIII.uilti 7 VI.borđ cū.III.caṛ 7 dimiđ.
Ibi.xv.ac̄ p̃ti.Valuit 7 ual.LX.ſolid.Vluuiñ libe tenuit T.R.E.
De feudo comit Roǵ teñ Rainald.v.hiđ in *STRATONE*.
Tṛạ.ẹ̄.VII.caṛ.In dñio ſunt.III.caṛ.7 VIII.ſerui.7 XX.uilti 7 VI.borđ
cū.XIIII.caṛ.Ibi.v.ac̄ p̃ti.Silua.III.q̃꞉ lḡ.7 úna laṭ.
Valuit.III.liƀ.7 poſt.c.ſoł.Modo.VI.liƀ.
De comite teñ idē.R.in *VLVRICETONE*.v.hiđ.Tṛạ.ẹ̄.XII.caṛ.
In dñio ſunt.IIII.7 VI.ſerui.7 XVIII.uilti cū p̃bro 7 XIX.borđ
hñt.XII.caṛ.Ibi moliñ de.VI.ſoł 7 IIII.deṇ.7 v.ac̄ p̃ti.
Valuit.LX.ſoł.7 poſt.XX.ſoł.Modo.c.ſoł.Æilmunḍ tenuit.h̄.II.Maṇ.
Idem teñ de cōm.v.hiđ in *LEILEFORDE*.Tṛạ.ẹ̄.VII.caṛ.In dñio
ẹ̄ una cū.II.ſcruis.7 IX.uilti 7 XVII.borđ 7 II.franciǵ cū.VI.caṛ.
Ibi moliñ de.X.ſoł.7 VI.deṇ.7 XI.ac̄ p̃ti.
Valuit.XL.ſoł.7 poſt.X.ſoł.Modo.L.ſolid.Chetelḅṭ tenuit.
De cōm teñ Wilts in *BELTONE*.v.hiđ.una v́ miñ.Tṛạ.ẹ̄.XI.caṛ.
In dñio ſunt.II.7 XXIII.uilti cū p̃bro 7 IX.borđ hñt.VIII.caṛ 7 dimiđ.
Ibi.VIII.ac̄ p̃ti.Valuit.IIII.liƀ.7 poſt.X.ſoł.Modo.III.liƀ.Vluuiñ
De cōm teñ Rainalḍ in *VLVESTONE* IN *STANLEI HVND*./tenuit.
una v́ trǣ Tṛạ.ẹ̄ dimiđ caṛ.Ibi.ẹ̄.I.uilts.Valet.v.ſoł.Elmunḍ tenuit.

[In MARTON Hundred]

2 The Earl also holds 4 hides less 1 virgate in FRANKTON.
Land for 6 ploughs. In lordship 3 ploughs;
    8 villagers and 6 smallholders with 3½ ploughs.
    Meadow, 15 acres.
The value was and is 60s.
    Wulfwin held it freely before 1066.

3 Reginald holds 5 hides in STRETTON (-on-Dunsmore) from Earl
Roger's Holding. Land for 7 ploughs. In lordship 3 ploughs; 8 slaves;
    20 villagers and 6 smallholders with 14 ploughs.
    Meadow, 5 acres; woodland 3 furlongs long and 1 wide.
The value was £3; later 100s; now £6.

4 Reginald also holds 5 hides in WOLSTON from the Earl.
Land for 12 ploughs. In lordship 4; 6 slaves.
    18 villagers with a priest and 19 smallholders have 12 ploughs.
    A mill at 6s 4d; meadow, 5 acres.
The value was 60s; later 20s; now 100s.
    Almund held these two manors.

5 He also holds 5 hides in (CHURCH) LAWFORD from the Earl.
Land for 7 ploughs. In lordship 1, with 2 slaves;
    9 villagers, 17 smallholders and 2 Frenchmen with 6 ploughs.
    A mill at 10s 6d; meadow, 11 acres.
The value was 40s; later 10s; now 50s.
    Ketelbern held it.

6 William holds 5 hides less 1 virgate in BILTON from the Earl.
Land for 11 ploughs. In lordship 2.
    23 villagers with a priest and 9 smallholders have 8½ ploughs.
    Meadow, 8 acres.
The value was £4; later 10s; now £3.
    Wulfwin held it.

In STONELEIGH Hundred

7 Reginald holds 1 virgate of land in WOLSTON from the Earl.
Land for ½ plough.
    1 villager.
Value 5s.
    Almund held it.

ᚠDe com̃ teñ Outi.III.hid in *QUATONE*.T̃ra.ē.XII.car̃.In dñio
funt.IIII.⁊ v.ſerui.⁊ XIX.uiłłi ⁊ XIIII.bord cū.X.car̃.Ibi.I.ac̃ p̃ti.
Silua.II.leūu l̄g.⁊ una lat̃ ⁊ moliñ de.II.ſoł.Valuit.VI.lib.m̃.c.ſoł.
ᚠDe com̃ teñ Walter.I.hid in *RAMESLEGE*.   ᚠIdē Outi libe tenuit.
T̃ra.ē.VII.car̃.In dñio.ē una.⁊ II.ſerui.⁊ VII.uiłłi ⁊ VII.bord cū
III.car̃.Silua.I.leūu l̄g.⁊ dimid leūu lat̃.Valuit.XXX.ſoł.m̃.XL.ſoł.
ᚠDe com̃ teñ Radulf.v.hid in *RIGGE*.   ᚠAchi libe tenuit.
T̃ra.ē.VII.car̃.In dñio.ē una.cū.I.ſeruo.⁊ III.uiłłi ⁊ IIII.bord cū.II.
car̃.Valuit.LX.ſoł.modo.XL.ſoł.Edric libe tenuit de Leurico
ᚠDe com̃ teñ Idē Rad in *SCIPLEI*.I.hid.T̃ra.ē.III.car̃.Ibi funt.II.uiłłi
⁊ una q̃rent quercuū.in l̄g ⁊ lat̃.Vał.v.ſoł.Alſi libe tenuit.T.R.E.

★ .XIII. TERRA HVGONIS COMITIS. *IN KEMELAV HVND.*
COMES HVGO ten.I.hid ⁊ III.virg træ in *PILARDETVNE*.⁊ Waleran
de eo.T̃ra.ē.II.car̃.In dñio.ē una.cū.I.ſeruo.⁊ II.uiłłi ⁊ II.bord
cū.I.car̃.Valuit.XX.ſoł.Modo.XXX.ſoł.Hugo camerar libe tenuit.

239 c
.XIIII. TERRA ALBERICI COMITIS. *IN COLESHELLE HD.*
COMES ALBERICVS tenuit de rege *ETONE*.Harding
tenuit T.R.E.T̃ra.ē.XX.VI.car̃.In dñio funt.III.⁊ III.ſerui.
⁊ XL.IIII.uiłłi ⁊ VI.colibti ⁊ X.bord cū.XVI.car̃.

[in STAFFORDSHIRE, later in SHROPSHIRE]

8 Auti holds 3 hides in QUATT from the Earl.
Land for 12 ploughs. In lordship 4; 5 slaves;
  19 villagers and 14 smallholders with 10 ploughs.
  Meadow, 1 acre; woodland 2 leagues long and 1 wide; a mill at 2s.
The value was £6; now 100s.
  Auti also held it freely.

9 Walter holds 1 hide in ROMSLEY from the Earl.
Land for 7 ploughs. In lordship 1; 2 slaves;
  7 villagers and 7 smallholders with 3 ploughs.
  Woodland 1 league long and ½ league wide.
The value was 30s; now 40s.
  Aki held it freely.

10 Ralph holds 5 hides in RUDGE from the Earl.
Land for 7 ploughs. In lordship 1, with 1 slave;
  3 villagers and 4 smallholders with 2 ploughs.
The value was 60s; now 40s.
  Edric held it freely from Earl Leofric.

11 Ralph also holds 1 hide in SHIPLEY from the Earl. Land for 3 ploughs.
  2 villagers.
  Oaks, 1 furlong in length and width.
Value 5s.
  Alfsi held it freely before 1066.

13   **LAND OF EARL HUGH**

In TREMLOW Hundred
1 Earl Hugh holds 1 hide and 3 virgates of land in PILLERTON (PRIORS)
  and Waleran from him. Land for 2 ploughs. In lordship 1, with 1 slave;
    2 villagers and 2 smallholders with 1 plough.
  The value was 20s; now 30s.
    Hugh the Chamberlain held it freely.

14   **LAND OF EARL AUBREY**   239 c

In COLESHILL Hundred
1 Earl Aubrey held NUNEATON from the King. Harding held it
  before 1066. Land for 26 ploughs. In lordship 3; 3 slaves;
    44 villagers, 6 freedmen and 10 smallholders with 16 ploughs.

Ibi moliñ de .xxxii. den..7 xx. ac p̃ti . Silua . ii . leuu lg̃.
7 i . leuu 7 dimid lat.

T.R.E. ualb.iiii. lib.7 poſt. iii. lib. Modo . c . ſolid.

Hanc trā ded Aluuin æcctæ de Co uentreu pro anima ſua T.R.E. cõ Albic abſtulit.

Ipſe cõm tenuit CLIPTONE . Aluuin *uicec'* IN MERETONE HD.
tenuit T.R.E.7 cū tra lib fuit . Ibi ſunt . v . hidæ. Tra. e. xvi.
car. In dñio ſunt. ii. car.7 xii. uiłłi cū pbro 7 xx. bord
hñt . vii . car. Ibi . ii . molini de.xi. ſolid.7 viii. ac p̃ti.
T.R.E.7 poſt. ualuit .xl. ſolid. Modo . iiii . lib.

Ipſe cõm tenuit SMITHA. Harding IN BOMELAV HD.
tenuit T.R.E.7 lib hō fuit. Ibi ſunt . vi. hidæ.Tra. e. xxv.
car. In dñio ſunt. ii. car.7 xxii. uiłłi 7 xxiii. bord cū
xii . car. Ibi ſunt. ii. libi hões . Silua.dimid leuu lg̃.
7 tñtd lat.7 ibi . l. ac p̃ti. Valuit. xl. ſolid. modo. vi . lib.

Ipſe cõm tenuit in BRANCOTE . i . hid 7 dimid.Tra.e. iii.car.
Salo tenuit 7 lib hō fuit. Ibi. e un uiłłs. Valuit. v. ſot.

Ipſe cõm tenuit in WAVRE . ii . hid 7 dim. Tra. e. iii. car.
Alric tenuit 7 lib cū tra fuit.Ibi. e un uiłłs 7 ii. bord.
Valuit. v. ſolid. Modo . iiii. denar plus. IN HONESBERIE HD.

Ipſe cõm tenuit in RODEWEI . ii . hid . Tra. e. iii. car.
Harding tenuit 7 cū ea lib fuit. Ibi ſunt. iiii. uiłłi 7 i. bord
cū . i. car. Ibi . viii.ac p̃ti. Valuit 7 ual. xx. ſolid.

~~Hæ træ Alberici ſunt in manu regis~~ *comit'* *de Wirce* . Goisfrid eas cuſtod.

239 c

A mill at 32d; meadow, 20 acres; woodland, 2 leagues
  long and 1½ leagues wide.
Value before 1066 £4; later £3; now 100s.

The Earl himself held
  in MARTON Hundred
2 CLIFTON (-upon-Dunsmore). Alwin the Sheriff held it before 1066;
  he was free, with the land. 5 hides. Land for 16 ploughs.
In lordship 2 ploughs.
    12 villagers with a priest and 20 smallholders have 7 ploughs.
    2 mills at 11s; meadow, 8 acres.
Value before 1066 and later 40s; now £4.
    Alwin gave this land to Coventry Church for his soul's sake
before 1066. Earl Aubrey took it away.

  in BRINKLOW Hundred
3 SMEETON. Harding held it before 1066; he was a free man. 6 hides.
  Land for 25 ploughs. In lordship 2 ploughs;
    22 villagers and 23 smallholders with 12 ploughs. 2 free men.
    Woodland ½ league long and as wide. Meadow, 50 acres.
The value was 40s; now £6.

4 in BRAMCOTE 1½ hides. Land for 3 ploughs. Salo held it;
  he was a free man.
    1 villager.
The value was 5s.

5 in (CHURCH)OVER 2½ hides. Land for 3 ploughs. Alric held it;
  he was free, with the land.
    1 villager and 2 smallholders.
The value was 5s; now 4d more.

  in HUNSBURY Hundred
6 in RADWAY 2 hides. Land for 3 ploughs. Harding held it;
  he was free, with the (land).
    4 villagers and 1 smallholder with 1 plough.
    Meadow, 8 acres.
The value was and is 20s.
    These lands of Earl Aubrey are in the King's hands.
Geoffrey of La Guerche has charge of them.

.XV. TERRA COMITISSÆ GODEVÆ. *IN COLESHELLE HD.*

COMITISSA GODEVA tenuit T.R.E. *AILESPEDE*. Ibi funt. IIII.

hidæ. Tra.ē. VIII. car. Ibi funt. VIII. uilti 7 I. bord cū. II. car

7 dimid. Silua ht. I. leūu 7 dim lg. 7 unā leūu lat.

T.R.E. ualb. XL. fot. 7 poft 7 modo. XXX. folid.

Ipfa comitiffa tenuit in *ADERESTONE*. III. hid. Tra.ē. V. car.

Ibi funt. XI. uilti 7 II. bord. 7 I. feruus cū. IIII. car.

Ibi. VI. ac pti. Silua. II. leūu lg. 7 II. leūu lat.

Valuit. XL. folid. Modo. LX. folid.

Ipfa comitiffa tenuit in *ARDRESHILLE* 7 *HANSLEI*. II. hid.

Tra.ē. VII. car. Ibi funt. XIII. uilti cū. V. car. Ibi. VI. ac pti.

Valuit. IIII. lib. Modo. C. folid.

Ipfa comitiffa tenuit *CHINESBERIE*. Ibi funt. VI. hidæ. Tra.ē

VII. car. In dnio funt. II. car. 7 I. feru. 7 XXXIII. uilti 7 III. bord.

cū. II. pbris hntes. XVI. car. Ibi molin de. IX. fot 7 IIII. den.

7 XII. ac pti. Silua. I. leūu lg. 7 tntd lat.

T.R.E. ualb. VI. lib. 7 poft. VII. lib. Modo. XIII. lib ad pondus.

Ipfa comitiffa tenuit *ANESTIE* 7 *FOCHESHELLE*. *IN BOMELAV HD.*

Ibi funt. IX. hidæ. Tra.ē. VII. car. In dnio funt. III. 7 II. ferui.

7 XXX. uilti 7 VI. bord cū. XI. car.

T.R.E. 7 poft. ualuit. X. lib. Modo. XII. lib.

Ipfa comitiffa tenuit *COVENTREV*. Ibi funt. V. hidæ. Tra.ē

XX. car. In dnio funt. III. car. 7 VII. ferui. 7 L. uilti 7 XII. bord.

cū. XX. car. Ibi molin de. III. folid. Silua. II. leūu lg.

7 tntd lat. T.R.E. 7 poft. ualuit. XII. lib. Modo XI. lib ad pond.

HAS TRAS GODIVÆ. tenet NICOLAVS ad firmā de rege.

In COLESHILL Hundred
1 Countess Godiva held ALSPATH before 1066. 4 hides. Land for 8 ploughs.
     8 villagers and 1 smallholder with 2½ ploughs.
     Woodland 1½ leagues long and 1 league wide.
   Value before 1066, 40s; later and now 30s.

The Countess herself held
2 in ATHERSTONE 3 hides. Land for 5 ploughs.
     11 villagers, 2 smallholders and 1 slave with 4 ploughs.
     Meadow, 6 acres; woodland 2 leagues long and 2 leagues wide.
   The value was 40s; now 60s.

3 in HARTSHILL and ANSLEY 2 hides. Land for 7 ploughs.
     13 villagers with 5 ploughs.
     Meadow, 6 acres.
   The value was £4; now 100s.

4 KINGSBURY. 6 hides. Land for 7 ploughs. In lordship 2 ploughs; 1 slave;
     33 villagers and 3 smallholders with 2 priests who have 16 ploughs.
     A mill at 9s 4d; meadow, 12 acres; woodland 1 league
       long and as wide.
   Value before 1066 £6; later £7; now £13 by weight.

in BRINKLOW Hundred
5 ANSTY and FOLESHILL. 9 hides. Land for 7 ploughs.
   In lordship 3; 2 slaves;
     30 villagers and 6 smallholders with 11 ploughs.
   Value before 1066 and later £10; now £12.

[in STONELEIGH Hundred]
6 COVENTRY. 5 hides. Land for 20 ploughs.
   In lordship 3 ploughs; 7 slaves;
     50 villagers and 12 smallholders with 20 ploughs.
     A mill at 3s; woodland 2 leagues long and as wide.
   Value before 1066 and later £12; now £11 by weight.

Nicholas holds these lands of Countess Godiva for the King's revenue.

.XVI TERRA COMITIS DE MELLENT. *IN STANLEI HVND'.*

COMES DE MELLEND teñ de rege *MVITONE*. Ibi funt
.II. hidæ. Tra.ē.VIII. car. Algar tenuit. In dñio.ē una.

7 II. ferui. 7 VI. uitti 7 XI. bord cū. III. car. Ibi. II. molini de
LXX. folid. 7 XII. ac pti.

T.R.E. ualb. III. lib. 7 post. XL. fot. Modo. VI. lib.

Ipfe cōm teñ in *MALVERTONE*. II. hid una v min. Leuuin
tenuit 7 lib hō fuit. Tra.ē.VIII. car. In dñio.ē una. 7 II. ferui.
7 un uitts 7 v. bord cū. I. car. Ibi moliñ de. L. folid. 7 xxx.ac
pti. Valuit. XL. folid. Modo. c. folid.

Ipfe cōm teñ *WIDECOTE*. Ibi.ē una hida. Tra. II. car. Cantuin
7 Turbn tenuer. 7 libi fuer. Ibi funt. IIII. uitti 7 v. bord cū. I. car.
T.R.E. ualb. x. fot. Modo. xxx. folid.

Ipfe cōm teñ in *RINCELE*. I. hid. Vafta.ē.
Silua ibi dimid leuu lg. 7 II. qrent lat. Cū onerat. ual. x. fot.

Ipfe cōm teñ in *DERCETO*. x. hid. Tres taini tenuer.
7 libi fuer. Tra.ē. XII. car. In dñio funt. III. car. 7 x. ferui.
7 XII. uitti cū pbro 7 v. bord hñt. VII. car. Ibi. L. ac pti.
T.R.E. ualb. x. lib. 7 post. XL. fot. Modo. VIII. lib.

Ipfe cōm teñ in *WARMINTONE*. XIII. hid. Azor tenuit
7 lib hō fuit. Tra.ē. XIIII. car. In dñio funt. IIII. 7 XII. ferui.
7 XXXVI. uitti 7 VIII. bord cū. XIIII. car. Ibi. LXIX. ac pti.
T.R.E. ualb. x. lib. Modo tntd.

Ipfe cōm teñ in *ERBVRBERIE*. IIII. hid 7 dimid. Leuuin
7 Alric tenuer. 7 uendere potuer. fed ñ difcedere cū tra.
Tra.ē. x. car. In dñio.ē una car cū. I. feruo. 7 IX. uitti 7 VI. bord
cū. IIII. car. T.R.E. ualb. c. fot. 7 post. LX. fot. Modo. c. folid.

LAND OF THE COUNT OF MEULAN

In STONELEIGH Hundred
1 The Count of Meulan holds MYTON from the King. 2 hides. Land
for 8 ploughs. Earl Algar held it. In lordship 1 (plough); 2 slaves;
    6 villagers and 11 smallholders with 3 ploughs.
    2 mills at 70s; meadow, 12 acres.
Value before 1066 £3; later 40s; now £6.

The Count himself holds
2 in MILVERTON 2 hides less 1 virgate. Leofwin held it; he was a
free man. Land for 8 ploughs. In lordship 1; 2 slaves;
    1 villager and 5 smallholders with 1 plough.
    A mill at 50s; meadow, 30 acres.
The value was 40s; now 100s.

3 WOODCOTE. 1 hide. Land for 2 ploughs. Kentwin and Thorbern
held it; they were free.
    4 villagers and 5 smallholders with 1 plough.
Value before 1066, 10s; now 30s.

4 in ROUNDSHILL. 1 hide. Waste.
    Woodland ½ league long and 2 furlongs wide; when exploited,
    value 10s.

[in HUNSBURY Hundred]
5 in (AVON) DASSETT 10 hides. 3 thanes held it; they were free.   5
Land for 12 ploughs. In lordship 3 ploughs; 10 slaves.
    12 villagers with a priest and 5 smallholders have 7 ploughs.
    Meadow, 50 acres.
Value before 1066 £10; later 40s; now £8.

6 in WARMINGTON 13 hides. Azor held it; he was a free man.   3
Land for 14 ploughs. In lordship 4; 12 slaves;
    36 villagers and 8 smallholders with 14 ploughs.
    Meadow, 69 acres.
Value before 1066 £10; now as much.

[in STONELEIGH Hundred]
7 in HARBURY 4½ hides. Leofwin and Alric held it and could
sell but could not depart with the land. Land for 10 ploughs.
In lordship 1 plough with 1 slave;
    9 villagers and 6 smallholders with 4 ploughs.
Value before 1066, 100s; later 60s; now 100s.

Ipſe com ten̄ *MORTONE*. Derman tenuit *IN ꝀEMESLAV HD̄.*

7 liƀ hō tenuit. Ibi ſunt. v. hidæ. Tra̅.ē.viii.car̅. In dn̄io

ſunt. iiii. car̅.7 xviii. ſerui.7 xx. uiƚƚi cū pƀro 7 i. borđ

hn̄t.vii. car̅. Ibi. xl. ac̅ p̄ti.

T.R.E.7 poſt. ualuit. vi. liƀ. modo. xi. liƀ.

Ipſe com ten̄ *WALTONE*. Saxi tenuit.7 liƀ hō fuit. Ibi ſunt

.v. hidæ. Tra̅.ē.vi.car̅. In dn̄io ſunt.iii.7 vi. ſerui.7 ix. uiƚƚi

7 i. borđ cū.iiii.car̅. Ibi moliñ de.vi. ſoliđ.

T.R.E.7 poſt. ualuit. vi. liƀ. Modo. vii. liƀ.

Ipſe com ten̄ *WALTONE*. Gida 7 Saied tenuer̅.7 liƀæ fuer̅.

Ibi ſunt. x. hidæ. Tra̅.ē.x. car̅. In dn̄io ſunt.ii.car̅.7 ix.

ſerui.7 xxxii. uiƚƚi 7 iii. borđ cū. x. car̅. Ibi. ii. molini

de. xii. ſoliđ.7 viii. ac̅ p̄ti. Silua. iiii. q̄rent̅ lg̅.7 ii. lat̅.

T.R.E. ualƀ. c. ſoƚ.7 poſt.iiii. liƀ. Modo. x. liƀ.

Ipſe com ten̄ *CONTONE*. Vluuard 7 Cantuin tenuer̅ 7 liƀi

fuer̅. Ibi. vii. hidæ ſunt. Tra̅.ē.viii. car̅. In dn̄io ſunt. iii.

7 vii. ſerui.7 xiiii. uiƚƚi cū pƀro 7 iii. borđ cū. v. car̅.

Ibi.x. ac̅ p̄ti. T.R.E. ualƀ. c. ſoƚ.7 poſt ſimiliꝉ. Modo. vi. liƀ.

Ipſe com ten̄ *CERLECOTE*. Saxi tenuit.7 liƀ hō fuit.

Ibi ſunt. iii. hidæ. Tra̅.ē. v. car̅. In dn̄io ſunt. ii.7 vii. ſerui.

7 xiiii. uiƚƚi 7 ii. borđ cū. v. car̅. Ibi. ii. molini de. xxi.

ſoliđ.7 xii. ac̅ p̄ti. T.R.E.7 poſt ualuit. l. ſoƚ. Modo. iiii. liƀ.

Ipſe com ten̄ *SCIREBVRNE*. Edric̃ *IN FERNECVBE HD̄.*

7 Leueget tenuer̅.7 liƀi fuer̅. Ibi ſunt. ii. hidæ 7 dim̄.

Tra̅.ē.vi. car̅. In dn̄io eſt. i.car̅.7 dim̄.7 iiii. ſerui.7 ix.

uiƚƚi cū pƀro 7 ii. borđ hn̄t. ii. car̅. Ibi. xvi. ac̅ p̄ti.

T.R.E. ualƀ. lx. ſoliđ.7 poſt. xl. ſoƚ. Modo. l. ſoliđ.

Ipſe com ten̄ *FVLEBROC*. Ælfled tenuit 7 liƀa fuit.

Ibi ſunt. ii. hidæ 7 dimiđ. Tra̅.ē.viii. car̅. In dn̄io.ē

una car̅ 7 dimiđ.7 iiii. ſerui.7 x. uiƚƚi 7 iii. borđ cū. v.

car̅. Ibi moliñ de. xii. ſoliđ.7 viii. ac̅ p̄ti.

T.R.E. ualƀ. lx. ſoƚ.7 poſt. xl. ſoƚ. Modo. lx. ſoliđ.

in TREMLOW Hundred

8 MORETON (MORRELL). Derman held it;. [he was]a free man. 5 hides.
Land for 8 ploughs. In lordship 4 ploughs; 18 slaves.
　　20 villagers with a priest and 1 smallholder have 7 ploughs.
　　Meadow, 40 acres.
Value before 1066 and later £6; now £11.

9 WALTON. Saxi held it; he was a free man. 5 hides.
Land for 6 ploughs. In lordship 3; 6 slaves;
　　9 villagers and 1 smallholder with 4 ploughs.
　　A mill at 6s.
Value before 1066 and later £3; now £7.

10 WALTON. Gytha and Saeith held it; they were free. 10 hides.
Land for 10 ploughs. In lordship 2 ploughs; 9 slaves;
　　32 villagers and 3 smallholders with 10 ploughs.
　　2 mills at 12s; meadow, 8 acres; woodland 4 furlongs
　　　long and 2 wide.
Value before 1066, 100s; later £4; now £10.

11 COMPTON (VERNEY). Wulfward and Kentwin held it; they were free.
7 hides. Land for 8 ploughs. In lordship 3; 7 slaves;
　　14 villagers with a priest and 3 smallholders with 5 ploughs.
　　Meadow, 10 acres.
Value before 1066, 100s; later the same; now £6.

12 CHARLECOTE. Saxi held it; he was a free man. 3 hides.
Land for 5 ploughs. In lordship 2; 7 slaves;
　　14 villagers and 2 smallholders with 5 ploughs.
　　2 mills at 21s; meadow, 12 acres.
Value before 1066 and later 50s; now £4.

in FERNCOMBE Hundred

13 SHERBOURNE. Edric and Leofgeat held it; they were free. 2½ hides.
Land for 6 ploughs. In lordship 1½ ploughs; 4 slaves.
　　9 villagers with a priest and 2 smallholders have 2 ploughs.
　　Meadow, 16 acres.
Value before 1066, 60s; later 40s; now 50s.

14 FULBROOK. Aelfled held it; she was free. 2½ hides. Land for 8 ploughs.
In lordship 1½ ploughs; 4 slaves;
　　10 villagers and 3 smallholders with 5 ploughs.
　　A mill at 12s; meadow, 8 acres.
Value before 1066, 60s; later 40s; now 60s.

★ Ipſe com̄ *SNITEFELD* . Sexi tenuit 7 lib̄ hō fuit . Ibi ſunt . IIII.ᵒʳ

hidæ . Tra . ē . XIIII . car̄ . In dn̄io ſunt . II . 7 x . ſerui . 7 XI . uiłłi

cū pb̄ro 7 IIII . bord̄ hn̄t . VI . car̄ . Ibi ſunt . XII . ac̄ p̄ti .

T . R . E . 7 poſt ualuit . IIII . lib̄ . Modo . c . ſolid̄ .

Ipſe com̄ ten *CLAVENDONE* . Boui tenuit . 7 lib̄ hō fuit .

Ibi ſunt . III . hidæ . Tra . ē . v . car̄ . In dn̄io . ē una . 7 XII . uiłłi

cū pb̄ro 7 XIIII . bord̄ hn̄t . v . car̄ . Ibi . III . ſerui . 7 XVI . ac̄

p̄ti . 7 una leŭu ſiluæ . cū onerat̄ . ual . x . ſoł .

Valuit . XL . ſolid̄ . Modo . IIII . lib̄ .

Ipſe com̄ ten *DONNELIE* . Aluuold tenuit 7 lib̄ hō fuit .

Ibi . ē una hida . Tra . II . car̄ . Ibi ſunt . VI . uiłłi 7 II . bord̄

cū . II . car̄ . Ibi haia hn̄s dimid̄ leŭu lḡ . 7 tn̄td̄ lat̄ .

Valuit . xx . ſolid̄ . Modo . xxx . ſolid̄ .

Ipſe com̄ ten *PRESTETONE* . Turbern tenuit 7 lib̄ hō fuit .

Ibi ſunt . v . hidæ . Tra . ē . III . car̄ . In dn̄io . ē una car̄ .

7 II . ſerui . 7 VII . bord̄ cū . I . franciḡ hn̄t . I . car̄ . Ibi mo

linū de . XVI . ſolid̄ . Silua . I . leŭu lḡ . 7 dim̄ leŭu lat̄ .

Cū onerat̄ . ual . x . ſolid̄ . Valuit . xxx . ſolid̄ . Modo . L . ſolid̄ .

Iſd̄ com̄ ten *CINTONE* . Britnod tenuit . 7 lib̄ hō fuit .

Ibi . ē una hida 7 dimid̄ . Tra . I . car̄ . Vaſta . ē . Val . v . ſolid̄ .

Silua ualet p̄ ann̄ . x . ſolid̄ . Tantd̄ ualuit T . R . E .

★ In Be | Ipſe com̄ ten *ILMEDONE* . Tres teini tenuer̄ 7 libi ferer̄ .
DRICES |
TON HD | Ibi ſunt . VII . hidæ . dimid̄ v træ min . Tra . ē . XII . car̄ .

In dn̄io ſunt . III . car̄ . 7 IX . ſerui . 7 XXIIII . uiłłi 7 III . bord̄

cū pb̄ro hn̄t . VIII . car̄ . Ibi . XL . ac̄ p̄ti .

T . R . E . ualb̄ . VII . lib̄ . 7 poſt . c . ſolid̄ . Modo . x . lib̄ .

Ipſe com̄ ten *WITECERCE* . p̄ . II . Maner̄ . Aluuin tenuit

7 potuit ire q̄ uoluit . Ibi ſunt . VII . hidæ . Tra . ē . XII . car̄ .

In dn̄io ſunt . III . car̄ . 7 VII . ſerui . 7 XVI . uiłłi 7 I . lib̄ hō

7 II . bord̄ cū pb̄ro . hn̄t . VIII . car̄ . Ibi . II . molini de . xx .

ſolid̄ . 7 xxx . ac̄ p̄ti . Valuit . VI . lib̄ . Modo . VIII . lib̄ 7 x . ſolid̄ .

15   SNITTERFIELD. Saxi held it; he was a free man. 4 hides.   240 a
    Land for 14 ploughs. In lordship 2; 10 slaves.
      11 villagers with a priest and 4 smallholders have 6 ploughs.
      Meadow, 12 acres.
    Value before 1066 and later £4; now 100s.

16   CLAVERDON. Bovi held it; he was a free man. 3 hides.
    Land for 5 ploughs. In lordship 1.
      12 villagers with a priest and 14 smallholders have 5 ploughs. 3 slaves.
      Meadow, 16 acres; woodland, 1 league; when exploited, value 10s.
    The value was 40s; now £4.

17   *DONNELIE.* Alfwold held it; he was a free man. 1 hide.
    Land for 2 ploughs.
      6 villagers and 2 smallholders with 2 ploughs.
      An enclosure which is ½ league long and as wide.
    The value was 20s; now 30s.

18   PRESTON (BAGOT). Thorbern held it; he was a free man. 5 hides.
    Land for 3 ploughs. In lordship 1 plough; 2 slaves.
      7 smallholders with 1 Frenchman have 1 plough.
      A mill at 16s; woodland 1 league long and ½ league
        wide; when exploited, value 10s.
    The value was 30s; now 50s.

19   The Count also holds KINGTON. Brictnoth held it; he was a free man.
    1½ hides. Land for 1 plough. Waste; value 5s.
      Woodland, value 10s a year; value before 1066 as much.

 The Count himself holds
  in BARCHESTON Hundred
20   ILMINGTON. 3 thanes held it; they were free. 7 hides less ½ virgate
of land. Land for 12 ploughs. In lordship 3 ploughs; 9 slaves.
      24 villagers and 3 smallholders with a priest have 8 ploughs.
      Meadow, 40 acres.
    Value before 1066 £7; later 100s; now £10.

21   WHITCHURCH, as two manors. Alwin held it and could go
where he would. 7 hides. Land for 12 ploughs.
In lordship 3 ploughs; 7 slaves.
      16 villagers, 1 free man and 2 smallholders with a priest
        have 8 ploughs.
      2 mills at 20s; meadow, 30 acres.
    The value was £6; now £8 10s.

★ Ipſe cõm ten̅ in *Cetitone* . II . hið 7 dimið *In Coleshelle hd̅* .
7 Leuuin̊ de eo . Celred 7 Godric tenuer̅ . 7 libi hões fuer̅ .
T̅ra . e̅ . III . car̅ . In dn̅io . e̅ una . 7 II . ſerui . 7 VII . uitti 7 IIII .
borð cū . II . car̅ . Ibi dimið molin̅ redð . v . ſot . 7 VIII . ac̅
p̅ti . Silua dimið leuu l̅g . 7 III . q̅rent̅ lat̅ .
Valet . xx . ſolið .
Ipſe cõm ten̅ in ead̅ uilla . II . hið 7 dimið . 7 Godric de eo .
Ide̅ tenuit T.R.E . 7 lib fuit . T̅ra . e̅ . v . car̅ . In dn̅io . e̅ una .
7 II . ſerui . 7 III . uitti 7 III . borð cū . I . car̅ . Ibi dimið molin̅
redð . v . ſolið . 7 VIII . ac̅ p̅ti . Silua dimið leuu l̅g . 7 III .
q̅rent̅ lat̅ . Valet . xx . ſolið .
Ipſe cõm ten̅ in *Wilmvndecote* . III . hið . 7 Ingenulf̊
7 Arnulf̊ de eo . Leuenot tenuit 7 lib hõ fuit . T̅ra . e̅ . vi .
car̅ . Ibi ſunt XI . uitti 7 v . borð cū . II . fabris hn̅tes . III .
car̅ 7 dimið . Silua . I . leuu l̅g . 7 dimið lat̅ . Vat . v . ſolið .
7 ferraria . v . ſolið . Valet . xxx . ſolið .
Ipſe cõm ten̅ in *Secintone* . II . hið 7 dimið . 7 Ingenulf
7 Arnulf̊ de eo . Godric tenuit 7 lib hõ fuit . T̅ra . e̅
v . car̅ . In dn̅io ſunt . II . car̅ . 7 VI . uitti 7 v . borð cū . III .
car̅ . Valet . xL . ſolið .
Ipſe cõm ten̅ in *Watitvne* . III . hið . 7 Hereuuard̊
de eo . Ide̅ tenuit T.R.E . 7 lib fuit . T̅ra . e̅ . vII . car̅ .
In dn̅io . e̅ una 7 dimið . 7 IIII . ſerui . 7 XII . uitti 7 v . borð .
cū . IIII . car̅ . Ibi . xx . ac̅ p̅ti . Silua . II . q̅rent̅ l̅g . 7 una
q̅rent̅ lat̅ . Valet . xxx . ſolið .

240 b

Ipſe cõm ten̅ in *Berchewelle* . I . hið . 7 Walt de eo . Leuenot
tenuit 7 lib fuit . Ibi . e̅ un̅ uitts cū dimið car̅ . Valet . v . ſolið .

in COLESHILL Hundred

22 in SHUTTINGTON 2½ hides. Leofwin holds from him. Ceolred
and Godric held it; they were free men. Land for 3 ploughs.
In lordship 1; 2 slaves;
    7 villagers and 4 smallholders with 2 ploughs.
    ½ mill which pays 5s; meadow, 8 acres; woodland ½ league
    long and 3 furlongs wide.
Value 20s.

23 in the same village 2½ hides. Godric holds from him; he also
held it before 1066; he was free. Land for 5 ploughs.
In lordship 1; 2 slaves;
    3 villagers and 3 smallholders with 1 plough.
    ½ mill which pays 5s; meadow, 8 acres; woodland ½ league
       long and 3 furlongs wide.
Value 20s.

24 in WILNECOTE 3 hides. Ingenwulf and Arnulf hold from him.
Leofnoth held it; he was a free man. Land for 6 ploughs.
    11 villagers and 5 smallholders with 2 smiths who have 3½ ploughs.
    Woodland 1 league long and ½ wide, value 5s;
       a forge, 5s.
Value 30s.

25 in SECKINGTON 2½ hides. Ingenwulf and Arnulf hold from him.
Godric held it; he was a free man. Land for 5 ploughs. In
lordship 2 ploughs;
    6 villagers and 5 smallholders with 3 ploughs.
Value 40s.

26 in WEDDINGTON 3 hides. Hereward holds from him; he also
held it before 1066; he was free. Land for 7 ploughs.
In lordship 1½; 4 slaves;
    12 villagers and 5 smallholders with 4 ploughs.
    Meadow, 20 acres; woodland 2 furlongs long and 1 furlong wide.
Value 30s.

27 in BERKSWELL 1 hide. Walter holds from him. Leofnoth held   240 b
it; he was free.
    1 villager with ½ plough.
Value 5s.

Ipſe com̄ teñ in *WERLAVESCOTE*.iii.v̆ træ̆.Saxi libere
tenuit T.R.E.Tră.ē.i.car̄.Ibi.ē ipſa cū.ii.uillis.7 iii.ac̄
p̃ti.Valet.ii.ſolid̄.

Ipſe com̄ teñ in *FRANCHETONE*.i.hid̄ 7 unā v̆ træ̆.7 Ran
nulf⁹ de eo.Tră.ē.iii.car̄.In dñio.ē una.7 ii.ſerui.7 iiii.
uilti 7 i.bord̄ cū.i.car̄.Ibi.x.ac̄ p̃ti.Valuit 7 ual.xx.ſol.
Chentuiñ⁹ libe tenuit.T.R.E.

Ipſe com̄ teñ in *BORTONE*.v.hid̄.7 Ingenulf⁹ de eo.Tră.ē
viii.car̄.In dñio ſunt.iii.7 vii.ſerui.7 xiii.uilti 7 xi.
bord̄ cū.iii.car̄ 7 dimid̄.7 uñ miles h̄t ibi.i.car̄ 7 dim̆.
Ibi.l.ac̄ p̃ti.Valuit.lx.ſol.Modo.lxx.ſol.
Leuuiñ⁹ libere tenuit T.R.E.

Ipſe com̄ teñ in *NEPTONE*.iii.hid̄ 7 iii.v̆ træ̆.7 Rob̄t⁹ de eo.
Tră.ē.viii.car̄.In dñio ſunt.ii.7 iiii.ſerui.7 xi.uilti
cū pb̄ro 7 viii.bord̄ h̄ñt.iiii.car̄ 7 dimid̄.Ibi.x.ac̄ p̃ti.
7 totid̄ paſturæ.Valuit.iiii.lib̄.Modo.iii.lib̄.
Leuenot 7 Bundi tenuer̄ libere.T.R.E.

Ipſe com̄ teñ in *SOCHEBERGE*.iiii.hid̄.7 Herleuiñ⁹ de eo.
Tră.ē.iiii.car̄.In dñio ſunt.ii.7 ii.ſerui.7 viii.uilti
7 vi.bord̄ cū.iii.car̄ 7 dimid̄.Ibi.vi.ac̄ p̃ti.
Valuit xl.ſol.7 poſt.xxx.ſol.Modo.l.ſol.
Leuuiñ⁹ libere tenuit T.R.E.

Ipſe com̄ teñ in *TORLAVESTONE*.ii.hid̄ 7 dim̄.7 Rob̄t⁹
de eo.Tră.ē.vi.car̄.In dñio.ē una.7 ii.ancillæ.7 iiii.
uilti 7 i.bord̄ cū.ii.car̄.Ibi.l.ac̄ p̃ti.7 ii.q̃rent̄ paſturæ.
Valuit xl.ſol.7 poſt.xxx.Modo.xxx.v.ſol.
Wlgar libe tenuit T.R.E.

28   in *WERLAVESCOTE* 3 virgates of land. Saxi held it freely before 1066.
Land for 1 plough. It is there, with
  2 villagers.
  Meadow, 3 acres.
Value 2s.

  [in MARTON Hundred]
29   in FRANKTON 1 hide and 1 virgate of land. Ranulf holds from him.
Land for 3 ploughs. In lordship 1; 2 slaves;
  4 villagers and 1 smallholder with 1 plough.
  Meadow, 10 acres.
The value was and is 20s.
  Kentwin held it freely before 1066.

30   in BOURTON (-on-Dunsmore) 5 hides. Ingenwulf holds from
him. Land for 8 ploughs. In lordship 3; 7 slaves;
  13 villagers and 11 smallholders with 3½ ploughs;
    1 man-at-arms has 1½ ploughs.
  Meadow, 50 acres.
The value was 60s; now 70s.
  Leofwin held it freely before 1066.

31   in NAPTON 3 hides and 3 virgates of land. Robert holds from
him. Land for 8 ploughs. In lordship 2; 4 slaves.
  11 villagers with a priest and 8 smallholders have 4½ ploughs.
  Meadow, 10 acres; pasture, as many.
The value was £4; now £3.
  Leofnoth and Bondi held it freely before 1066.

32   in SHUCKBURGH 4 hides. Herlwin holds from him. Land for 4 ploughs.
In lordship 2; 2 slaves;
  8 villagers and 6 smallholders with 3½ ploughs.
  Meadow, 6 acres.
The value was 40s; later 30s; now 50s.
  Leofwin held it freely before 1066.

33   in THURLASTON 2½ hides. Robert holds from him.
Land for 6 ploughs. In lordship 1; 2 female slaves;
  4 villagers and 1 smallholder with 2 ploughs.
  Meadow, 50 acres; pasture, 2 furlongs.
The value was 40s; later 30s; now 35s.
  Wulfgar held it freely before 1066.

Ipſe com̄ ten̄ in *HODENELLE* .IIII.hiđ.7 Giſlebt de eo.

Tra.ē.IIII.car̄.In dn̄io.ē una.7 un̄ miles cū VI.uiłłis

7 III.borđ hт̄.III.car̄.Ibi.xx.ac̄ p̄ti.

Valuit.xx.ſoł.7 poſt.xL.Modo.Lx.Ordric libere tenuit T.R.E.

Ipſe com̄ ten̄ in *MORTONE*.I.hiđ 7 dim̄.7 Mereuin de eo.

Tra.ē.VI.car̄.In dn̄io.ē una.7 I.ſeru.7 v.uiłłi 7 VI.borđ

cū.III.car̄.Ibi.xII.ac̄ p̄ti.Valuit.xxx.ſoł.7 poſt xxv.ſoł.

Modo.xxx.ſoliđ.Mereuuin 7 Scrotin 7 Wallef libe tenueŕ.

Ipſe com̄ ten̄ in eađ uilla.I.hiđ 7 I.v træ.7 Wallef de eo.

Tra.ē.VI.car̄.In dn̄io.ē una.cū.I.ſeruo.7 x.uiłłi 7 VII.

borđ cū.IIII.car̄.Ibi.xII.ac̄ p̄ti.Valuit.L.ſoł.7 poſt 7 modo

xL.v.ſoliđ.Scroti libe tenuit T.R.E.

Ipſe com̄ ten̄ in *MORTONE* dimiđ hidā.7 Wallef de eo.

Tra.ē.II.car̄.Ibi ſunt.III.uiłłi cū.I.borđ 7 I.ſeruo.hn̄t.I.car̄.

7 VI.ac̄ p̄ti ibi.Valuit.xv.ſoliđ.Modo.x.ſoliđ.

Wallef iđē tenuit libe T.R.E.   *IN BOMELAV HVNĐ.*

Ipſe com̄ ten̄ in *WESTONE*.II.hiđ.7 Fulco de eo.Tra.ē.VII.

car̄.In dn̄io.ē una.7 VI.uiłłi 7 VII.borđ cū.III.car̄.Ibi.VIII.

ac̄ p̄ti.Valuit 7 uał.xL.ſoliđ.

Ipſe com̄ ten̄ in *WIBETOT* 7 in *WELEI* dimiđ hiđ.7 Fulco

de eo.Tra.ē.IIII.car̄.In dn̄io ſunt.II.7 III.uiłłi 7 IIII.borđ

cū.II.car̄.Ibi.xL.ac̄ p̄ti.Valuit 7 uał.xxx.ſoliđ.

34 in HODNELL 4 hides. Gilbert holds from him.
Land for 4 ploughs. In lordship 1.
    1 man-at-arms with 6 villagers and 3 smallholders has 3 ploughs.
    Meadow, 20 acres.
The value was 20s; later 40s; now 60s.
    Ordric held it freely before 1066.

35 in (HILL)MORTON 1½ hides. Merwin holds from him. Land for 6 ploughs.
In lordship 1; 1 slave;
    5 villagers and 6 smallholders with 3 ploughs.
    Meadow, 12 acres.
The value was 30s; later 25s; now 30s.
    Merwin, Scroti, and Waltheof held it freely.

36 in the same village 1 hide and 1 virgate of land.
Waltheof holds from him. Land for 6 ploughs.
In lordship 1, with 1 slave;
    10 villagers and 7 smallholders with 4 ploughs.
    Meadow, 12 acres.
The value was 50s; later and now 45s.
    Scroti held it freely before 1066.

37 in (HILL)MORTON ½ hide. Waltheof holds from him. Land for 2 ploughs.
    3 villagers with 1 smallholder and 1 slave have 1 plough.
    Meadow, 6 acres.
The value was 15s; now 10s.
    Waltheof also held it freely before 1066.

   in BRINKLOW Hundred
38 in WESTON (-in-Arden) 2 hides. Fulk holds from him.
Land for 7 ploughs. In lordship 1;
    6 villagers and 7 smallholders with 3 ploughs.
    Meadow, 8 acres.
The value was and is 40s.

39 in WIBTOFT and in WILLEY ½ hide. Fulk holds from him.
Land for 4 ploughs. In lordship 2;
    3 villagers and 4 smallholders with 2 ploughs.
    Meadow, 40 acres.
The value was and is 30s.

Ipſe cõm teñ in ead uilla.ii.hiđ 7 dimiđ.7 Robt de eo.
Tra.ē.v.car̃.In dñio ſunt.ii.7 v.uilli 7 iii.borđ cũ.ii.francig
hñt.iii.car̃.Ibi.xxx.aͨ p̃ti.Valuit 7 ual.l.ſoliđ.
Has.iii.tras tenuit Sexi libere.T.R.E.

Ipſe cõm teñ in BOCHINTONE.iiii.hiđ 7 unã v̾ træ.7 Salo de eo.
Tra.ē.viii.car̃.In dñio.ē una.7 ii.ſerui.7 v.uilli cũ.i.car̃.
Ibi.c.aͨ p̃ti.Valuit 7 ual xx.ſoliđ.Aliet 7 Alſi libe tenuer̃.

Ipſe cõm teñ in ESTLEIA.i.hiđ.7 Godric de eo.Tra.ē.ii.car̃.

240 c

In dñio.ē una car̃.7 v.uilli 7 iii.borđ cũ.i.car̃.Silua.i.leuŭ
lg̃.7 dim leuŭ lat̃.Cũ onerat̃.ual.x.ſol.Valuit 7 ual.xx.ſol.
Alſi libere tenuit.T.R.E.

★ Ipſe cõm in SMERECOTE 7 in SOVLEGE.i.hiđ.7 Godric de eo.
Tra.ē.ii.car̃.Ibi ſunt.ii.uilli.Silua.i.leuŭ lg̃.7 dim leu lat̃.
Cũ onerat̃.ual.x.ſoliđ.Valuit.xv.ſol.Modo.v.ſoliđ.
Sexi libere tenuit.T.R.E.

Ipſe cõm teñ in BEDEWORD.iiii.hiđ.7 Vlſchetel de eo.
Tra.ē.vi.car̃.In dñio.ē una.7 ii.ſerui.7 v.uilli 7 iii.borđ.
cũ.ii.car̃.Ibi.xvi.aͨ p̃ti.Silua.i.leu lg̃.7 dim leu lat̃.
Val.x.ſol cũ onerat̃.Valuit 7 ual.xl.ſol.Eduin tenuit.

Ipſe cõm teñ in SCELFTONE.ii.hiđ.7 Wallef de eo.Tra.ē
.iii.car̃.In dñio.ē.i.car̃.7 vi.uilli 7 ii.borđ cũ.ii.car̃.
Ibi.iiii.aͨ p̃ti.Silua.ii.q̃rent lg̃.7 una q̃rent lat̃.

Valuit 7 ual.xl.ſoliđ.Idẽ Wallef libe tenuit.T.R.E.

240 b, c

40 in the same village 2½ hides. Robert holds from him.
Land for 5 ploughs. In lordship 2.
    5 villagers and 3 smallholders with 2 Frenchmen have 3 ploughs.
    Meadow, 30 acres.
The value was and is 50s.
    Saxi held these three lands freely before 1066.

41 in BULKINGTON 4 hides and 1 virgate of land. Salo holds from him.
Land for 8 ploughs. In lordship 1; 2 slaves;
    5 villagers with 1 plough.
    Meadow, 100 acres.
The value was and is 20s.
    Alfgeat and Alfsi held it freely.

42 in ASTLEY 1 hide. Godric holds from him. Land for 2 ploughs.
In lordship 1 plough;   240 c
    5 villagers and 3 smallholders with 1 plough.
    Woodland 1 league long and ½ league wide; when exploited, value 10s.
The value was and is 20s.
    Alfsi held it freely before 1066.

43 in SMERCOTE and in 'SOLE' 1 hide. Godric holds from him.
Land for 2 ploughs.
    2 villagers.
    Woodland 1 league long and ½ league wide; when exploited, value 10s.
The value was 15s; now 5s.
    Saxi held it freely before 1066.

44 in BEDWORTH 4 hides. Ulfketel holds from him. Land for 6 ploughs.
In lordship 1; 2 slaves;
    5 villagers and 3 smallholders with 2 ploughs.
    Meadow, 16 acres; woodland 1 league long and ½ league wide;
      value 10s when exploited.
The value was and is 40s.
    Earl Edwin held it.

45 in SHILTON 2 hides. Waltheof holds from him. Land for 3 ploughs.
In lordship 1 plough;
    6 villagers and 2 smallholders with 2 ploughs.
    Meadow, 4 acres; woodland 2 furlongs long and 1 furlong wide.
The value was and is 40s.
    Waltheof also held it freely before 1066.

Ipse cõm teñ in _MERSTONE_.i.hiđ.7 Hereuuard de eo.Tra

ē.iiii.car. In dñio funt.ii.7 una ancilla.7 xii.uitti 7 viii.

borđ cũ.iiii.car.Ibi.vi.ac pti.Valuit 7 uat.iii.liƀ.

Idem Hereuuard tenuit.T.R.E. _IN MERETONE HĐ_

Ipse cõm teñ in _LODBROC_.ii.hiđ.Tra.ē.iii.car. In dñio.ē una.

Witts ten de eo.Ibi funt.iiii.uitti 7 i.borđ.cũ.ii.car.7 x.ac pti.

Valuit.xx.foliđ.Modo.l.foliđ.

Ipse cõm teñ in _BERNHANGRE_.iii.virg træ.7 Hereuuard

de eo.Tra.ē.ii.car.Ibi funt.ii.uitti 7 ii.borđ cũ.i.car.

Silua.iiii.qrent lg.7 iii.lat.Valuit 7 uat.xx.foliđ.

Idē Hereuuard liƀe tenuit T.R.E.

Ipse cõm teñ 7 Gisleƀt de eo.ii.hiđ 7 una v træ quæ ptiñ

ad Stanlei M comitis.Ibi.ē.i.car in dñio.Valet.xx.fot.

Ipse cõm teñ in _ILLINTONE_.iiii.hiđ.7 Wariñ 7 Roger de eo.

Tra.ē.iiii.car. In dñio.ē una.7 iiii.ferui.7 ii.uitti 7 iii.borđ

cũ.i.car.Ibi moliñ de.vi.fot 7 viii.deñ.Ibi.ix.ac pti.

Silua.i.leuu lg.7 dimiđ lat.Valuit.xx.fot.Modo.xl.fot.

Edric libere tenuit T.R.E.

Ipse cõm teñ in _WIDECOTE_.i.hiđ.7 Gisleƀt de eo.Tra.ē.i.car.

Ibi.i.miles cũ.ii.uittis 7 ix.borđ ht.i.car 7 dimiđ.Silua

ht.i.leuu lg.7 dimiđ lat.Valuit.x.foliđ.Modo.xx.fot.

Leuric liƀe tenuit.T.R.E.

46 in MARSTON (JABBETT). 1 hide. Hereward holds from him.
Land for 4 ploughs. In lordship 2; 1 female slave;
12 villagers and 8 smallholders with 4 ploughs.
Meadow, 6 acres.
The value was and is £3.
Hereward also held it freely before 1066.

in MARTON Hundred
47 in LADBROKE 2 hides. Land for 3 ploughs. In lordship 1.
William holds from him.
4 villagers and 1 smallholder with 2 ploughs.
Meadow, 10 acres.
The value was 20s; now 50s.

[in BRINKLOW Hundred]
48 in BARNACLE 3 virgates of land. Hereward holds from him.
Land for 2 ploughs.
2 villagers and 2 smallholders with 1 plough.
Woodland 4 furlongs long and 3 wide.
The value was and is 20s.
Hereward also held it freely before 1066.

49 [in....] 2 hides and 1 virgate of land which belong to the Count's
manor of Stoneleigh. Gilbert holds from him. In lordship 1 plough.
Value 20s.

[in STONELEIGH Hundred]
50 in LILLINGTON 4 hides. Warin and Roger hold from him.
Land for 4 ploughs. In lordship 1; 4 slaves;
2 villagers and 3 smallholders with 1 plough.
A mill at 6s 8d; meadow, 9 acres; woodland 1 league
long and ½ wide.
The value was 20s; now 40s.
Edric held it freely before 1066.

51 in WOODCOTE 1 hide. Gilbert holds from him. Land for 1 plough.
1 man-at-arms with 2 villagers and 9 smallholders have 1½ ploughs.
The woodland is 1 league long and ½ league wide.
The value was 10s; now 20s.
Leofric held it freely before 1066.

Ipſe com̄ ten̄ in *WESTONE* . III . hid̄ . tcia parte v̄ min̄.

7 Robt de eo . Tra . e̅ . v . car̄ . In dn̄io ſunt . II . 7 II . ancillæ.

Ibi . I . miles 7 III . uiłłi . 7 VII . bord̄ cū . II . car̄ . 7 XII . ac̄ p̄ti.

Spinetū . II . q̄rent lḡ . 7 una lat̄ . Valuit . xxx . ſol̄ . M . L . ſolid̄.

Ipſe com̄ ten̄ in *CVBITONE* . III . hid̄ . Vlf tenuit libe . T.R.E.

7 Boſcher de eo . Tra . e̅ . III . car̄ . In dn̄io . e̅ una car̄ cū . III .

bord̄ . Ibi . VIII . ac̄ p̄ti . Valuit . xL . ſolid̄ . Modo . xxx . ſolid̄.

Leuuin 7 Chetelbern libe tenue̅r . T.R.E. *IN HONESBERIE HD̄.*

Ipſe com̄ ten̄ in *WIMERESTONE* . I . hid̄ 7 dimid̄ . Tra . e̅

. v . car̄ . Gislebt ten̄ de eo . In dn̄io ſunt . II . car̄ . 7 vI . ſerui.

7 xv . uiłłi 7 II . bord̄ cū . vII . car̄ . 7 p̄bro . Ibi . Ix . ac̄ p̄ti.

Valuit . xxx . ſoł . 7 poſt . xx . ſoł . Modo . IIII . lib̄ 7 x . ſolid̄.

Leuric libere tenuit T.R.E.

Ipſe com̄ ten̄ in *WARMINTONE* . II . hid̄ 7 dimid̄ . 7 q̇d̄a miles

de eo . Azor libe tenuit T.R.E. Valet . xx . ſolid̄ . V̄rata ſuṅ.

Quæ hic miles ibi ht̄ . cū hōum pecunia qui in M̄ comit̄ nume̅

Ipſe com̄ ten̄ in *ORLAVESCOTE* . v . hid̄ 7 S Petrus p̄tellens

de eo . Tra . e̅ . v . car̄ . In dn̄io . e̅ una car̄ 7 dimid̄ . 7 II . ſerui . 7 IIII .

uiłłi 7 III . bord̄ cū . II . car̄ . Ibi . xII . ac̄ p̄ti . Valuit 7 uał . III . lib̄.

Boui tenuit libe T.R.E.

Ipſe com̄ ten̄ in *CONTONE* . IIII . hid̄ 7 III . virg træ . 7 Gislebt de

eo . Tra . e̅ . vI . car̄ . In dn̄io ſunt . II . car̄ . 7 vII . ſerui . 7 vIII . uiłłi

cū p̄bro 7 vI . bord̄ cū . IIII . car̄ . Ibi . xL . ac̄ p̄ti . Valuit . Lx . ſoł.

Modo . IIII . lib̄ . Aluricus libere tenuit . T.R.E.

52 in WESTON (-under-Wetherley) 3 hides less a third part of one virgate.
Robert holds from him. Land for 5 ploughs. In lordship 2;2 female slaves.
    1 man-at-arms, 3 villagers and 7 smallholders with 2 ploughs.
    Meadow, 12 acres; a spinney 2 furlongs long and 1 wide.
The value was 30s; now 50s.
    Ulf held it freely before 1066.

53 in CUBBINGTON 3 hides. Bosker holds from him. Land for 3 ploughs.
In lordship 1 plough, with
    3 smallholders.
    Meadow, 8 acres.
The value was 40s; now 30s.
    Leofwin and Ketelbern held it freely before 1066.

   in HUNSBURY Hundred
54 in WORMLEIGHTON 1½ hides. Land for 5 ploughs. Gilbert holds
from him. In lordship 2 ploughs; 6 slaves;
    15 villagers and 2 smallholders with 7 ploughs and
      with a priest.
    Meadow, 9 acres.
The value was 30s; later 20s; now £4 10s.
    Leofric held it freely before 1066.

55 in WARMINGTON 2½ hides. A man-at-arms holds from him.
Azor held it freely before 1066.
Value 20s.
 What this man-at-arms has there is enumerated with the stock of the
men who are in the Count's manor.

56 in ARLESCOTE 5 hides. St. Peter's of Preaux holds from him.
Land for 5 ploughs. In lordship 1½ ploughs; 2 slaves;
    4 villagers and 3 smallholders with 2 ploughs.
    Meadow, 12 acres.
The value was and is £3.
    Bovi held it freely before 1066.

57 in (FENNY) COMPTON 4 hides and 3 virgates of land. Gilbert holds
from him. Land for 6 ploughs. In lordship 2 ploughs; 7 slaves;
    8 villagers with a priest and 6 smallholders with 4 ploughs.
    Meadow, 40 acres.
The value was 60s; now £4.
    Aelfric held it freely before 1066.

Ipſe coɱ ten in *TACESBROC*.viii.hiđ.una v̅ min.7 Roger
de eo.Tra.e̅.vi.car.In dɳio.e̅ dimiđ car.7 v.uiłłi 7 vii.
borđ cū.iii.car.Ibi.xii.ac̅ p̅ti.Valuit.lx.ſoł.M̥.xl.
Baldeuin liƀe tenuit T.R.E.

Ipſe coɱ ten in *NIWEBOLD*.ii.hiđ.7 Gisleƀt de eo.Tra.e̅
iiii.car.In dɳio ſunt.ii.7 vi.uiłłi 7 iiii.borđ cū.iiii.car.
Ibi.xii.ac̅ p̅ti.Valuit.xxx.ſoliđ.Modo.l.ſoł.

Alſi Ailred 7 Tube liƀe tenuer̅.T.R.E. *IN PATELAV HĐ.*
Ipſe coɱ ten in *LVDITONE*.xii.hiđ.7 iiii.milites de eo.
Tra.e̅.ix.car.In dɳio ſunt.v.car.7 xx.uiłłi 7 ix.borđ
cū.v.car.Ibi.xlii.ac̅ p̅ti.Valuit.viii.liƀ.Modo.vi.liƀ.
Quattuor teini liƀe tenuer̅.T.R.E. p.ii.Maner.

Ipſe coɱ ten in *LOCHESLEI*.iiii.hiđ.7 Hugo de eo.una v̅
min.Tra.e̅.viii.car.In dɳio ſunt.ii.7 iii.ſerui.7 xi.uiłłi
cū pƀro 7 xi.borđ hɳt.vi.car.Valuit xxx.ſoł.Modo.iiii.
liƀ 7 x.ſoliđ.Eſtan liƀe tenuit T.R.E.

Ipſe coɱ ten in *PRESTETONE*.v.hiđ.7 Hugo de eo.Tra.e̅
iii.car.In dɳio.e̅ dim car.7 ii.ſerui.7 i.uiłłs 7 iii.borđ
cū.i.car.Valuit.xxx.ſoł.Modo.xl.Britnod liƀe tenuit.T.R.E.

Ipſe coɱ ten in *OVESLEI*.iii.hiđ 7 Fulco de eo.Tra.e̅.iiii.
car.In dɳio.e̅ una.7 v.uiłłi 7 v.borđ cū.ii.car.Ibi mo
linū de.iiii.ſoł 7 vi.ac̅ p̅ti.Silua.iii.q̅rent lg̅.7 una lat̅.

[in STONELEIGH Hundred]

58 in TACHBROOK(MALLORY) 8 hides less 1 virgate. Roger holds   240 d
from him. Land for 6 ploughs. In lordship ½ plough;
     5 villagers and 7 smallholders with 3 ploughs.
     Meadow, 12 acres.
The value was 60s; now 40s.
Baldwin held it freely before 1066.

59 in NEWBOLD (COMYN) 2 hides. Gilbert holds from him.
Land for 4 ploughs. In lordship 2;
     6 villagers and 4 smallholders with 4 ploughs.
     Meadow, 12 acres.
The value was 30s; now 50s.
Alfsi, Aelred and Tubbi held it freely before 1066.

in PATHLOW Hundred
60 in LUDDINGTON 12 hides. 4 men-at-arms hold from him.
Land for 9 ploughs. In lordship 5 ploughs;
     20 villagers and 9 smallholders with 5 ploughs.
     Meadow, 42 acres.
The value was £8; now £6.
Four thanes held it freely before 1066 as two manors.

61 in LOXLEY 4 hides less 1 virgate. Hugh holds from him.
Land for 8 ploughs. In lordship 2; 3 slaves.
     11 villagers with a priest and 11 smallholders have 6 ploughs.
The value was 30s; now £4 10s.
Alstan held it freely before 1066.

[in FERNCOMBE Hundred]

62 in PRESTON (BAGOT) 5 hides. Hugh holds from him. Land for 3 ploughs.
In lordship ½ plough; 2 slaves;
     1 villager and 3 smallholders with 1 plough.
The value was 30s; now 40s.
Brictnoth held it freely before 1066.

63 in OVERSLEY 3 hides. Fulk holds from him. Land for 4 ploughs.
In lordship 1;
     5 villagers and 5 smallholders with 2 ploughs.
     A mill at 4s; meadow, 6 acres; woodland 3 furlongs long
       and 1 wide.

Valuit 7 ual̃.xl.fol̃.Britmar libe tenuit.T.R.E.   ⌐HD̃.

Ipſe com̃ ten̄ in *ILMEDONE*.i.hid̃ 7 dim̃ virg̃ *IN BERRICES⌐*
7 Qdard de eo.Ibi h̄t in dñio.ii.car̃.7 vi.feru.7 vi.uitti
cũ dimid̃ car̃.Valet.xl.folid̃.H̃ tra.ē in m̃ comitis *ILMEDON*.
In *WITECERCE* m̃ comitis ten̄ Walter de eo.i.hid̃.7 ibi
h̄t.i.car̃.7 ualet.x.folid̃.Aluuin̄ libe tenuit T.R.E.
Ipſe com̃ ten̄ in *VLWARDA*.iiii.hid̃ 7 dimid̃.7 Radulf̄ de
eo.Tra.ē.iiii.car̃.In dñio.ē una.7 ii.ferui.7 iii.uitti
7 v.bord̃.cũ.i.car̃.Valuit.xxx.fol̃.Modo.xl.folid̃.
Aluric tenuit libe T.R.E.

.XVII. TERRA TVRCHIL DE WARWIC. *IN COLESHELLE HVND̃*.

Tvrchil ten̄ de rege *CREDEWORDE*.Ibi funt.iiii.hidæ.
Tra.ē.vii.car̃.In dñio funt.iii.car̃.7 iii.ferui.7 xii.uitti
7 vii.bord̃ cũ.v.car̃.Ibi.xvi.ac̃ p̃ti.Silua dim̃ leuu
lg̃.7 tntd̃ lat̃.Valuit.xl.folid̃.Modo.l.folid̃.Vluuin̄
Idem Turchil ten̄ *BICHEHELLE*.Ibi ⌐libere tenuit.T.R.E.
funt.ii.hidæ.Tra.ē.iiii.car̃.In dñio.ē dimid̃ car̃.7 vii.uitti
7 iiii.bord̃ cũ.iii.car̃.Ibi.iii.ac̃ p̃ti.Silua.iiii.q̃rent̃ lg̃.7 tntd̃
lat̃.Valuit 7 ual̃.xxx.folid̃.Aluuard libe tenuit.T.R.E.
Id̃e.T.ten̄ alia *BICHEHELLE*.Ibi funt.ii.hidæ.Tra.ē.iiii.
car̃.Ibi funt.viii.uitti cũ.ii.car̃ Silua ibi.xii.q̃rent̃ lg̃.
7 vi.lat̃.Valuit.xx.fol̃.Modo.x.fol̃.Aluric libe tenuit T.R.E.

The value was and is 40s.
Brictmer held it freely before 1066.

in BARCHESTON Hundred

64 in ILMINGTON 1 hide and ½ virgate. Odard holds from him.
He has in lordship 2 ploughs; 6 slaves;
6 villagers with ½ plough.
Value 40s.
This land is in the Count's manor of Ilmington.

65 In WHITCHURCH, a manor of the Count's, Walter holds 1 hide
from him; he has 1 plough.
Value 10s.
Alwin held it freely before 1066.

66 The Count himself holds 4½ hides in WOLFORD. Ralph holds
from him. Land for 4 ploughs. In lordship 1; 2 slaves;
3 villagers and 5 smallholders with 1 plough.
The value was 30s; now 40s.
Aelfric held it freely before 1066.

17   LAND OF THORKELL OF WARWICK

In COLESHILL Hundred

1 Thorkell holds CURDWORTH from the King. 4 hides.
Land for 7 ploughs. In lordship 3 ploughs; 3 slaves;
12 villagers and 7 smallholders with 5 ploughs.
Meadow, 16 acres; woodland ½ league long and as wide.
The value was 40s; now 50s.
Wulfwin held it freely before 1066.

Thorkell also holds

2 BICKENHILL. 2 hides. Land for 4 ploughs. In lordship ½ plough;
7 villagers and 4 smallholders with 3 ploughs.
Meadow, 3 acres; woodland 4 furlongs long and as wide.
The value was and is 30s.
Alfward held it freely before 1066.

3 the other BICKENHILL. 2 hides. Land for 4 ploughs.
8 villagers with 2 ploughs.
Woodland 12 furlongs long and 6 wide.
The value was 20s; now 10s.
Aelfric held it freely before 1066.

Idē.T.teñ in *MENEWORDE*.I.hiđ.Tra.ē.I.car.Ibi.ē uñ
uitts cū dimiđ car.7 v.ac pti.Silua dim leuu lg.7 III.qrent
lat.Valuit 7 uat.v.soliđ.Godric libe tenuit T.R.E.

Idē.T.teñ *VLFELMESCOTE*.Ibi funt *IN MERETONE HĐ*
IIII.hidæ 7 dimiđ.Tra.ē.III.car.In dñio.ē una.7 IIII.ferui.
7 VII.uitti cū pbro 7 x.borđ hñt.IIII.car.Ibi.v.ac pti.
Valuit 7 uat.XL.soliđ.Afchil libe tenuit.T.R.E.

Idem.T.teñ in *RIETONE*.III.hiđ¡Tra.ē.x.car. *IN STANLEI HĐ.*
Ibi funt.XXIII.uitti cū pbro 7 VIII.borđ hñtes.VIII.car
7 ibi moliñ đe.XII.soliđ.7 XII.ac pti.Silua dimid leuu
lg.7 II.qrent lat.Valuit.c.fot.Modo.LX.soliđ.
Aluuiñ pat ej libe tenuit.T.R.E.

De Turchil teñ Gudmund *PATITONE*.
Ibi funt.IIII.hidæ.Tra.ē.III.car.In dñio.ē una.7 VII.
uitti 7 VIII.borđ cū.III.car.Ibi.II.molini de.II.fot
7 x.ac pti.Silua.I.leuu lg.7 I.lat.uat.xx.fot
cū onerat.Totū ualuit 7 uat.XXX.fot.Aluuard tenuit.

De.T.teñ Almar *LANGEDONE*.Ibi funt.II.hidæ 7 dim.
Tra.ē.II.car.In dñio.ē dimiđ.7 VI.uitti 7 III.borđ hñt
.I.car 7 dim.Ibi.VI.ac pti.Silua.I.leuu lg.7 dim lat.
Valuit 7 uat.xx.foliđ.Arnul tenuit T.R.E.

De.T.teñ Alnod *MACHITONE*.Ibi funt.v.hidæ.una v
min.Tra.ē.v.car.Ibi funt.x.uitti 7 IIII.borđ cū.III.car.
7 II.ac pti.Silua.I.leuu lg.7 dimiđ lat.Valuit.xx.
fot.Modo.XL.foliđ.Ailmund libe tenuit T.R.E.

4   in MINWORTH. 1 hide. Land for 1 plough.
      1 villager with ½ plough.
      Meadow, 5 acres; woodland ½ league long and 3 furlongs wide.
    The value was and is 5s.
      Godric held it freely before 1066.

    in MARTON Hundred
5   WOLFHAMPCOTE.4½ hides. Land for 3 ploughs. In lordship 1; 4 slaves.
      7 villagers with a priest and 10 smallholders have 4 ploughs.
      Meadow, 5 acres.
    The value was and is 40s.
      Askell held it freely before 1066.

    in STONELEIGH Hundred
6   in RYTON (-on-Dunsmore). 3½ hides. Land for 10 ploughs.
      23 villagers with a priest and 8 smallholders who have 8 ploughs.
      A mill at 12s; meadow, 12 acres; woodland ½ league
        long and 2 furlongs wide.
    The value was 100s; now 60s.
      His father, Alwin, held it freely before 1066.

    From Thorkell
    [in COLESHILL Hundred]   241 a
7   his brother, Godmund, holds PACKINGTON.   4 hides.
    Land for 3 ploughs. In lordship 1;
      7 villagers and 8 smallholders with 3 ploughs.
      2 mills at 2s; meadow, 10 acres; woodland 1 league long
        and 1 wide; value 20s when exploited.
    The total value was and is 30s.
      Alfward held it; he was free.

8   Aelmer holds LONGDON. 2½ hides. Land for 2 ploughs. In lordship ½.
      6 villagers and 3 smallholders have 1½ ploughs.
      Meadow, 6 acres; woodland 1 league long and ½ wide.
    The value was and is 20s.
      Arnulf held it before 1066.

9   Alnoth holds MACKADOWN. 5 hides less 1 virgate. Land for 5 ploughs.
      10 villagers and 4 smallholders with 3 ploughs.
      Meadow, 2 acres; woodland 1 league long and ½ wide.
    The value was 20s; now 40s.
      Almund held it freely before 1066.

De.T.ten Roger MERSTONE . Ibi funt.III.hidæ.Tra

ē.III.car̄ . In dn̄io.ē una.7 IIII.uilti 7 II.bord̄ cū.III.car̄.

Ibi.II.ac̄ p̄ti.Valuit.xx.fol.Modo.xxx.Eduin uicecom̄ 9 libe. tenuit.

De.T.ten id̄ Rog in ELMEDONE dim̄ hid̄.Tra.ē dim̄

car̄.Ibi tam̄.ē in dn̄io.I.car̄.7 v.ac̄ p̄ti.Silua.I.q̄rent

lḡ.7 alta lat̄.Valuit 7 uat̄.v.folid̄.Tochi libe tenuit.

De.T.ten Bruning in WINCHICELLE.III.virg tre.

Tra.ē.I.car̄.Ipfa.ē in dn̄io ibi 7 VIII.ac̄ p̄ti.Silua.

II.q̄rent lḡ.7 tn̄td̄ lat̄.Valuit 7 uat̄.v.fot.Id̄ libe tenuit.

De.T.ten.R.de olgi in DERCELAI.II.hid̄ in uadim̄.

Tra.ē.III.car̄.Ibi funt.VII.uilti cū.II.car̄.7 II.ferui.

7 molin̄ de xxxII.denar̄.7 x.ac̄ p̄ti.Silua.II.q̄rent

lḡ.7 tn̄td̄ lat̄.Valuit.xxx.fol.Modo.xL.fot.Vntain tenuit.

De.T.ten Eduin 9 in WITECORE.II.hid̄ una v̄ min̄. 9

Tra.ē.I.car̄.In dn̄io.ē ipfa.cū.II.uiltis 7 v.bord̄.7 ibi

II.ac̄ æ p̄ti.Silua.I.leuu lḡ.7 dim̄ lat̄.Valuit 7 uat̄.x.fot.

Duo Vlurici libe tenuer̄ T.R.E.

De.T.ten.R.de olgi BERTANESTONE in uadim̄.Ibi funt

IX.hidæ.Tra.ē.xI.car̄.In dn̄io.ē una car̄.7 vI.libi hōes

cū.IX.uiltis 7 IIII.bord̄ hn̄t.x.car̄.Ibi molin̄ de.IIII.fot,

Silua dim̄ leuu lḡ.7 III.q̄rent lat̄.Valuit 7 uat̄.c.fot.

Ailmar 9 tenuit.7·lictia regis uendid̄ Aluuino pat’ Turchil uicecomiti.

10 Roger holds MARSTON. 3 hides. Land for 3 ploughs. In lordship 1;
  4 villagers and 2 smallholders with 3 ploughs.
  Meadow, 2 acres.
The value was 20s; now 30s.
  Edwin the Sheriff held it freely.

11 Roger also holds ½ hide in ELMDON. Land for ½ plough.
In lordship, however, 1 plough.
  Meadow, 5 acres; woodland 1 furlong long and another wide.
The value was and is 5s.
  Toki held it freely.

12 Browning holds 3 virgates of land in WIGGINS HILL.
  Land for 1 plough; it is in lordship.
  Meadow, 8 acres; woodland 2 furlongs long and as wide.
The value was and is 5s.
  He also held it, freely.

13 Robert d'Oilly holds 2 hides in pledge in DOSTHILL. Land for 3 ploughs.
  7 villagers with 2 ploughs; 2 slaves.
  A mill at 32d; meadow, 10 acres; woodland 2 furlongs
    long and as wide.
The value was 30s; now 40s.
  Untan held it.

14 Edwin holds 2 hides less 1 virgate in (NETHER?) WHITACRE.
Land for 1 plough; it is in lordship, with
  2 villagers and 5 smallholders.
  Meadow, 2 acres; woodland 1 league long and ½ wide.
The value was and is 10s.
  Two Wulfrics held it freely before 1066.

15 Robert d'Oilly holds BARSTON in pledge. 9 hides.
Land for 11 ploughs. In lordship 1 plough.
  5 free men with 9 villagers and 4 smallholders have 10 ploughs.
  A mill at 4s; woodland ½ league long and 3 furlongs wide.
The value was and is 100s.
  Aelmer held it and with the King's permission sold it
to Alwin the Sheriff, Thorkell's father.

De.T.ten̅ Wiłłs *BEDESLEI*.Ibi ſunt.ii.hidæ.Tra.e̅.ii.

car̅.Ibi ſunt.iii.uiłłi 7 v.bord̅ 7 ii.ſerui cu̅.i.car̅.

Silua.i.leuu̅ 7 dim̅ l̅g̅.7 dimid̅ leuu̅ lat̅.Valuit 7 uał x.ſoł.

Huj træ.v.parte̅ p̅occupauit hic.W.ſup̅.W.rege̅.7 ibi

manet q̣da̅ Brictric q̣ teneb̅ ea̅ T.R.E.

Alia̅ tra̅ tenuer̅ Archil 7 Cerret ho̅es Turchil.

De.T.ten̅.iiii.fr̅s in Wlfeſineſcot.i. hid̅ 7 dim̅ v træ.

Tra.e̅.ii.car̅.7 tam̅ ſunt ibi.iii.car̅.7 iii.ac̅ p̊ti.

Valuit 7 uał.xx.ſolid̅.Idem ipſi tenuer̅ 7 lib̅i fuer̅.

De.T.ten̅ Herm̅frid in *LODBROCH*.i.hid̅ 7 una̅ v træ.

Tra.e̅.ii.car̅.Ibi ſunt.iii.ho̅es h̅ntes.ii.car̅.7 vi.ac̅s p̊ti.

Valuit.xv.ſoł.Modo.xx.ſoł.Eduin̅ tenuit.

De.T.ten̅ Erm̅frid in *CALDECOTE* dimid̅ hid̅.Tra.e̅.ii.car̅.

In d̅nio.e̅ una.7 viii.ac̅ p̊ti.Valuit.iiii.ſoł.Modo.viii.ſoł.

De.T.ten̅ Ricard̅ in *CALDECOTE* dim̅ hid̅.Tra.e̅.i.car̅.Ibi

e̅ ipſa cu̅.ii.ho̅ib.7 viii.ac̅ p̊ti.Valuit 7 uał.iiii.ſolid̅.

De.T.ten̅ Almar in *LODBROC* 7 *REDBORNE*.i.hid̅ 7 dim̅.

Tra.e̅.iiii.car̅.In d̅nio ſunt.iii.7 vi.ſerui.7 ix.uiłłi 7 ii.bord̅

cu̅.iii.car̅.7 ibi.vi.ac̅ p̊ti.Valuit.xxx.ſoł.Modo.xl.ſoł.

De.T.ten̅ Almar in *CALVESTONE*.i.hid̅ 7 dim̅.Tra.e̅.iii.car̅.

In d̅nio.e̅ una.cu̅.i.ſeruo.7 iiii.uiłłi 7 ii.bord̅.h̅nt.i.car̅.Valuit

ʃx.ſoł.M̊ xvi.ſoł.

16 William holds BADDESLEY (ENSOR). 2 hides. Land for 2 ploughs.
3 villagers, 5 smallholders and 2 slaves with 1 plough.
Woodland 1½ leagues long and ½ league wide.
The value was and is 10s.
This William misappropriated a fifth part of this land in King William's despite; one Brictric, who held it before 1066, lives there. Arkell and Ceolred, Thorkell's men, held the rest of the land.

[in MARTON Hundred]
17 in WOLFHAMPCOTE 4 brothers hold 1 hide and ½ virgate of land.
Land for 2 ploughs. However, 3 ploughs there.
Meadow, 3 acres.
The value was and is 20s.
They also held it themselves; they were free.

18 Ermenfrid holds 1 hide and 1 virgate of land in LADBROKE.
Land for 2 ploughs.
3 men who have 2 ploughs.
Meadow, 6 acres.
The value was 15s; now 20s.
Edwin held it.

19 Ermenfrid holds ½ hide in CALCUTT. Land for 2 ploughs.
In lordship 1.
Meadow, 8 acres.
The value was 4s; now 8s.

20 Richard holds ½ hide in CALCUTT. Land for 1 plough.
It is there, with
2 men.
Meadow, 8 acres.
The value was and is 4s.

21 Aelmer holds 1½ hides in LADBROKE and RADBOURN.
Land for 4 ploughs. In lordship 3; 6 slaves;
9 villagers and 2 smallholders with 3 ploughs.
Meadow, 6 acres.
The value was 30s; now 40s.

22 Aelmer holds 1½ hides in CAWSTON. Land for 3 ploughs.
In lordship 1, with 1 slave.
4 villagers and 2 smallholders have 1 plough.
The value was 10s; now 16s.

⌐De.T.ten̅ Wills in *LODBROC*.II.hid̅ 7 una̅ v̇ træ.Tra.e̅.II.car̊.
Ibi ſunt.IIII.uilti 7 III.bord̅.7 II.ſerui.7 un̅ miles.cu̅.II.car̊
int̊ om̅s.ibi.II.a̅c p̊ti.Valuit.xx.ſol.Modo.xl.ſol.

⌐De.T.ten̅ un̅ p̊br.I.virg̊ træ.in ipſa uilla.Ibi.e̅.I.car̊ cu̅.I.
uilto.7 ibi.II.a̅c p̊ti.Valuit.v.ſol.Modo.x.ſol.

⌐De.T.ten̅ Eddulf in *ROCHEBERIE*.II.hid̅ 7 dim̅.Tra.e̅.vi.car̊.
In dn̅io.e̅.I.car̊.7 II.ſerui.7 xi.uilti 7 v.bord̅ cu̅.v.car̊.
Ibi molin̅ de.xiii.ſol.7 IIII.denar̊.7 xvi.a̅c p̊ti.Valuit.l.ſol.
Modo.xl.ſolid̅.

⌐De.T.ten̅ Vlf in *CALVESTONE*.I.hid̅.Tra.e̅.I.car̊.Ipſa.e̅
in dn̅io.7 IIII.uilt 7 I.bord̅ 7 I.ſeru̅.Valuit.x.ſol.Modo.xII.ſol.
Has.ix.t̊ras p̅dict̊as tenuit Eduin 7 potuit ire quo uoluit.

⌐De.T.ten̅ Goſlin in *BERDINGEBERIE*.I.hid̅ 7 dim̅ uirg̊ træ.
Tra.e̅.III.car̊.Ibi ſunt.III.francones ho̅es cu̅.IIII.uiltis 7 III.
bord̅ hn̅tes.III.car̊.Valuit.xx.ſol.Modo.xl.ſol.Ipſi ho̅es
francones tenuer̅ libe T.R.E.   *IN MERETONE HVND̅.*

⌐De.T.ten̅ Rob̅t in *EPTONE*.III.v̇ træ.Tra.e̅.v.car̊.In dn̅io
e̅ una.7 IIII.uilti 7 v.bord̅ hn̅t.II.car̊.Ibi.vIII.a̅c p̊ti..
Valuit.x.ſol.Modo.xxx.ſolid̅.Eduin tenuit

⌐De.T.ten̅ Oſlach in *FLECHENOC*.II.hid̅ 7 dim̅.Tra.e̅.IIII.car̊.
In dn̅io.e̅ una 7 dim̅.7 III.ſerui.7 x.uilti 7 III.bord̅ cu̅.III.car̊
7 dimid̅.Valuit 7 ual̅ xxx.ſol.Eduin tenuit.

23 William holds 2 hides and one virgate of land in LADBROKE.   241 b
Land for 2 ploughs.
   4 villagers, 3 smallholders, 2 slaves and 1 man-at-arms
      with 2 ploughs between them all.
   Meadow, 2 acres.
The value was 20s; now 40s.

24 a priest holds 1 virgate of land in this village. 1 plough, with
      1 villager.
   Meadow, 2 acres.
The value was 5s; now 10s.

25 Edwulf holds 2½ hides in RUGBY.   Land for 6 ploughs.
In lordship 1 plough; 2 slaves;
   11 villagers and 5 smallholders with 5 ploughs.
   A mill at 13s 4d; meadow, 16 acres.
The value was 50s; now 40s.

26 Ulf holds 1 hide in CAWSTON.   Land for 1 plough; it is in lordship;
      4 villagers, 1 smallholder and 1 slave.
The value was 10s; now 12s.

   Edwin held the above nine lands; he could go where he would.

27 Jocelyn holds 1 hide and ½ virgate of land in BIRDINGBURY.
Land for 3 ploughs.
   3 freemen with 4 villagers and 3 smallholders, who have 3 ploughs.
The value was 20s; now 40s.
   These freemen held it freely before 1066.

   in MARTON Hundred
28 Robert holds 3 virgates of land in NAPTON. Land for 5 ploughs.
In lordship 1.
   4 villagers and 5 smallholders have 2 ploughs.
   Meadow, 8 acres.
The value was 10s; now 30s.
   Edwin held it.

29 Oslac holds 2½ hides in FLECKNOE. Land for 4 ploughs.
In lordship 1½; 3 slaves;
   10 villagers and 3 smallholders with 3½ ploughs.
The value was and is 30s.
   Edwin held it.

ꝑDe.T.teñ Harding in *HODENHELLE* . IIII . hiđ . Tra.ē . IIII.

caŕ . In dñio . ē una . 7 XI . uitti 7 II . borđ cũ . II . caŕ . 7 XX . ac̃ ꝑti .

Valuit 7 ual . XL . fot . Vlnod tenuit liƀe . T.R.E.

ꝑDe.T.teñ Goduin in eađ uilla . I . hiđ . Tra.ē . I . caŕ . In dñio . ē

ipfa . cũ . I . feruo . 7 IIII . borđ cũ dim caŕ . 7 IIII . ac̃ ꝑti . Valuit

X . fot . Modo . XX . foliđ . Ordric liƀe tenuit . T.R.E.

ꝑDe.T.teñ Ailric in *FLECHENHO* . I . hiđ 7 dim v̊ træ . Tra.ē

II . caŕ . In dñio . ē una . 7 I . uitts 7 IIII . borđ cũ . I . caŕ . Ibi . IIII . ac̃

ꝑti . Valuit XX . fot . modo . XXX . foliđ . Aluuiñ pat . T.tenuit.

ꝑDe.T.teñ Gifleƀt in *LODBROC* . III . v̊ træ . Tra.ē dim caŕ . In dñio

tam̃ . ē . I . caŕ . 7 II . ferui . 7 II . ac̃ ꝑti . Valuit . v . fot . Modo . X . fot.

ꝑDe.T.teñ Vluric in *WILEBERE* .   ꝑHereuuard tenuit.

unã v̊ træ 7 dim . Tra.ē . I . caŕ . In dñio . ē ipfa . 7 II . uitti cũ . I . borđ .

7 una ac̃ ꝑti . Valuit 7 ual . X . foliđ . Idē Vluric liƀe tenuit.

ꝑDe.T.teñ Vlfi . III . v̊ træ 7 dim . Tra.ē . I . caŕ 7 dimiđ . In dñio . ē

dimiđ . 7 II . uitti 7 III . borđ cũ . I . caŕ . 7 IIII . ac̃ ꝑti . Valuit 7 ual . X . fot.

ꝑDe.T.teñ Gifleƀt in *BENTONE* . I . v̊ træ . Tra.ē dim caŕ.

Valuit . v . fot . Modo . II . fot.

30   Harding holds 4 hides in HODNELL. Land for 4 ploughs.
In lordship 1;
    11 villagers and 2 smallholders with 2 ploughs.
    Meadow, 20 acres.
The value was and is 40s.
    Wulfnoth held it freely before 1066.

31   Godwin holds 1 hide in the same village. Land for 1 plough.
It is in lordship, with 1 slave;
    4 smallholders with ½ plough.
    Meadow, 4 acres.
The value was 10s; now 20s.
    Ordric held it freely before 1066.

32   Alric holds 1 hide and ½ virgate of land in FLECKNOE.
Land for 2 ploughs. In lordship 1;
    1 villager and 4 smallholders with 1 plough.
    Meadow, 4 acres.
The value was 20s; now 30s.
    Alwin, Thorkell's father, held it.

33   Gilbert holds 3 virgates of land in LADBROKE. Land for ½ plough.
In lordship, however, 1 plough and 2 slaves.
    Meadow, 2 acres.
The value was 5s; now 10s.
    Hereward held it.

34   Wulfric holds 1½ virgates of land in WILLOUGHBY.
Land for 1 plough. It is in lordship;
    2 villagers with 1 smallholder.
    Meadow, 1 acre.
The value was and is 10s.
    Wulfric also held it freely.

35   Wulfsi holds 3½ virgates of land. Land for 1½ ploughs.
In lordship ½;
    2 villagers and 3 smallholders with 1 plough.
    Meadow, 4 acres.
The value was and is 10s.

36   Gilbert holds 1 virgate of land in BILTON. Land for ½ plough.
The value was 5s; now 2s.

⅄De.T.ten Ordric in *WALECOTE* 7 *WILEBENE* 7 *CALDECOTE*.II.hiđ.
Tra.ē.I.cař. In dñio tam̃.ē una cař.7 II.ſerui.7 IIII.uiłłi 7 VI.
borđ cũ.I.car 7 dim̃.Ibi.VI.ãc p̃ti.Valuit.xx.ſoł.m̃.xxx.ſoliđ.
Idem Ordric libe tenuit.

⅄De.T.ten Vlchetel in *EPTONE* dim̃ hiđ.Tra.ē.III.cař.In dñio
ē dim̃ cař.7 IIII.uiłłi 7 II.borđ cũ.I.car 7 dim̃.7 VI.ãc p̃ti.
Valuit.xx.ſoliđ.Modo.xxx.ſoliđ.Idē Vlchetel libe tenuit.

⅄De.T.ten Aluuin in *SOCHEBERGE* dim̃ v træ.Tra.ē dim̃ cař.
Ibi.ē in dñio cũ.II.borđ.7 II.ãc p̃ti.Valuit 7 uał.v.ſoliđ.
Vluuin libe tenuit.

⅄De.T.ten Leuiet 7 Goduin in *WILEBEI* dim̃ hiđ.Tra.ē.I.cař.
Ipſa.ē in dñio.7 II.ãc p̃ti.Valuit 7 uał.x.ſoł.Idem ipſi tenueř.

⅄De.T.ten Godric in *NIWETONE*.II.hiđ.Tra.ē.II.cař.In dñio
ē una.7 IIII.uiłłi 7 II.borđ.7 II.ãc p̃ti.Valuit 7 uał.xx.ſoliđ.
Wlſtàn libe tenuit T.R.E.

⅄De.T.ten Alde in *NIWETONE* dimiđ hiđ.Tra.ē dimiđ cař.
Ibi.ē tam̃.I.cař.cũ.II.borđ.Valuit 7 uał.x.ſoł.Godeua libe tenuit.

⅄De.T.ten Radulf in *NIWETONE* dimiđ hiđ.Tra.ē.I.cař.
Ibi ſunt.II.uiłłi 7 dimiđ ãc p̃ti.Valuit 7 uał.II.ſoliđ.

37 Ordric holds 2 hides in 'WALCOTE', WILLOUGHBY and CALCUTT.
Land for 1 plough. In lordship, however, 1 plough; 2 slaves;
    4 villagers and 6 smallholders with 1½ ploughs.
    Meadow, 6 acres.
The value was 20s; now 30s.
    Ordric also held it freely.

38 Ulfketel holds ½ hide in NAPTON.　Land for 3 ploughs.
In lordship ½ plough;
    4 villagers and 2 smallholders with 1½ ploughs.
    Meadow, 6 acres.
The value was 20s; now 30s.
    Ulfketel also held it freely.

39 Alwin holds ½ virgate of land in SHUCKBURGH.　Land for ½ plough.
It is in lordship, with
    2 smallholders.
    Meadow, 2 acres.
The value was and is 5s.
    Wulfwin held it freely.

40 Leofgeat and Godwin hold ½ hide in WILLOUGHBY.　Land for 1 plough.
It is in lordship.
    Meadow, 2 acres.
The value was and is 10s.
    They also held it themselves.

[in BRINKLOW Hundred]

41 Godric holds 2 hides in NEWTON.　Land for 2 ploughs.
In lordship 1;
    4 villagers and 2 smallholders.
    Meadow, 2 acres.
The value was and is 20s.
    Wulfstan held it freely before 1066.

42 Aldith holds ½ hide in NEWTON.　Land for ½ plough.
However, 1 plough, with
    2 smallholders.
The value was and is 10s.
    Godiva held it freely.

43 Ralph holds ½ hide in NEWTON. Land for 1 plough.
    2 villagers.
    Meadow, ½ acre.
The value was and is 2s.

⁊ De.T.ten Vluric in *HOLME*.I.hiđ.Tra.ē dimiđ car.Ibi.ē

taṁ.I.car cū.II.uiłłis.⁊ I.borđ ⁊ I.ſeruo.⁊ III.ãc p̃ti.

Valuit.v.ſol.Modo.x.ſoliđ.Idē Vluric liƀe tenuit.

241 c

⁊ De.T.ten Raduł⁹ in *HOLME*.I.hiđ.Tra.ē.I.car.Ibi.ē

u ı borđ cū dimiđ car.⁊ III.ãc p̃ti.Valuit.v.ſol.Modo

III.ſoliđ.Vlſtan liƀe tenuit.T.R.E.

⁊ De.T.ten idē Rađ in *WAVRA* dimiđ hiđ.Tra.ē dimiđ

car.Ibi.ē un uiłłs.⁊ dimiđ ãc p̃ti.Valuit ⁊ ual.III.ſol.

⁊ De.T.ten Leueua in *LILLEFORD*.II.hiđ.Tra.ē.I.car

⁊ dim.Ibi ſunt.vI.uiłłi cū.I.car.⁊ I.ſeruo.⁊ moliñ de

IIII.ſoliđ.⁊ una ãc p̃ti.⁊ dimiđ.Valuit.xx.ſol.ṁ.x.ſol

⁊ vIII.den.Aluuin libere tenuit T.R.E.

⁊ De.T.ten.R.de olgi in *MERSTONE*.I.hiđ.Tra.ē.I.car

Vaſta.ē.Ibi.III.ãc p̃ti.Valuit.x.ſoliđ.Modo.xvI.den.

Algar tenuit.

⁊ De.T.ten Ermenfrid in *ASCESHOT*.II.hiđ.Tra.ē.IIII.car.

Ibi ſunt.Ix.uiłłi ⁊ xIIII.borđ cū.IIII.car.⁊ II.molini de.xx.

ſoliđ.⁊ xvI.ãc p̃ti.Silua dim leuu łg.⁊ III.q̃rent lat.

Valuit.xx.ſol.Modo.xL.ſoliđ.Turchil liƀe tenuit.

⁊ De.T.ten Wiłłs in *ERBVRGEBERIE*.IIII.hiđ.Tra.ē.Ix.

car.Ibi ſunt xII.uiłłi cū p̃bro ⁊ v.borđ h̃ntes.IIII.car.

Ibi.vI.ãc p̃ti.Valuit ⁊ ual.Lx.ſol.Orđric liƀe tenuit.

44 Wulfric holds 1 hide in BIGGIN. Land for ½ plough.
    However, 1 plough, with
        2 villagers, 1 smallholder and 1 slave.
        Meadow, 3 acres.
    The value was 5s; now 10s.
        Wulfric also held it freely.

45 Ralph holds 1 hide in BIGGIN. Land for 1 plough.   241 c
        1 smallholder with ½ plough.
        Meadow, 3 acres.
    The value was 5s; now 3s.
        Wulfstan held it freely before 1066.

46 Ralph also holds ½ hide in (CHURCH)OVER. Land for ½ plough.
        1 villager.
        Meadow, ½ acre.
    The value was and is 3s.

47 Leofeva holds 2 hides in (LITTLE) LAWFORD. Land for 1½ ploughs.
        6 villagers with 1 plough and 1 slave.
        A mill at 4s; meadow, 1½ acres.
    The value was 20s; now 10s 8d.
        Alwin held it freely before 1066.

    [in COLESHILL Hundred?]
48 Robert d'Oilly holds 1 hide in (LEA?)MARSTON. Land for 1 plough. Waste.
        Meadow, 3 acres.
    The value was 10s; now 16d.
        Earl Algar held it.

    [in STONELEIGH Hundred]

49 Ermenfrid holds 2 hides in ASHOW. Land for 4 ploughs.
        9 villagers and 13 smallholders with 4 ploughs.
        2 mills at 20s; meadow, 16 acres; woodland ½ league
            long and 3 furlongs wide.
    The value was 20s; now 40s.
        Thorkell held it freely.

50 William holds 4 hides in HARBURY. Land for 9 ploughs.
        12 villagers with a priest and 5 smallholders who have
            4 ploughs.
        Meadow, 6 acres.
    The value was and is 60s.
        Ordric held it freely.

De.T.teñ Aluuin in *BADECHITONE* . IIII . hid . Tra . ē
IIII . car . In dñio funt . II . 7 VII . uilti 7 VIII . borđ cū . II . car.
Ibi moliñ de . x . fol 7 VIII . deñ . 7 xxvii . ac p̃ti . Valuit
xxx . fol . Modo . L . folid . Archil libe tenuit T.R.E.

De.T.teñ Hadulf in *BILNEI* . II . hid . Tra . ē . III . car.
In dñio . ē una . 7 v . uilti 7 VII . borđ cū . II . car . Ibi II . ferui.
7 moliñ de . xL . deñ . 7 VIII . ac p̃ti . Silua . IIII . q̃rent lḡ.
7 II . q̃rent lat . Valuit xx . fol . Modo xxxv . fol . Idē tenuit

De.T.teñ Robt in *WESTONE* . I . v træ   qui nc teñ.
7 dimiđ . Tra . ē dimiđ car . Valta . ē . Ibi . IIII . ac p̃ti.
Valuit . vi . folid . modo nil reddit . Vluui libe tenuit.

De.T.teñ Wlfi in *BRANDVNE* dimiđ hiđ . Tra . ē . IIII.
car . Ibi funt . x . uilti cū . I . feruo . hñt . III . car . Ibi moliñ
de . xx.vi . deñ . 7 xvi . ac p̃ti . Silua . IIII . q̃rent lḡ . 7 II . q̃
lat . Valuit . xx . folid . Modo . xxv . fol . Turchil libe tenuit.

De.T.teñ . R . de olgi in *LILLINTONE* dim hiđ . Tra . ē dim
car . Vna tam ibi . ē cū . vi . borđ 7 I . ancilla q̃ hñt alia car.
Ibi . IIII . ac p̃ti . Valuit . x . fol . Modo . xx . fol . Bruning

De.T.teñ Ermenfrid in *REDEFORD* . v . hiđ. libe tenuit.
Tra . ē . xIII . car . In dñio funt . III . car . 7 VIII . ferui . 7 xIx.
uilti 7 VIII . borđ cū . Ix . car . Ibi moliñ de . vi . fol 7 VIII . deñ.
7 xII . ac p̃ti . Valuit . c . fol . 7 poft . xL . fol . Modo . vi . lib.
Eduin tenuit libe T.R.E. Ermfrid emit a Chetelbto
licentia . 7 teñ de rege in feudo . ut teftat breuis regis.

51 Alwin holds 4 hides in BAGINTON. Land for 4 ploughs. In lordship 2;
7 villagers and 8 smallholders with 2 ploughs.
A mill at 10s 8d; meadow, 27 acres.
The value was 30s; now 50s.
Arkell held it freely before 1066.

52 Adolf holds 2 hides in BINLEY. Land for 3 ploughs. In lordship 1;
5 villagers and 7 smallholders with 2 ploughs. 2 slaves.
A mill at 40d; meadow, 8 acres; woodland 4 furlongs long
and 2 furlongs wide.
The value was 20s; now 35s.
The former holder now holds it.

53 Robert holds 1½ virgates of land in WESTON (-under-Wetherley)
Land for ½ plough. Waste.
Meadow, 4 acres.
The value was 6s; now it pays nothing.
Wulfwy held it freely.

54 Wulfsi holds ½ hide in BRANDON. Land for 4 ploughs.
10 villagers with 1 slave have 3 ploughs.
A mill at 26d; meadow, 16 acres; woodland 4 furlongs
long and 2 furlongs wide.
The value was 20s; now 25s.
Thorkell held it freely.

55 Robert d'Oilly holds ½ hide in LILLINGTON. Land for ½ plough.
There is however 1, with
6 smallholders and 1 female slave who have another plough.
Meadow, 4 acres.
The value was 10s; now 20s.
Browning held it freely.

56 Ermenfrid holds 5 hides in RADFORD (SEMELE). Land for 13 ploughs.
In lordship 3 ploughs; 8 slaves;
19 villagers and 8 smallholders with 9 ploughs.
A mill at 6s 8d; meadow, 12 acres.
The value was 100s; later 40s; now £6.
Edwin held it freely before 1066; Ermenfrid bought it from
Ketelbern with [the King's] permission and holds it as a Holding
from the King, as the King's writ testifies.

⨍ De.T.ten Almar in *ROTELEI*.v.hid. *IN HONESBERIE HD̅.*

Tra.e̅.vii.car. In d̅nio ſunt.ii.7 vi.ſerui.7 xviii.uilti

7 vii.bord cū.vii.car̅.Ibi.xxiiii.ac̅ p̅ti.Valuit.iii.lib̅.

7 poſt.iiii.lib̅.Modo.c.ſolid.Ordric libe tenuit T.R.E.

⨍ De.T.ten Almar in *CONTONE*.ii.hid.Tra.e̅.ii.car.In

d̅nio.e̅.i.car 7 dimid.7 iiii.ſerui.7 vi.uilti 7 ii.bord cū

.i.car 7 dimid.Ibi.xvi.ac̅ p̅ti.Valuit.xx.ſol.M̊.xl.ſol.

⨍ De.T.ten Rogeri in ead uilla.iii.hid 7 unā v̅ træ.

Tra.e̅.vi.car̅.In d̅nio ſunt.ii.cū.i.ſeruo.7 viii.uilti

7 iiii.bord cū.iiii.car̅.Ibi.xxxiiii.p̅ti.Valuit.xl.ſol.

Modo.l.ſolid.Ordric 7 Aluuin 7 Vlſi libe tenuer̅.T.R.E.

241 d

⨍ De feudo.T.ten comes de mellend *MOITONE*.Ibi ſunt

ii.hidæ.Tra.e̅.ii.car̅.In d̅nio.e̅ una.7 ii.ſerui.7 vii.

uilti 7 vii.bord cū.iiii.car̅.Ibi.ii.molini de.lxx.ſol.

7 viii.hoēs reddent.xxxii.den.Valuit.c.ſol.7 poſt

xl.ſol.Modo.vi.lib̅.Eduin tenuit.

Hanc trā emit.R.Halebold.

⨍ De.T.ten Warin in *WIMENESTONE*.iii.hid.Tra.e̅

viii.car̅.In d̅nio ſunt.iiii.7 xv.uilti 7 iiii.bord 7 ii.

franc.int̅ oms hn̅t.vii.car̅.Ibi.xxx.vi.ac̅ p̅ti.

De hac tra ten.ii.milit.i.hid 7 unā.v̅.7 hn̅t.ii.car

cū.iii.bord.Tot̅ T.R.E.ualb̅.iiii.lib̅.7 poſt tntd̅.

Modo.x.lib̅.Ordric 7 Vluuin 7 Vluric libe tenuer̅.

in HUNSBURY Hundred

57 Aelmer holds 5 hides in RATLEY. Land for 7 ploughs.
In lordship 2; 6 slaves;
   18 villagers and 7 smallholders with 7 ploughs.
   Meadow, 24 acres.
The value was £3; later £4; now 100s.
   Ordric held it freely before 1066.

58 Aelmer holds 2 hides in (FENNY) COMPTON. Land for 2 ploughs.
In lordship 1½ ploughs; 4 slaves;
   6 villagers and 2 smallholders with 1½ ploughs.
   Meadow, 16 acres.
The value was 20s; now 40s.

59 Roger holds 3 hides and 1 virgate of land in the same village.
Land for 6 ploughs. In lordship 2, with 1 slave;
   8 villagers and 4 smallholders with 4 ploughs.
   Meadow, 34 [acres].
The value was 40s; now 50s.
   Ordric, Alwin and Wulfsi held it freely before 1066.

[In STONELEIGH Hundred]
60 From Thorkell's Holding the Count of Meulan holds MYTON. 2 hides. 241 d
Land for 2 ploughs. In lordship 1; 2 slaves;
   7 villagers and 7 smallholders with 3 ploughs.
   2 mills at 70s; 8 men who pay 32d.
The value was 100s; later 40s; now £6.
   Earl Edwin held it.
   R. Halebold bought this land.

From Thorkell
   [in HUNSBURY Hundred]
61 Warin holds 3 hides in WORMLEIGHTON. Land for 8 ploughs.
In lordship 4.
   15 villagers, 4 smallholders and 2 freemen have 7 ploughs
      between them all.
   Meadow, 36 acres; 2 men-at-arms hold 1 hide and 1 virgate
      of this land; they have 2 ploughs, with 3 smallholders.
Total value before 1066 £4; later, as much; now £10.
   Ordric, Wulfwin and Wulfric held it freely.

╓De.T.ten͗ Tonne in *BERICOTE* .II.hid. *IN STANLEI HD.*

Tra.e̅.III.car͗.In dn̅io.e̅ una.7 II.serui.7 IIII.uilli

7 III.bord cu̅.II.car.Ibi moliñ de.IIII.sol.7 VI.ac̅ p̅ti.

Valuit.xx.sol.Modo.xL.sol.Aluuin͗ pat͗.T.tenuit.

╓De.T.ten͗ æccla S̅ MARIÆ de Waruuic.I.hid in *MOITONE.*

Tra.e̅.I.car͗.Ibi sunt.III.bord cu̅.I.car͗.7 una Ancilla.

Ibi.IIII.ac̅ p̅ti.Valuit.v.sol.Modo.x.sol.Æduin tenuit.

╓De.T.ten͗ Algar.I.hid 7 dim͗.Tra.e̅.III.car͗.In dn̅io

st̅.II.car.7 VI.serui.7 IIII.uilli 7 IIII.bord cu̅.I.car͗.

Ibi.xII.ac̅ p̅ti.Valuit.xxx.sol.Modo.xL.sol.Aluric

╓De.T.ten͗ Ermenfrid *IN KEMELAV HVND.* ╓libe tenuit.

una̅ hid in *FVLREI*.7 alta̅m in *ETENDONE*.Tra.e̅.I.

car͗.In dn̅io.e̅ ipsa cu̅.I.bord.Valuit.x.solid.

Modo.xxv.sol.Almar libe tenuit T.R.E.

╓De.T.ten͗ Aluuin͗ in *CONTONE*.III.hid.Tra.e̅.VI.car͗.

In dn̅io sunt.II.7 IIII.serui.7 IX.uilli 7 x.bord cu̅

.v.car͗.Ibi.xxx.ac̅ p̅ti.Valuit 7 ual.IIII.lib.

╓De.T.ten͗ abb de Abendone.I.hid in *CESTRETON.*

Tra.e̅.VII.car͗.7 II.serui.7 x.uilli 7 VIII.bord cu̅.VI.

car͗.Ibi.xvI.ac̅ p̅ti.Valuit.Lx.sol.Modo.c.sol.

╓De.T.ten͗ ide̅ abb in *CESTRETON*.╓Aluuol tenuit.

.I.hid in uadim͗.Tra.e̅.II.car͗.Ibi sunt.v.milit͗ angli

in STONELEIGH Hundred

62 Tonni holds 2 hides in BERICOTE. Land for 3 ploughs.
In lordship 1; 2 slaves;
   4 villagers and 3 smallholders with 2 ploughs.
   1 mill at 4s; meadow, 6 acres.
The value was 20s; now 40s.
   Alwin, Thorkell's father, held it.

63 St. Mary's Church, Warwick, holds 1 hide in MYTON.
Land for 1 plough.
   3 smallholders with 1 plough; 1 female slave.
   Meadow, 4 acres.
The value was 5s; now 10s.
   Earl Edwin held it.

64 Algar holds 1½ hides. Land for 3 ploughs. In lordship 2 ploughs; 6 slaves;
   4 villagers and 4 smallholders with 1 plough.
   Meadow, 12 acres.
The value was 30s; now 40s.
   Aelfric held it freely.

in TREMLOW Hundred

65 Ermenfrid holds 1 hide in FULLREADY and another in ETTINGTON.
Land for 1 plough. It is in lordship, with
   1 smallholder.
The value was 10s; now 25s.
   Aelmer held it freely before 1066.

66 Alwin holds 3 hides in COMPTON (VERNEY). Land for 6 ploughs.
In lordship 2; 4 slaves;
   9 villagers and 10 smallholders with 5 ploughs.
   Meadow, 30 acres.
The value was and is £4.

67 the Abbot of Abingdon holds 1 hide in CHESTERTON.
Land for 7 ploughs. 2 slaves;
   10 villagers and 8 smallholders with 6 ploughs.
   Meadow, 16 acres.
The value was 60s; now 100s.
   Alfwold held it.

68 the Abbot also holds 1 hide in pledge in CHESTERTON.
Land for 2 ploughs.
   5 English men-at-arms who have 4½ ploughs.

hñtes . IIII . caɍ 7 dimiđ . Ibi . VIII . aᴄ p̃ti . Valuit . xx . ſoɫ.

Modo . L . ſoɫ . Alnod Briꜩuin 7 Turi liɓe tenueɍ . T.R.E.

ꝼDe . T . ten̾ Witts in *COCꝨꝨNE* . *IN FERNECꝨBE HꝨNĐ*.

.IIII . hiđ . Tra . ē . VI . caɍ . Ibi ſu̇nt . II . liɓi hōes 7 VII . borđ

7 IIII . ſerui cū . III . caɍ . Ibi moᷣñ de . XXXII . den̾ 7 in

Waruuic . I . dom̾ redđ . VIII . den̾ . Ibi . x . aᴄ p̃ti.

Silua . VI . qɍent̾ lḡ . 7 IIII . q̃ꝫ lat̾ . Paſc . L . porꝛ.

Valuit . xL . ſoɫ . 7 poſt . xx . ſᴄɫ . Modo . L . ſoliđ . Vntoni⁹

ꝼDe . T . ten̾ . R . de olgi in *ETꝨNE* . I̓ᷓ hiđ . ꝼliɓe tenuit.

Tra . ē . v . caɍ . In dñio ſunt . III . caɍ . 7 v . ſerui . 7 IX . uitti

7 VIII . borđ cū . VIII . caɍ . Ibi . v . aᴹᴄ p̃ti . Silua . I . leùu

in lḡ 7 lat̾ . Valuit . xL . ſoɫ . Modo . IIII . liɓ.

Aluuin⁹ liɓe tenuit T.R.E.

242 a

.XVIII TERRA HꝨGONIS DE GRENTEMAISNIL.

Hugo De Grentemaiſnil ten̾ de rege in cuſtodia

.I . hiđ . 7 ᶜᵃ̃ VI . parte̾ . I . hidæ . in *MORTONE* 7 in *WILEBEĐ*.

Tra . ē . II . caɍ . Ibi ſunt . v . uitti cū . I . borđ . hñtes . II . caɍ.

Valuit . xx . ſoɫ . Modo . xxx . ſoɫ . Grinchet 7 Suain tenueɍ.

Idē Hugo ten̾ in *MERSETONE* . x . hiđ . *IN KEMELAV HĐ*.

Tra . ē . x . caɍ . In dñio ſunt . IIII . 7 VI . ſerui . 7 XXX . uitti
7 · II · ancille

7 II . borđ cū p̃bro h̾nt . VII . caɍ . Ibi . II . molini de . XI . ſoɫ.

7 II . franeig ibi . 7 II . ɓurḡſes in Waruuic redđ . XVI . den̾.

Valuit . x . liɓ . Modo . xv . liɓ . Baldeuin⁹ liɓe tenuit.

Meadow, 8 acres.
The value was 20s; now 50s.
Alnoth, Brictwin and Thori held it freely before 1066.

in FERNCOMBE Hundred
69 William holds 4 hides in COUGHTON. Land for 6 ploughs.
2 free men, 7 smallholders and 4 slaves with 3 ploughs.
A mill at 32d; in Warwick 1 house which pays 8d; meadow, 10
acres; woodland 6 furlongs long and 4 furlongs wide;
pasture-land, 50 pigs.
The value was 40s; later 20s; now 50s.
Untan held it freely.

70 Robert d'Oilly holds 3 hides in NUNEATON. Land for 5 ploughs.
In lordship 3 ploughs; 5 slaves;
9 villagers and 8 smallholders with 8 ploughs.
Meadow, 5 acres; woodland 1 league in length and width.
The value was 40s; now £4.
Alwin held it freely before 1066.

18   LAND OF HUGH OF GRANDMESNIL   242 a

[In MARTON Hundred]
1 Hugh of Grandmesnil holds in charge from the King 1 hide and the sixth
part of 1 hide in (HILL) MORTON and in WILLOUGHBY. Land for 2 ploughs.
5 villagers with 1 smallholder who have 2 ploughs.
The value was 20s; now 30s.
Grimkell and Swein held it.

Hugh also holds
in TREMLOW Hundred
2 in (BUTLERS) MARSTON 10 hides. Land for 10 ploughs.
In lordship 3; 6 male and 2 female slaves.
30 villagers and 2 smallholders with a priest have 7 ploughs.
2 mills at 11s.
2 Frenchmen and 2 burgesses in Warwick who pay 16d.
The value was £10; now £15.
Baldwin held it freely.

Idē.H.teñ in *PILARDETONE*.x.hid̃ Tra.ē.x.car̃.
In dñio funt.III.7 VIII.ferui 7 IIII.ancillæ.7 xxIII.uitti
cũ pɓro 7 I.milite 7 v.bord̃ hñtes IX.car̃. Ibi moliñ
de.v.folid̃.Silua.I.leuũ lg̃.7 I.lat̃.7 in Waruuic.I.
mafura redd̃.IIII.denar̃.7 xx.ac̃ p̃ti.
Valuit.x.liɓ.Modo.xvII.liɓ.Baldeuin liɓe tenuit.
Idē.H.teñ in *MIDELTONE*.IIII.hid̃.Tra.ē.IIII.car̃.
In dñio.ē una 7 dimid̃ car̃.7 III.ferui.7 xII.uitti cũ
pɓro 7 v.bord̃ hñt.II.car̃ 7 dimid̃.Ibi moliñ de
xx.folid̃.7 vI.ac̃ p̃ti.Valuit.IIII.liɓ.Modo.vI.liɓ.
Palliñ liɓe tenuit T.R.E.   *IN FEXHOLE HVND.*
Idē.H.teñ *OCTESELVE*.Ibi funt.x.hidæ Tra.ē
vIII.car̃. In dñio funt.III.7 xI.ferui.7 xx.uitti 7 xII.
bord̃ cũ.vII.car̃. Ibi moliñ de.xvI.den.7 xx.ac̃ p̃ti.
Valuit.x.liɓ.Modo.xI.liɓ.Toli liɓe tenuit T.R.E.
Idē.H.teñ in *SERVELEI*.III.hid̃.Tra.ē.xII.car̃.
In dñio.ē una.7 III.ferui.7 vIII.uitti 7 vI.bord̃ cũ.II.
car̃ 7 dimid̃.Ibi.x.ac̃ p̃ti Silua.I.leuũ lg̃.7 dim lat̃.
Valuit.xx.fot.Modo xxx.fot.Toli liɓe tenuit.
Idē.H.teñ in *LAPEFORDE* dimid̃ hid̃.Tra.ē.I.car̃.
Ibi funt.III.uitti.Silua.II.leuũ lg̃.7 I.leuũ lat̃.
Valuit.x.fot.Modo xx.folid̃.Baldeuin liɓe tenuit.

De ipfo Hvg̃ teñ Huɓt.II.hid̃ 7 dimid̃ in *TORLA*
VESTONE.Tra.ē.vII.car̃.In dñio funt.II.7 IX.uitti
7 I-II.bord̃ cũ.III.car̃.Ibi xL.ac̃ p̃ti.7 una q̃rent pastæ.
Valuit.xL.fot.Modo.Lx.fot.Baldeuin tenuit.

3   in PILLERTON (HERSEY) 10 hides. Land for 10 ploughs. In lordship 3;
8 male and 4 female slaves;
     23 villagers with a priest, 1 man-at-arms and 5 smallholders
        who have 9 ploughs.
     A mill at 5s; woodland 1 league long and 1 wide; in Warwick
        1 dwelling which pays 4d; meadow, 20 acres.
   The value was £10; now £17.
   Baldwin held it freely.

[in COLESHILL Hundred]
4   in MIDDLETON 4 hides. Land for 4 ploughs. In lordship 1½
ploughs and 3 slaves.
     12 villagers with a priest and 5 smallholders have 2½ ploughs.
     1 mill at 20s; meadow, 6 acres.
   The value was £4; now £6.
   Palli held it freely before 1066.

in FEXHOLE Hundred
5   OXHILL. 10 hides. Land for 8 ploughs. In lordship 3; 11 slaves;
     20 villagers and 11 smallholders with 7 ploughs.
     A mill at 16d; meadow, 20 acres.
   The value was £10; now £11.
   Toli held it freely before 1066.

[in FERNCOMBE Hundred]
6   in SHREWLEY 3 hides. Land for 12 ploughs. In lordship 1; 3 slaves;
     8 villagers and 6 smallholders with 2½ ploughs.
     Meadow, 10 acres; woodland 1 league long and ½ wide.
   The value was 20s; now 30s.
   Toli held it freely.

7   in LAPWORTH ½ hide. Land for 1 plough.
     3 villagers.
     Woodland 2 leagues long and 1 league wide.
   The value was 10s; now 20s.
   Baldwin held it freely.

[in MARTON Hundred]
8   From Hugh himself Hubert holds 2½ hides in THURLASTON.
   Land for 7 ploughs. In lordship 2;
     9 villagers and 4 smallholders with 3 ploughs.
     Meadow, 40 acres; pasture, 1 furlong.
   The value was 40s; now 60s.
   Baldwin held it.

ᚿ De . H . teñ Witts . II⁊ . v̅ træ in *LODBROC* . Tra . e̅ . I.
car̅ . Ibi p̅b̅r 7 I . uiłts c̅ī⁊ . II . bord . h̅nt dim̅ car̅ . 7 moliñ
de . III . sol . 7 III . a̅c p̅ti . Valuit ﹒ v ﹒ sot . Modo . x . solid᷄﹒

ᚿ De . H . teñ Robt . I . hid in *ETEDONE*.
Tra . e̅ . I . car̅ . Ibi . I . uiłts c̅u . I . bord h̅t dim̅ car̅.
Valuit 7 uał . x . solid . Baldeuin̊ tenuit.

ᚿ De . H . teñ abbatia S̅ Ebrulfi ﹒ VI . hid 7 uñā v̅ træ
in *PILARDETVNE* . Tra . e̅ . x . car̅ . In d̅ñio sunt . III᷄﹒
7 XIII . uiłti 7 XXIII . bord c̅u ﹒ I . francig 7 III⁊᷄ . tainis
h̅nt . VIII . car̅ . Ibi . XII . a̅c p̅ti . Valuit . VI . lib̅ . M̊ . x . lib̅᷄﹒
Quattuor⁊ taini lib̅e tenue̅r . T.R.E.

★ ᚿ De . H . teñ Roger̊ in . . . *ATERCOTE* . v . hid . Tra . e̅ . v᷄﹒
car̅ . In d̅ñio sunt . IIII . 7 VII . uiłti c̅u p̅b̅ro 7 XIX bord᷄
h̅nt . III . car̅ . Valuit ﹒ c . solid . Modo . VII . lib̅ . Toli lib̅e

ᚿ De . H . teñ id̅e Rog̅ . III . hid in *ROCHINTONE* . ſtenuit᷄﹒
Tra . e̅ . VIII . car̅ . Ibi . XXVII . uiłti c̅u p̅b̅ro 7 XXIIII . bord
h̅nt . IX . car̅ . Silua . I . leuu᷄ 7 dim̅ l̅g̅ . 7 VIII᷄ q̅rent lat᷄﹒
Valuit 7 uał . c . solid . Balduin̊ tenuit lib̅e T.R.E.

ᚿ De . H . teñ Osb̅n̊ . v . hid in *BILLESLEI* . Tra . e̅ . VIII . car̅᷄﹒
In d̅ñio sunt . III . ea̅r . 7 VIII . serui . 7 VIII . uiłti c̅u p̅b̅ro

242 b
7 IX . bord h̅ntes . IIII . car̅᷄ . 7 In Waruuic ﹒ I . dom̊ū
de . VIII . denar᷄ . Valuit 7 uał . c . solid . Baldeuin̊ tenuit.

From Hugh
9 William holds 3 virgates of land in LADBROKE. Land for 1 plough.
A priest and 1 villager with 2 smallholders have ½ plough.
A mill at 3s; meadow, 3 acres.
The value was 5s; now 10s.

[in TREMLOW Hundred]
10 Robert holds 1 hide in ETTINGTON. Land for 1 plough.
1 villager with 1 smallholder has ½ plough.
The value was and is 10s.
Baldwin held it.

11 St. Evroul's Abbey holds 6 hides and 1 virgate of land in PILLERTON (PRIORS).
Land for 10 ploughs. In lordship 3;
13 villagers and 23 smallholders with 1 Frenchman and 3 thanes
have 8 ploughs.
Meadow, 12 acres.
The value was £6; now £10.
4 thanes held it freely before 1066.

[in FEXHOLE Hundred]
12 Roger holds 5 hides in WHATCOTE. Land for 5 ploughs. In lordship 4.
7 villagers with a priest and 19 smallholders have 3 ploughs.
The value was 100s; now £7.
Toli held it freely.

[in FERNCOMBE Hundred]
13 Roger also holds 3 hides in ROWINGTON. Land for 8 ploughs.
27 villagers with a priest and 24 smallholders have 9 ploughs.
Woodland 1½ leagues long and 8 furlongs wide.
The value was and is 100s.
Baldwin held it freely before 1066.

14 Osbern holds 5 hides in BILLESLEY. Land for 8 ploughs.
In lordship 3 ploughs; 8 slaves;
8 villagers with a priest and 9 smallholders who have 4 ploughs.   242 b
In Warwick 1 house at 8d.
The value was and is 100s.
Baldwin held it.

⌐De . H . teñ Hugo : f . c̄ſtaǹtij . unā v̇ træ in *LOCHESLEI*.
Tra . ē dimid car̄ . Ibi . ē . I . uiłłs . Valuit 7 uał . v . ſol.
Manegot libe tenuit.   *IN COLESHELLE HD*.
⌐De . H . teñ Walter dimid hid in *WITACRE* . Tra . ē
dimid car̄ : Ibi . ē . I . uiłłs cū . II . boƀ₂ arans : Valuit
7 uał . II . ſol . Balduin tenuit.

XIX. TERRA HENRICI DE FERIER *IN COLESHELLE HD*.
HENRICVS De Fereires teñ . v . hid 7 dim in *GREN*
DONE . 7 Turſtiṅ de eo . Tra . ē . XVI . car̄ . Ibi ſunt
XXIIII . uiłłi 7 XVI . bord cū . VIII : car̄ . Ibi moliñ de . v . ſol.
7 XXX.VI . ãc p̃ti : Silua . I . leuū 7 dim łḡ . 7 una leuū lat̄.
Valuit 7 uał . XL : ſol : Siuuard barn tenuit.
De . H . teñ Radulf . IIII : hid in *BORTONE* . *IN BOMELAV HD*.
Tra . ē . VIII . car̄ . In dñio ſunt . II . 7 XIII . uiłłi cū p̃bro 7 VII.
bord hñt . VI . car̄ . Ibi . II : molini de . VII ſolid 7 VIII . denar̄.
Valuit . IIII . lib . Modo . XL . ſolid . Siuuard tenuit.
De . H . teñ Waʒelin : II . hid in *ERBVRBERIE* . *IN STANLEI HD*.
Tra . ē . v . car̄ : In dñio ſunt . II . 7 II . ſerui . 7 IIII . uiłłi cū . I . car̄.
Valuit . XL . ſol . Modo . IIII . lib . Siuuard tenuit . *IN REMELAV HD*.
De . H . teñ Saſuualo . XVII . hid in *ETENDONE* . Tra . ē
XII . car̄ . In dñio ſunt . IIII . car̄ . 7 x . ſerui . 7 XXXII . uiłłi cū
p̃bro 7 XXV . bord 7 I . milite 7 II . tainis hñt XVI . car̄ 7 dim̄.
Ibi moliñ de . XVIII . ſol . 7 XXX : ãc p̃ti.
Valuit . VI . lib . 7 poſt . IIII . lib . Modo . XX . lib.

242 b

[in PATHLOW Hundred]
15 Hugh son of Constantine holds 1 virgate of land in LOXLEY.
   Land for ½ plough.
       1 villager.
   The value was and is 5s.
       Manegot held it freely.

   in COLESHILL Hundred
16 Walter holds ½ hide in (OVER?)WHITACRE. Land for ½ plough.
       1 villager who ploughs with 2 oxen.
   The value was and is 2s.
       Baldwin held it.

19   **LAND OF HENRY OF FERRERS**   *A COMPANION OF WILLIAM OF NORMANDY ? WHERE IS FERRERS ON THE CONTINENT ?*

   In COLESHILL Hundred
1 Henry of Ferrers holds 5½ hides in GRENDON and Thurstan
   from him. Land for 16 ploughs.
       24 villagers and 16 smallholders with 8 ploughs.
       A mill at 5s; meadow, 36 acres; woodland 1½ leagues
           long and 1 league wide.
   The value was and is 40s.
       Siward Bairn held it.

From Henry
   in BRINKLOW Hundred
2 Ralph holds 4 hides in BURTON (HASTINGS). Land for 8 ploughs.
   In lordship 2.
       13 villagers with a priest and 7 smallholders have 6 ploughs.
       2 mills at 7s 8d.
   The value was £4; now 40s.
       Siward held it.

   in STONELEIGH Hundred
3 Wazelin holds 2 hides in HARBURY. Land for 5 ploughs.
   In lordship 2; 2 slaves;
       4 villagers with 1 plough.
   The value was 40s; now £4.
       Siward held it.

   in TREMLOW Hundred
4 Saswalo holds 17 hides in ETTINGTON. Land for 12 ploughs.
   In lordship 4 ploughs; 10 slaves.
       32 villagers with a priest, 25 smallholders,
           1 man-at-arms and 2 thanes have 16½ ploughs.
       A mill at 18s; meadow, 30 acres.
   The value was £6; later £4; now £20.

De.H.ten̄ Wazelin dimiđ hiđ in *CESTEDONE*.Tra.ē.I.car̄
7 dim̄.Ibi.ē.I.car̄ cū.I.bouar̄ 7 I.ać p̄ti. Valuit 7 ual.x.sol.
De.H.ten̄ Nigell.II.hiđ 7 dimiđ
in *ALDVLVESTREV*.Tra.ē.II.car̄.In dn̄io.ē una.7 VII.uitli.
7 III.borđ hn̄t.II.car̄.Valuit 7 ual.xx.sol.

.XX. TERRA ROGERIJ DE IVERI. *IN STANLEI HVND.*

ROGERIVS de IVRI.ten̄ de rege.v.hiđ in *CVBINTONE*.
Tra.ē.IIII.car̄.In dn̄io sunt.II.7 III.serui.7 II.uitli 7 II.borđ
cū.I.car̄.Ibi.xv.ać p̄ti. Valuit 7 ual.xL.soliđ. Turbern
liħe tenuit T.R.E. H.ē de feudo ep̄i baioc̄sis.

.XXI.TERRA ROBERTI DE OILGI. *IN COLESHELLE HĐ.*

ROBERTVS de OILGI ten̄.II.hiđ in *MERSTONE*.7 Robt⁹de eo.
Tra.II.car̄.In dn̄io.ē una.7 II.serui.7 IIII.uitli hn̄t.II.car̄.
Ibi.vI.ać p̄ti. Silua.IIII.q̄rent lḡ.7 una q̄q̄ lat̄. Valuit.x.sol.
Modo.xx.soliđ. Aluric̄ liħe tenuit.T.R.E. Hanc tr̄a emit ab eo
Robtus.licentia regis.W.

242 c

.XXII.TERRA ROBERTI DE STATFORD. *IN BOMELAV HĐ.*

ROBERTVS De Stadford ten̄ de rege.vII.hiđ in *WARA*.
Tra.ē.xII.car̄.In dn̄io sunt.IIII.7 XIIII.uitli 7 v.borđ
hn̄t.v.car̄.Ibi molin̄ de.II.sol.7 IIII.ać p̄ti.
Valuit.xx.sol.Modo.c.sol.Waga libere tenuit.T.R.E.

5 Wazelin holds ½ hide in CHESTERTON. Land for 1½ ploughs.
1 plough there, with 1 ploughman.
    Meadow, 1 acre.
The value was and is 10s.

[in COLESHILL Hundred]
6 Nigel holds 2½ hides in AUSTREY. Land for 2 ploughs. In lordship 1.
    7 villagers and 3 smallholders have 2 ploughs.
The value was and is 20s.

20   **LAND OF ROGER OF IVRY** *FRENCH ?*

In STONELEIGH Hundred
1 Roger of Ivry holds 5 hides in CUBBINGTON from the King, as he states.
Land for 4 ploughs. In lordship 2; 3 slaves;
    2 villagers and 2 smallholders with 1 plough.
    Meadow, 15 acres.
The value was and is 40s.
    Thorbern held it freely before 1066. It is of the Bishop of
Bayeux's Holding.

21   **LAND OF ROBERT D'OILLY** *NORMAN ?*

In COLESHILL Hundred
1 Robert d'Oilly holds 2 hides in (LEA) MARSTON and Robert Hunter
from him. Land for 2 ploughs. In lordship 1; 2 slaves.
    4 villagers have 2 ploughs.
    Meadow, 6 acres; woodland 4 furlongs long and 1 furlong wide.
The value was 10s; now 20s.
    Aelfric held it freely before 1066. Robert bought this
land from him with King William's permission.

22   **LAND OF ROBERT OF STAFFORD**   242 c

In BRINKLOW Hundred
1 Robert of Stafford holds 7 hides in (CHURCH)OVER from the King.
Land for 12 ploughs. In lordship 4.
    14 villagers and 5 smallholders have 5 ploughs.
    A mill at 2s; meadow, 4 acres.
The value was 20s; now 100s.
    Waga held it freely before 1066.

Idē Robt̄ ten . vii . hiđ in *VOLWARDE* . Tra . ē . x . cař.

★ In dn̄io funt . 7 iiii . ferui . 7 viii . uiłłi 7 viii . borđ cū pb̄ro hn̄t . vi . cař . Ibi molin̄ de . xx . denar.

Valuit . xx . fol . Modo . c . fol . Waga lib̄e tenuit.

Idē . R . ten . v . hiđ in *BVRDINTONE* . Tra . ē . viii . cař.

In dn̄io funt . ii . 7 xii . uiłłi 7 viii . borđ cū . vi . cař.

★ Ibi molin̄ de . x . fol . 7 xii . ac̄ p̄ti . Valuit . lx . fol . m̊ . c . fol.

Idē . R . ten *TIHESHOCHE* . Ibi fuɲ xxiii . hidæ . *IN FEXHOLE* Tra . ē . xxxii . cař . In dn̄io funt . xi . 7 ix . ferui . *HVND*.

7 liii . uiłłi cū pb̄ro 7 xxviii . borđ hn̄t xxiii . cař.

Ibi . xvi . ac̄ p̄ti . 7 In Waruuic . iii . dom redđ . xviii . den.

Valuit . xx . lib̄ . Modo . xxx . lib̄ . Waga libere tenuit.

Idē . R . ten . v . hiđ in *ETELINCOTE* . Tra . ē . ix . cař . In dn̄io funt . iii . cař . 7 vii . ferui . 7 xxvi . uiłłi 7 iii . borđ cū . viii . cař . Valuit . iiii . lib̄ . Modo . viii . lib̄ . Auegrin 7 Ordec libere tenueř . *IN FERNECVMBE HVND.*

Idē . R . ten . i . hiđ in *HOLEHALE* . Tra . ē . xv . cař.

Ibi funt . xvii . uiłłi 7 xi . borđ cū . vi . cař . Silua dim̄ leuū lḡ . 7 i . q̄rent lať . Valuit 7 uał . iii . lib̄ . Waga te

Idē . R . ten in *OFFEWORDE* . v . hiđ . Tra . ē . vi . cař . nuit.

Ibi funt . iii . cař 7 dim̄ cū . iii . feruis 7 x . borđ . Ibi molin̄ de . iiii . foliđ . Silua . i . leuū lḡ . 7 dimiđ leuū lať.

Valuit . iii . lib̄ . Modo . iiii . lib̄ . Waga lib̄e tenuit . T.R.E.

Idē . R . ten in *EDRICESTONE* . v . hiđ . Tra . ē . v . cař.

In dn̄io funt . ii . 7 ii . ferui . 7 iiii . uiłłi 7 vi . borđ cū . i . cař.

Robert also holds
[in BARCHESTON Hundred]
2 in WOLFORD 7 hides. Land for 10 ploughs.
   In lordship [... ploughs] ; 4 slaves.
      8 villagers and 8 smallholders with a priest have 6 ploughs.
      A mill at 20d.
   The value was 20s; now 100s.
      Waga held it freely.

3 in BURMINGTON 5 hides. Land for 8 ploughs. In lordship 2;
      12 villagers and 8 smallholders with 6 ploughs.
      A mill at 10s; meadow, 12 acres.
   The value was 60s; now 100s.
      Godwin held it freely.

   in FEXHOLE Hundred
4 TYSOE. 23 hides. Land for 32 ploughs. In lordship 11; 9 slaves.
      53 villagers with a priest and 28 smallholders have 23 ploughs.
      Meadow, 16 acres; in Warwick 3 houses which pay 18d.
   The value was £20; now £30.
      Waga held it freely.

5 in IDLICOTE 5 hides. Land for 9 ploughs.
   In lordship 3 ploughs; 7 slaves;
      26 villagers and 3 smallholders with 8 ploughs.
   The value was £4; now £8.
      Hafgrim and Ordheah held it freely.

   in FERNCOMBE Hundred
6 in ULLENHALL 1 hide. Land for 15 ploughs.
      17 villagers and 11 smallholders with 6 ploughs.
      Woodland ½ league long and 1 furlong wide.
   The value was and is £3.
      Waga held it.

7 in 'OFFORD' 5 hides. Land for 6 ploughs. 3½ ploughs, with 3 slaves;
      10 smallholders.
      A mill at 4s; woodland 1 league long and ½ league wide.
   The value was £3; now £4.
      Waga held it freely before 1066.

8 in EDSTONE 5 hides. Land for 5 ploughs. In lordship 2; 2 slaves;
      4 villagers and 6 smallholders with 1 plough.

7 in Waruuic . I . dom̃ redđ . v . den̷ . Silua dim̃ leuu̷

lg̅ . 7 dimiđ q̃rent lat̷ . Valet . III . lib̃ . Ailric 7 Vluuin̷

libere tenuer̅ . *IN PATELAV HVND̅.*

Idē . R . ten̷ . VII . hiđ in *WOTONE* . Tra . ē . IX . car̷ . Ibi fuꝗ

XXIII . uilti cũ pb̃ro 7 XXII . borđ hn̄tes . VI . car̷ .

R uenator
obt' ten' de eo
in *BRANCOTE*.
.I . hiđ . Tra.II.car̷.
ꝗ ibi . ē c̄ . I . uillo
Val . x .foliđ.

Ibi . II . molini de . XI . fot̷ . 7 VIII . ftich anguilt . Silua . II .

leuu̷ lg̅ . 7 una lat̷ . Valet . IIII . lib̃ . Waga libe tenuit .

De eođ Rob̃to ten̷ Aluric . v . hiđ *IN STANLEI HD̅.*   *

in *BVBENHALLE* . Tra . ē . v . car̷ . In dñio . ē una car̷ 7 dim̃ .

cũ . I . feruo . 7 VI . uilti 7 IꞂ . borđ cũ . II . car̷ 7 dim̃ . Ibi molin̄

de . IIII . foliđ . Silua . II . q̃rent lg̅ . 7 tn̄tđ lat̷ . Valet . L . fot̷ .

De . R . ten̷ Grim dimiđ hiđ in *BERTONE*. Idem libe tenuit .

Tra . ē . I . car̷ . Ibi . ē ipfa in dñio . 7 v . ferui . 7 II . uilti 7 III . borđ .

Valuit 7 uat̷ . XX . foliđ . H̄ tra . ē *IN BEDRICESTONE HD̅.*

De . R . ten̷ Orduui . II . hiđ in *WORWARDE* . Tra . ē . VI . car̷ .

In dñio funt . II . 7 IIII . uilti 7 IIII . borđ cũ . I . car̷ . Valet . L . fot̷ .

Aluui libe tenuit .

De . R . ten̷ Aluuin̷ . II . hiđ in eađ uilla . Tra . ē . II . car̷ . In

dñio . ē una . cũ . I . feruo . 7 IIII . uilti 7 III . borđ cũ . I . car̷ .

Valuit . XX . fot̷ . modo . XXX . fot̷ . Aluuin̷ libere tenuit .

In Warwick 1 house which pays 5d; woodland ½ league long
and ½ furlong wide.
Value £3.
Aelfric and Wulfwin held it freely. *Saxon's* !

in PATHLOW Hundred
9　in WOOTTON (WAWEN)　7 hides.　Land for 9 ploughs.
23 villagers with a priest and 22 smallholders who
have 6 ploughs.
2 mills at 11s and 8 sticks of eels; woodland 2 leagues
long and 1 wide.
Value £4.
Waga held it freely.

[in BRINKLOW Hundred]
10　Robert Hunter holds 1 hide from him in BRAMCOTE.　Land for 2
ploughs, which [are] there, with
1 villager.
Value 10s.

in STONELEIGH Hundred
11　also from Robert, Aelfric holds 5 hides in BUBBENHALL.
Land for 5 ploughs.　In lordship 1½ ploughs, with 1 slave;
6 villagers and 2 smallholders with 2½ ploughs.
A mill at 4s; woodland 2 furlongs long and as wide.
Value 50s.
He also held it freely.

From Robert
[in BARCHESTON Hundred]
12　Grim holds ½ hide in BARTON (-on-the Heath).　Land for 1 plough.
It is there, in lordship; 5 slaves;
2 villagers and 3 smallholders.
The value was and is 20s.
This land is in BARCHESTON Hundred.

13　Ordwy holds 2 hides in WOLFORD.　Land for 6 ploughs.　In lordship 2;
4 villagers and 4 smallholders with 1 plough.
Value 50s.
Alfwy held it freely.

14　Alwin holds 2 hides in the same village.　Land for 2 ploughs.
In lordship 1, with 1 slave;
4 villagers and 3 smallholders with 1 plough.
The value was 20s; now 30s.
Alwin held it freely.

ꝟ De . R . ten Iuuein . I . hiđ 7 dimiđ in *VLLAVINTONE*.

Tra . ē . II . car . In dñio . ē una . 7 II . ſerui . cū . I . uillo 7 I . borđ.

Valuit 7 uał xx . ſoliđ . Dodo 7 Leuric libere tenueꝛ.

ꝟ De . R . ten Brion . II . hiđ in *DICFORDE* . Tra . ē . VII . car.

In dñio ſunt . II . 7 IX . ſerui . 7 VIII . uilli 7 III . borđ cū . III.

car . Ibi moliñ de . LXVIII . denaꝛ . Valuit . XL . ſoł . modo

IIII . liƀ . Leuric libere tenuit . T.R.E.   ꝼ caꝛ.

ꝟ De . R . ten Wariñ . v . hiđ in parua *CONTONE* . Tra . ē . VI.

In dñio ſunt . III . car . 7 VIII . ſerui . 7 VIII . uilli 7 II . borđ cū . VI.

car Ibi . VI . ac ꝓti . Valuit LX . ſoł . Modo . c . ſoł . Brictric liƀe ten.

ꝟ De . R . ten Aluuiñ . I . hiđ in *CONTONE* . Tra . ē . I . caꝛ.   ꝼ tenuit.

Ibi ſunt . II . borđ . Valuit 7 uał . x . ſoliđ . Duo fꝛs liƀe tenueꝛ.

ꝟ De . R . ten Hugo . II . hiđ in *MORTONE* . *IN FERNECŬBE HĐ*.

Tra . ē . IIII . car . In dñio . ē una . 7 II . ſerui . 7 v . uilli 7 ꝛ . borđ

cū . II . caꝛ . Ibi ꝓtū . III . qꝛent lg . 7 VI . ptic lať . Silu₂ dimiđ

leuu lg . 7 I . qꝛent . lat . Valuit . xxx . ſoł . Modo . I . ſoliđ.

Grimulf liƀe tenuit.   *IN BERRICⱭSTONE HĐ*.

ꝟ De . R . ten Ailric . I . hiđ in *EDELMITONE* . Tra . ē . I . caꝛ . Ipſa . ē

ibi in dñio . cū . II . ſeruis 7 I . uillo . Valuit . x . ſoł . Modo . xv . ſoł.

ꝟ De . R . ten Hugo . I . hiđ *IN PATELAV HVNDꝟ* Ailric liƀe tenuit.

7 unā v træ in *CLIFORDE* Tra . ē . II . caꝛ . In dñio ꞏ ē una . 7 II.

ſerui . 7 III . uilli 7 III . borđ cū . I . caꝛ . Valuit 7 uał xxx . ſoliđ.

Sauuard liƀe tenuit . T.R.E.

15 Ewein holds 1½ hides in WILLINGTON. Land for 2 ploughs.
In lordship 1; 2 slaves, with
1 villager and 1 smallholder.
The value was and is 20s.
Doda and Leofric held it freely.

16 Brian holds 2 hides in DITCHFORD. Land for 7 ploughs.
In lordship 2; 9 slaves;
8 villagers and 3 smallholders with 3 ploughs.
A mill at 68d.
The value was 40s; now £4.
Leofric held it freely before 1066.

17 Warin holds 5 hides in LITTLE COMPTON. Land for 6 ploughs.
In lordship 3 ploughs; 8 slaves;
8 villagers and 2 smallholders with 6 ploughs.
Meadow, 6 acres.
The value was 60s; now 100s.
Brictric held it freely.

242 d

18 Alwin holds 1 hide in COMPTON (SCORPION). Land for 1 plough.
2 smallholders.
The value was and is 10s.
Two brothers held it freely.

in FERNCOMBE Hundred
19 Hugh holds 2 hides in MORTON (BAGOT). Land for 4 ploughs.
In lordship 1; 2 slaves;
5 villagers and 5 smallholders with 2 ploughs.
Meadow, 3 furlongs long and 6 perches wide; woodland ½
league long and 1 furlong wide.
The value was 30s; now 50s.
Grimulf held it freely.

in BARCHESTON Hundred
20 Alric holds 1 hide in ILMINGTON. Land for 1 plough. It is there,
in lordship, with 2 slaves;
1 villager.
The value was 10s; now 15s.
Alric held it freely.

in PATHLOW Hundred
21 Hugh holds 1 hide and 1 virgate of land in (RUIN) CLIFFORD.
Land for 2 ploughs. In lordship 1; 2 slaves;
3 villagers and 3 smallholders with 1 plough.
The value was and is 30s.
Saeward held it freely before 1066.

De.R.ten Wills.v.hiđ in *CLOTONE*.Tra.ē.iii.car.In dñio
ē una.cū.i.feruo.7 vii.uilli 7 iii.borđ cū.ii.car.Valuit
7 uat.lx.foliđ.Odo 7 Aileua liđe tenueř.T.R.E.
De.R.teñ Herueus.i.hiđ in *MORTONE*.Tra.ē.ii.car.
In dñio tam funt.ii.7 iiii.ferui.7 v.uilli 7 ii.borđ cū.ii.car.
Va'uit.xx.fot.Modo.xl.fot.Waga liđe tenuit T.R.E.
De.R.ten Vrfer.i.hiđ 7 unā v.7.iii.partē.i.uirgæ
in *VLWARDITONE*.Tra.ē.ii.car.In dñio.ē una.cū.i.feruo.
7 ii.uillis.7 i.q̃rent p̃ti.Valuit.x.fot.Modo.xx.fot.
Simund dan liđe tenuit T.R.E.
De.R.ten Drogo.iii.hiđ in *WITELEIA*.Tra.ē.vi.car.In dñio
ē una.7 ii.ferui.7 iii.uilli 7 vi.borđ cū.ii.car.Ibi moliñ de.ii.
foliđ.7 x.ač p̃ti.Silua dimiđ leuu lḡ.7 ii.q̃rent lat.
Valuit.xx.foliđ.modo.xl.fot.Tres fřs tenueř.
De.R.ten Ludichel.i.hiđ 7 dimiđ in *LONGELEI*.Tra.ē.ii.car.
In dñio funt.ii.cū.i.feruo.7 iii.uilli 7 iiii.borđ cū.ii.car.
Ibi.xii.ač p̃ti.Silua.i.leuu lḡ.7 dim leuu lat.Valuit.xxx.
fot.modo.xl.fot.Ernui liđe tenuit.
De.R.ten Ailric.i.hiđ in *BVRLEI*.Tra.ē.i.car.Ibi.ē uñ
uills 7 i.feru.7 i.ač p̃ti.Valuit.xx.fot.Modo.x.fot.Iđē tenuit.
Leuing ten in *OFFEWORDE* trā.i.car de inland.7 ibi hť.i.
car.Valuit 7 uat x.fot.

22 William holds 5 hides in CLOPTON. Land for 3 ploughs.
In lordship 1, with 1 slave;
    7 villagers and 3 smallholders with 2 ploughs.
The value was and is 60s.
    Odo and Aelfeva held it freely before 1066.

[in FERNCOMBE Hundred]
23 Hervey holds 1 hide in NORTON (LINDSEY). Land for 2 ploughs.
In lordship, however, 2; 4 slaves;
    5 villagers and 2 smallholders with 2 ploughs.
The value was 20s; now 40s.
    Waga held it freely before 1066.

24 Urfer holds 1 hide, 1 virgate and the third part of 1 virgate in
WOLVERTON. Land for 2 ploughs. In lordship 1, with 1 slave ;
    2 villagers.
Meadow, 1 furlong.
The value was 10s; now 20s.
    Sigmund the Dane held it freely before 1066.

25 Drogo holds 3 hides in WHITLEY. Land for 6 ploughs.
In lordship 1; 2 slaves;
    3 villagers and 6 smallholders with 2 ploughs.
    A mill at 2s; meadow, 10 acres; woodland ½ league long
      and 2 furlongs wide.
The value was 20s; now 40s.
    Three brothers held it.

26 Iudichael holds 1½ hides in LANGLEY. Land for 2 ploughs.
In lordship 2, with 1 slave;
    3 villagers and 4 smallholders with 2 ploughs.
    Meadow, 12 acres; woodland 1 league long and ½ league wide.
The value was 30s; now 40s.
    Ernwy held it freely.

27 Alric holds 1 hide in BEARLEY. Land for 1 plough.
    1 villager and 1 slave.
    Meadow, 1 acre.
The value was 20s; now 10s.
    He also held it [before 1066].

28 In 'OFFORD' Leofing holds land for 1 plough, of *inland;*
he has 1 plough.
The value was and is 10s.

.XXIII. TERRA ROBERTI DISPENSATOŘ *IN COLESHELLE HĐ.*

*fr   ROBERTVS Diſpenſator ten de rege VIIII.hiđ in *MERSTON.*
Tra.ē.VIII.car. In dñio ſunt.ii.7 ii.ſerui.7 XXIIII.uiłłi cũ
VI.car̄.Ibi moliñ de.x.ſoliđ.7 VI.ac̄ p̄ti.Valuit 7 uał.IIII.liɓ.
Ailmar liɓe tenuit T.R.E.Similit 7 hanc ſequentē trā.
Idem.Ro.ten dimiđ hiđ in *FILINGELEI*.Tra.ē.ii.car̄.Ibi
ſunt.IIII.uiłłi cũ pɓro 7 i.borđ hñtes.ii.car̄.Ibi.i.ac̄ p̄ti.
Silua.ii.leuu łḡ.7 i.leu lat̄.Valuit.x.ſoł.Modo.xx.ſoł
Idem.R.ten.i.hiđ in *LETH*.Tra.ē.i.car̄.Ibi.i.miles cũ.i.
car̄.7 IIII.uiłłi 7 i.borđ 7 ii.ſerui.cũ.i.car̄.Ibi.ii.ac̄ p̄ti.
Valuit.x.ſoliđ.Vał.xv.ſoliđ.Aluuin liɓe tenuit.
Idē.R.ten.x.hiđ in *BERTANESTONE*.Tra.ē.x.car̄.
Ibi ſunt.VI.liɓi hões 7 IX.uiłłi 7 IIII.borđ cũ.x.car̄.
Ibi moliñ de.IIII.ſoliđ.Silua dimiđ leuu łḡ.7 III.q̃z lat̄.
Valuit 7 uał.c.ſoliđ.Ailmar liɓe tenuit.7 lic̄tia regis.W.
uendiđ Aluuino uicecomiti.

.XXII. TERRA ROBERTI DE VECI.   *IN BOMELAV HVNĐ.*

★   ROBERTVS ten de rege.v.hiđ 7 dim.in *VLVEĿA.*
Tra.ē.VIII.car̄.In dñio ſunt.ii.7 IIII.ſerui.7 xv.uiłłi
cũ pɓro 7 ii.borđ hñt.VII.car̄.Ibi.L.ac̄ p̄ti.Paſturæ
dimiđ leuu in łḡ 7 lat̄.Valuit..iɓ.Modo.L.ſoł.
Alric filius Meriet liɓe tenuit.T.R.E.
Iđ Roɓt ten.III.virḡ træ in *WITECORE*.Tra.ē.i.car̄.7 ibi.ē cũ.i.
uiłło.7 ii.ac̄ p̄ti.Valuit.x.ſoł.M.ii.ſoł.Ailric liɓe tenuit.

23   LAND OF ROBERT THE BURSAR *-- WHERE IS BURSAR?*

In COLESHILL Hundred

fr 1   Robert the Bursar holds 9 hides in (LEA) MARSTON from the King.
Land for 8 ploughs. In lordship 2; 2 slaves;
    24 villagers with 6 ploughs.
    A mill at 10s; meadow, 6 acres.
The value was and is £4.
    Aelmer held it freely before 1066, and the following land likewise.

2   Robert also holds ½ hide in FILLONGLEY. Land for 2 ploughs.
    4 villagers with a priest and 1 smallholder who have 2 ploughs.
    Meadow, 1 acre; woodland 2 leagues long and 1 league wide.
The value was 10s; now 20s.

3   Robert also holds 1 hide in LEA (MARSTON). Land for 1 plough.
    1 man-at-arms with 1 plough; 4 villagers, 1 smallholder
      and 2 slaves with 1 plough.
    Meadow, 2 acres.
The value was 10s; the value is 15s.
    Alwin held it freely.

4   Robert also holds 10 hides in BARSTON. Land for 10 ploughs.
    6 free men, 9 villagers and 4 smallholders with 10 ploughs.
    A mill at 4s; woodland ½ league long and 3 furlongs wide.
The value was and is 100s.
    Aelmer held it freely and with King William's permission
sold it to Alwin the Sheriff.

24   LAND OF ROBERT OF VESSEY   *WHERE IS VESSEY?*

In BRINKLOW Hundred

1   Robert of Vessey holds 5½ hides in WOLVEY from the King.
Land for 8 ploughs. In lordship 2; 4 slaves.
    15 villagers with a priest and 2 smallholders have 7 ploughs.
    Meadow, 50 acres; pasture ½ league in length and width.
The value was £3?; now 50s.
    Alric son of Mergeat held it freely before 1066.

[in COLESHILL Hundred]

2   Robert also holds 3 virgates of land in (NETHER?) WHITACRE.
Land for 1 plough. It is there, with
    1 villager.
    Meadow, 2 acres.
The value was 10s; now 2s.
    Alric held it freely.

.XXV. TERRA RADVLFI DE MORTEMER. *IN BOMELAV HD.*

RADVLFVS De Mortemer teñ *STRATONE*. 7 Roger
de eo. Ibi funt. III. hidæ. Tra. ē. vi. cař. In dñio funt. II
7 VIII. uitti 7 IIII. borđ cū. IIII. cař. Ibi. v. ač pti.
Valuit. XL. fol. Modo. XXX. fol. Edricus libe tenuit.

.XXVI. TERRA RADVLFI DE LIMESI.

RADVLFVS De Limefi teñ de rege *IN BVDEBROC*
v. hiđ. Tra. ē. XII. cař. In dñio funt. III. cař. 7 VII. ferui.
7 XXII. uitti 7 XIII. borđ cū. vi. cař. Ibi moliñ de. II. fol.
7 XXX. ač pti. Silua. I. leuū lḡ. 7 III. q̃rent lať.
In Waruuic. VII. dom. redđt VII. fol p annū.
Valuit 7 uat. VIII. liƀ. Eduin tenuit.

.XXVII. TERRA WILLI FILIJ ANSCVLFI.

WILLELM filius Anfculfi teñ de rege *ESTONE*.
7 Godmund de eo. Ibi funt. VIII. hidæ. Tra. ē. XX. cař.
In dñio. ē tra. vi. cař. f; carucæ ibi ñ fuÿ. Ibi. XXX.
uitti cū pƀro 7 I. feruo 7 XII. borđ hñt. XVIII. cař.
Ibi moliñ de. III. fol. Silua. III. leuū lḡ. 7 dim leū lať.
Valuit. IIII. liƀ. Modo. c. fol. Eduin tenuit.

De. W. teñ Stannechetel. I. hiđ in *WITONE*. Tra. ē
IIII. cař. In dñio. ē una. 7 II. ferui. 7 I. uitts 7 II. borđ
cū. II. cař. Valuit. x. fol. Modo. xx. Idē. S. libe tenuit.

De. W. teñ Petrus. III. hiđ in *HARDINTONE*. Tra. ē. vi.
cař. In dñio. ē una. 7 II. ferui. 7 IX. uitti 7 III. borđ cū. IIII.
cař. Ibi moliñ de. III. fol. 7 v. ač pti. Silua. I. leuū lḡ.
7 dimiđ lať. f; in defenfo regis. ē. Valuit. xx. fol. m̄. xxx.
Eduin tenuit.

25   LAND OF RALPH OF MORTIMER

In BRINKLOW Hundred

1   Ralph of Mortimer holds STRETTON (BASKERVILLE) and Roger
     from him. 3 hides. Land for 6 ploughs. In lordship 2;
        8 villagers and 4 smallholders with 4 ploughs.
        Meadow, 5 acres.
     The value was 40s; now 30s.
        Edric held it freely.

26   LAND OF RALPH OF LIMESY

[In FERNCOMBE Hundred]

1   Ralph of Limesy holds 5 hides in BUDBROOKE from the King.
     Land for 12 ploughs. In lordship 3 ploughs; 7 slaves;
        22 villagers and 13 smallholders with 6 ploughs.
        A mill at 2s; meadow, 30 acres; woodland 1 league long
          and 3 furlongs wide; in Warwick 7 houses which pay 7s a year.
     The value was and is £8.
        Earl Edwin held it.

27   LAND OF WILLIAM SON OF ANSCULF

[In COLESHILL Hundred]

1   William son of Ansculf holds ASTON from the King and Godmund
     from him. 8 hides. Land for 20 ploughs. In lordship land
     for 6 ploughs, but the ploughs are not there.
        30 villagers with a priest, 1 slave and 12 smallholders
          have 18 ploughs.
        A mill at 3s; woodland 3 leagues long and ½ league wide.
     The value was £4; now 100s.
        Earl Edwin held it.

From William

2   Stanketel holds 1 hide in WITTON. Land for 4 ploughs.
     In lordship 1; 2 slaves;
        1 villager and 2 smallholders with 2 ploughs.
     The value was 10s; now 20s.
        Stanketel also held it freely.

3   Peter holds 3 hides in ERDINGTON. Land for 6 ploughs.
     In lordship 1; 2 slaves;
        9 villagers and 3 smallholders with 4 ploughs.
        A mill at 3s; meadow, 5 acres; woodland 1 league long
          and ½ wide, but it is within the King's Enclosure.
     The value was 20s; now 30s.
        Earl Edwin held it.

⟋De.W.teñ Drogo.II.hiđ in *CELBOLDESTONE*.Tra.ē

IIII.caŕ.In dñio.ē.I.caŕ 7 dim.7 III.uilłi 7 VII.borđ

cū.v.caŕ.Silua.III.q̃rent lat.7 dim leuu lḡ.

Valuit.xx.fot.Modo.xxx.Afchi 7 Aluui libe tenueŕ.

⟋De.W.teñ Ricoard.IIII.hiđ in *BERMINGEHA*.Tra

ē.VI.caŕ.In dñio.ē.una.7 v.uilłi 7 IIII.borđ cū.II.caŕ.

Silua dim leuu lḡ.7 II.q̃rent lat.Valuit 7 uał.xx.fot.

Vluuin libe tenuit.T.R.E. *IN CVDVLVESTAN HĎ.*

⟋De.W.teñ Roger.II.hiđ in *ESENINGETONE*.Tra.ē.VI.

caŕ.In dñio.ē una.7 II.ferui.7 xv.uilłi 7 II.borđ cū.III.caŕ.

Silua.I.leuu lḡ.7 tntđ lat.In Bifcopefberie.ē una v

tre ptineȝ ad hanc trā.f; vafta.ē.Valuit 7 uał.xx.fot.

★ XXVIII TERRA WILLI FILIJ CORBUCION.

Wilłs filius Corbucion teñ de rege *ERMENDONE*.

7 Robtus de eo in uadimoñ.Ibi funt.IIII.hidæ.

Tra.ē.v.caŕ.In dñio funt.II.7 VI.ferui.7 VI.uilłi 7 III.

borđ cū.II.caŕ 7 dim.Ibi.x.ać p̃ti.Silua.IIII.q̃rent

lḡ.7 II.q̃rent lał.Valuit 7 uał.L.fot.Turchil libe tenuit..

⟋De.W.teñ Ailmar.II.hiđ in *CINTONE*.Tra.ē.II.caŕ.

Ibi funt.v.uilłi hñtes eas.Silua dim leuu lḡ.7 IIII.q̃ȝ

lał.Valuit 7 uał.x.fot.Turchil libe tenuit.T.R.E.

⟋De.W.teñ Juhell.II.hiđ 7 dim in *SECHINTONE*.Tra.ē

IIII.caŕ.In dñio.ē una.7 VI.uilłi 7 IIII.borđ cū.II.caŕ.

Ibi.I.ać p̃ti 7 dimiđ.Valuit 7 uał.xxx.fot.Ernui tenuit.

4 Drogo holds 2 hides in EDGBASTON. Land for 4 ploughs.
In lordship 1½ ploughs;
   3 villagers and 7 smallholders with 5 ploughs.
   Woodland 3 furlongs wide and ½ league long.
The value was 20s; now 30s.
   Aski and Alfwy held it freely.

5 Richard holds 4 hides in BIRMINGHAM. Land for 6 ploughs.
In lordship 1;
   5 villagers and 4 smallholders with 2 ploughs.
   Woodland ½ league long and 2 furlongs wide.
The value was and is 20s.
   Wulfwin held it freely before 1066.

  in CUTTLESTONE Hundred (in Staffordshire)
6 Roger holds 2 hides in ESSINGTON. Land for 6 ploughs.
In lordship 1; 2 slaves;
   15 villagers and 2 smallholders with 3 ploughs.
   Woodland 1 league long and as wide; in Bushbury is
      1 virgate of land which belongs to this land, but it is waste.
The value was and is 20s.

28   LAND OF WILLIAM SON OF CORBUCION

[In COLESHILL Hundred]
1 William son of Corbucion holds AMINGTON from the King and
Robert from him, in pledge. 4 hides. Land for 5 ploughs.
In lordship 2; 6 slaves;
   6 villagers and 3 smallholders with 2½ ploughs.
   Meadow, 10 acres; woodland 4 furlongs long and 2 furlongs wide.
The value was and is 50s.
   Thorkell Battock held it freely.

From William
2 Aelmer holds 2 hides in KINETON (GREEN). Land for 2 ploughs.
   5 villagers who have them.
   Woodland ½ league long and 4 furlongs wide.
The value was and is 10s.
   Thorkell held it freely before 1066.

3 Iudhael holds 2½ hides in SECKINGTON. Land for 4 ploughs.
In lordship 1;
   6 villagers and 4 smallholders with 2 ploughs.
   Meadow, 1½ acres.
The value was and is 30s.
   Ernwy held it.

╱De . W . teñ Ordric . II . hiđ in *WITSCAGA* . Tra . ē . II . cař.

Ibi ſunt . III . uiłłi cũ p̃ro 7 IIII . borđ . Silua . III . q̃rent

lg̃ . 7 una lať . Valuit . xxx . ſol . Modo . x . ſol . Idē Ordric

╱De . W . teñ Roger . I . hiđ *IN MERETON HĎ* ╱ libe tenuit.

in *HODENELLE* . . . . . ē . I . cař . Ipſa ibi . ē cũ . II . uiłłis 7 II . borđ.

Ibi . VI . ãc p̃ti . Valuit . x . ſol . Modo . xx . ſol . Aluui libe tenuit.

╱De . W . teñ Oſmund . II . hiđ in *HƲNINGEHA* . Tra . ē . IIII . cař.

In dñio . ē una . 7 II . ſerui . 7 IIII . uiłłi 7 II . borđ cũ . I . cař . Ibi . VI.

ãc p̃ti . Valuit . XL . ſol . modo . xxx . ſol . Erneuui . libe tenuit . T.R.E.

╱De . W . teñ Chetel . I . hiđ 7 dim in eađ uilla . 7 dim v̄ træ.

Tra . ē . III . cař . In dñio . ē una . cũ . I . ſeruo . 7 III . uiłłi 7 v . borđ

cũ . II . cař . Ibi . VI . ãc p̃ti . Valuit 7 uał xxx . ſol . Saulf libe tenuit.

╱De . W . teñ Johais . II . virg træ 7 dim in *WESTONE* . *IN STANLEI HĎ*.

Tra . ē . I . cař 7 dimiđ . In dñio . ē una . cũ . I . uiłło 7 I . borđ.

Ibi . x . ãc p̃ti . Valuit 7 uał . x . ſol . Sauuold libe tenuit.

╱De . W . teñ Roger unā v̄ træ in *CONDELME* . Tra . ē . I . cař.

Ibi ſunt . II . borđ . Silua dim leu lg̃ . 7 IIII . q̃rent lať . Valuit

v . ſol . Modo . IIII . ſol .   *IN BERRICESTONE HƲND*.

╱De . W . teñ Johais . II . hiđ 7 dim in *BERRICESTONE* . Tra . ē

III . cař 7 dimiđ . In dñio ſunt . II . 7 v . uiłłi 7 VII . borđ cũ . I . cař

4 Ordric holds 2 hides in WISHAW. Land for 2 ploughs.
   3 villagers with a priest and 4 smallholders.
   Woodland 3 furlongs long and 1 wide.
The value was 30s; now 10s.
   Ordric also held it freely.

in MARTON Hundred

5 Roger holds 1 hide in HODNELL. [Land for] 1 plough.
It is there, with
   2 villagers and 2 smallholders.
   Meadow, 6 acres.
The value was 10s; now 20s.
   Alfwy held it freely.

6 Osmund holds 2 hides in HUNNINGHAM. Land for 4 ploughs.   243 b
In lordship 1; 2 slaves;
   4 villagers and 2 smallholders with 1 plough.
   Meadow, 6 acres.
The value was 40s; now 30s.
   Ernwy held it freely before 1066.

7 Ketel holds 1½ hides and ½ virgate of land in the same village.
Land for 3 ploughs. In lordship 1, with 1 slave;
   3 villagers and 5 smallholders with 2 ploughs.
   Meadow, 6 acres.
The value was and is 30s.
   Saewulf held it freely.

in STONELEIGH Hundred

8 Johais holds 2½ virgates of land in WESTON (-under-Wetherley).
Land for 1½ ploughs. In lordship 1, with
   1 villager and 1 smallholder.
   Meadow, 10 acres.
The value was and is 10s.
   Saewold held it freely.

9 Roger holds 1 virgate of land in COUNDON. Land for 1 plough.
   2 smallholders.
   Woodland ½ league long and 4 furlongs wide.
The value was 5s; now 4s.

in BARCHESTON Hundred

10 Johais holds 2½ hides in BARCHESTON. Land for 3½ ploughs.
In lordship 2;
   5 villagers and 7 smallholders with 1½ ploughs.

7 dimid. Ibi moliñ de. c. deñ. 7 xii. ac p̃ti. Valuit. xl. folid.
Modo. l. folid. Wiching libe tenuit. T.R.E.

⌐ De. W. teñ Goisfrid. i. hid in MAPELBERGE. Tra. e̅. iii. car.
In dñio. e̅ una. cu̅. i. feruo. 7 ii. uilli cu̅. i. car. Ibi. x. ac p̃ti.
Silua. i. q̃rent lg. 7 i. lat. Valuit. xx. fol. modo. xv. folid.

⌐ De. W. teñ Turchil. i. hid 7 dimid   ⌐ Leuiet libe tenuit.
in ECLESHELLE. Tra. e̅. i. car. Ibi funt. ii. bord. 7 x. ac p̃ti.
Valuit. x. fol. Modo. v. fol. Suain libe tenuit T.R.E.

⌐ De. W. teñ Leuric 7 Eileua. iii. hid 7 una v træ in GRASTON.
Tra. e̅. ii. car. In dñio. e̅ una. 7 ii. ferui. 7 uñ uills 7 iii. bord
cu̅. i. car. Ibi. iiii. ac p̃ti. Valuit. xl. fol. Modo. xxx. folid.

⌐ De. W. teñ Wills. ii. hid in BENINTON. ⌐ Ide̅ ipfi libe tenuer̃.
Tra. e̅. ii. car. In dñio. e̅ una. cu̅. i. feruo 7 v. bord.
Ibi. iii. ac p̃ti. De parte molini. iiii. fu̅mas annonæ. 7 viii.
ftich anguill. 7 de Wich. iii. fu̅mas falis. Valuit. xx. fol.
Modo. xxx. folid. Edric libe tenuit T.R.E. IN KEMELAV

Ipfe Wills ten. i. hid in BEREFORD de rege.   ⌐ HVND.
Tra. e̅. ii. car. Ibi funt. ii. ferui. 7 ix. ac p̃ti.
Valuit. xx^{ti}. fol. Modo. v. folid. Saulf tenuit T.R.E.

A mill at 100d; meadow, 12 acres.
The value was 40s; now 50s.
Wicking held it freely before 1066.

[in FERNCOMBE Hundred]

11 Geoffrey holds 1 hide in MAPPLEBOROUGH. Land for 3 ploughs.
In lordship 1, with 1 slave;
2 villagers with 1 plough.
Meadow, 10 acres; woodland 1 furlong long and 1 wide.
The value was 20s; now 15s.
Leofgeat held it freely.

12 Thorkell holds 1½ hides in EXHALL. Land for 1 plough.
2 smallholders.
Meadow, 10 acres.
The value was 10s; now 5s.
Swein held it freely before 1066.

13 Leofric and Aelfeva hold 3 hides and 1 virgate of land in (ARDENS)
GRAFTON. Land for 2 ploughs. In lordship 1; 2 slaves;
1 villager and 3 smallholders with 1 plough.
Meadow, 4 acres.
The value was 40s; now 30s.
They also held it themselves freely.

14 William holds 2 hides in BINTON. Land for 2 ploughs.
In lordship 1, with 1 slave;
5 smallholders.
Meadow, 3 acres; from part of a mill 4 packloads of corn
and 8 sticks of eels; from Droitwich 3 packloads of salt.
The value was 20s; now 30s.
Edric held it freely before 1066.

In TREMLOW Hundred

15 William holds 1 hide himself from the King in BARFORD.
Land for 2 ploughs. 2 slaves;
Meadow, 9 acres.
The value was 20s; now 5s.
Saewulf held it before 1066.

Idē. W . ten . IIII . hiđ in *STODLEI*. *IN FERNECŪBE HVND*. ii7dˡ.*

Tra . ē . XI . car̄ . In dn̄io ſunt . II . 7 III . ſerui 7 XIX . uitti cū

p̄ro 7 XII . borđ hn̄t . IX . car̄ . Ibi moliñ de . V . ſoliđ . 7 XXIIII. or

ac p̄ti . Salina redđ . XIX . ſūmas ſalis . Silua . I . leuū lḡ.

7 dim leu lat . Valuit 7 uat . C . ſoliđ . Suain libe tenuit.

Idē . W . ten . II . hiđ 7 dim 7 II . part uni v in *VLWARDITONE*. as

Tra . ē . V . car̄ . In dn̄io . ē una . 7 IIII . ſeruī . 7 X . uitti 7 VII . borđ v.v̄*

cū . V . car̄ . Ibi . XX . ac p̄ti . Silua . I . q̄rent lḡ . 7 dim lat.

In Waruuic . I . dom redđ . VIII . denar . Valuit XXX . ſoliđ. 9

Modo . LX . ſot . Ernuin libe tenuit . T.R.E.

Idē . W . ten . IIII . hiđ in *BVRLEI* . Tra . ē . IIII . car̄ . In dn̄io . ē una . ii7dv̄*

7 II . ſerui . 7 IX . uitti 7 VI . borđ cū . V . car̄ . Ibi . IIII . ac p̄ti.

In Waruuic . I . dom redđ . VIII . den . Valuit . LX . ſot . m̄ . XL . ſot. 9

Erneuin 7 mat ej libe tenuer̄ . *IN COLVESTAN HĐ*. 9

Idē . W . ten *CILLENTONE* . Ibi ſuꝼ . III . hidæ . Tra . ē . VI . car̄ . In

dn̄io . ē una car̄ . 7 IX . ſerui . 7 XIII . uitti 7 VI . borđ cū . V . car̄.

Ibi . II . ac p̄ti . Silua . II . leuū lḡ . 7 dim leu lat . Valuit . IIII . libꝑ.

Modo . XXX . ſoliđ . Eps de Ceſtre calūniat hanc tra.

XXIX. TERRA WILLI Buenuaſleth *IN ꝰEMELAV HVND*.

Witts Buenuaſleth ten de rege *LISTECORNE* . Ibi ſunt

. V . hidæ p̄t inland . Tra . ē . XVIII . car̄ . In dn̄io ſunt . II . car̄.

7 VII . ſerui . 7 XIX . uitti 7 IX . borđ cū p̄ro hn̄t . VI . car̄.

Ibi . XXX . ac p̄ti . 7 una Graua . II . q̄rent lḡ . 7 XX . ptic lat. coiñ 9

Valuit . C . ſoliđ . Modo . VII . libꝑ . Radulf tenuit.

243 b

William also holds
　in FERNCOMBE Hundred
16　in STUDLEY 4 hides. Land for 11 ploughs. In lordship 2; 3 slaves.　　　　2½
　　　19 villagers with a priest and 12 smallholders have 9 ploughs.
　　　A mill at 5s; meadow, 24 acres; a salt-house which pays 19
　　　　packloads of salt; woodland 1 league long and ½ league wide.
　　The value was and is 100s.
　　　Swein held it freely.

17　in WOLVERTON 2½ hides and 2 parts of 1 virgate.
　　Land for 5 ploughs. In lordship 1; 4 slaves;　　　　　　　　　　　　5 v
　　　10 villagers and 7 smallholders with 5 ploughs.
　　　Meadow, 20 acres; woodland 1 furlong long and ½
　　　　wide; in Warwick 1 house which pays 8d.
　　The value was 30s; now 60s.
　　　Ernwin held it freely before 1066.

18　in BEARLEY 4 hides. Land for 4 ploughs. In lordship 1; 2 slaves;　　2½ v
　　　9 villagers and 6 smallholders with 5 ploughs.
　　　Meadow, 4 acres; in Warwick 1 house which pays 8d.
　　The value was 60s; now 40s.
　　　Ernwin and his mother held it freely.

　in CUTTLESTONE Hundred (in Staffordshire)
19　CHILLINGTON. 3 hides. Land for 6 ploughs.
　In lordship 1 plough; 9 slaves;
　　　13 villagers and 6 smallholders with 5 ploughs.
　　　Meadow, 2 acres; woodland 2 leagues long and ½ league wide.
　　The value was £4; now 30s.
　　　The Bishop of Chester claims this land.

29　　　　　　LAND OF WILLIAM BONVALLET

In TREMLOW Hundred
1　William Bonvallet holds LIGHTHORNE from the King. 5 hides,
　besides the *inland*. Land for 18 ploughs. In lordship 2 ploughs;
　7 slaves.
　　　19 villagers and 9 smallholders with a priest have 6 ploughs.
　　　Meadow, 30 acres; a copse 2 furlongs long and 20 perches wide.
　　The value was 100s; now £7.
　　　Earl Ralph held it.

Idē Wills ten´.iii.v´ træ in *Erbvrberie*. I*N Stanlei* H̅D̅.
Tra.e̅.ii.car̅. Ibi sunt.ii.uilli. Valuit.x.sol.modo.v.sol.
Aluuin´ libe tenuit.T.R.E. I*N Fernecvbe* H̅D̅

⌐De.W.ten´ Roger´.iiii.hid 7 dimid in *Optone*. Tra est
viii.car̅. In dn̅io.e̅ una 7 dimid.7 iiii.serui.7 x.uilli
7 v.bord cu̅.iiii.car̅. Ibi.xxx.ac̅ p̅ti. Silua.x.qrent´
7 xviii.ptic lg̅.7 v.qrent´ lat̅. Valet.lxx.sol. Valuit.x.
solid. Tres hōes Leurici libe tenuer̅.

⌐De.W.ten´ Hugo.ii.hid in *Spernore*. Tra.e̅.iiii.car̅.
In dn̅io.e̅ una.7 iiii.uilli 7 vii.bord cu̅.iii.car̅. Ibi mo
linu̅ de.iiii.solid.7 vii.stich anguill.7 viii.ac̅ p̅ti.
Silua.iii.qrent´ lg̅.7 una lat̅. Valet.xl.sol.

⌐De.W.ten´ Wills.i.hid in *Stodlei*. Tra.e̅.ii.car̅.
In dn̅io.e̅ una car̅.7 iiii.ac̅ p̅ti. Silua.iii.qrent´ lg̅.
7 ii.qrent´ lat̅. Valet.x.solid. Godric libe tenuit.

.XXX. T*ERRA* G*oisfridi* D*e* M*annevile*.

Goisfrid´ De Manneuile ten de rege *Cvntone*.
Ibi sunt.xxx.hidæ. Tra.e̅.xx.car̅. In dn̅io sunt.vii.
7 xxv.serui.7 xlv.uilli cu̅ p̅bro 7 xiii.bord.7 ii.milit´
hn̅t.x.car̅. Ibi molin̅ de.x.solid.7 p̅ti.iii.qrent´ lg̅.
7 tntd lat̅. Silua.ii.qrent´ in lg̅ 7 lat̅. Valuit.xv.lib.
Modo.xxx.lib. Asgar stalre tenuit. I*N Honesberie* H̅D̅.

*i.7 q̅´p De eod Goisfrido ten´ Wills dimid hid 7.iiii.parte̅
uni´ hid in *Wimelestone*. Tra.e̅.i.car̅ 7 dim. In dn̅io
e̅ una car̅.cu̅.ii.bord. Valuit.xx.sol. Modo.xv.sol.

In STONELEIGH Hundred
2   William also holds 3 virgates of land in HARBURY. Land for 2 ploughs.
2 villagers.
The value was 10s; now 5s.
Alwin held it freely before 1066.

In FERNCOMBE Hundred
3   Roger holds 4½ hides in UPTON from William. Land for 8 ploughs.
In lordship 1½; 4 slaves;
10 villagers and 5 smallholders with 4 ploughs.
Meadow, 30 acres; woodland 10 furlongs and 18 perches
long and 5 furlongs wide.
Value 70s; the value was 10s.
Three of Earl Leofric's men held it freely.

4   Hugh holds 2 hides in SPERNALL from William. Land for 4 ploughs.
In lordship 1;
4 villagers and 7 smallholders with 3 ploughs.
A mill at 4s and 7 sticks of eels; meadow, 8 acres;
woodland 3 furlongs long and 1 wide.
Value 40s.

5   William holds 1 hide in STUDLEY from William. Land for 2 ploughs.
In lordship 1 plough.
Meadow, 4 acres; woodland 3 furlongs long and 2 furlongs wide.
Value 10s.
Godric held it freely.

30   LAND OF GEOFFREY DE MANDEVILLE

[In BARCHESTON Hundred]
1   Geoffrey de Mandeville holds (LONG) COMPTON from the King. 30 hides.
Land for 20 ploughs. In lordship 7; 25 slaves.
45 villagers with a priest, 13 smallholders and 2 men-at-arms
have 10 ploughs.
A mill at 10s; meadow, 3 furlongs long and as wide;
woodland 2 furlongs in length and width.
The value was £15; now £30.
Asgar the Constable held it.

In HUNSBURY Hundred
2   Also from Geoffrey, William holds ½ hide and the fourth   1¼
part of 1 hide in WORMLEIGHTON. Land for 1½ ploughs.
In lordship 1 plough, with
2 smallholders.
The value was 20s; now 15s.

*vii.   GOISFRID de Wirce ten de rege *CHIRCHEBERIE.*

Ibi funt. xv. hidæ. Tra. ē. xx. caŕ. In dnio funt. vii.

7 vi. ſerui. 7 ii. ancillæ. 7 xli. uiłł 7 ii. borđ cū. ii. pbris

hntes xxi. caŕ. Ibi. xl. ac pti.

In hoc m̄ hnt monachi S Nicolai. ii. caŕ. 7 xxii. uiłłos

7 vi. borđ cū. v. caŕ.   ʃ libe tenuit.

Toŕ ualuit. c. ſoł. 7 poſt. xl. ſoł. Modo. x. liɓ. Leuuin

*iiii.   Idē. Go. ten *NEWEBOLD*. Ibi funt. viii. hidæ. Tra. ē. xvi.

caŕ. In dnio funt. iii. 7 ii. ſerui. 7 xxv. uiłłi 7 viii. borđ

cū. xi. caŕ. Valuit 7 uał. c. ſoliđ. Leuuin liɓe tenuit.

*.iiii.   Idē G. ten *FENINIVVEBOLD*. Ibi funt. viii. hidæ. Tra

eſt. xvi. caŕ. In dnio funt. iiii. caŕ. 7 viii. ſerui. 7 xxvi.

uiłłi 7 iii. borđ cū. x. caŕ. Ibi. x. ac pti.   ʃ HVND.

Valuit 7 uał. vii. liɓ. Leuuin liɓe tenuit. *IN MERETON*

*ii.   Idē. G. ten. v. hiđ in *LELLEFORD*. Tra. ē. xiiii. caŕ. In

dnio. ē una. 7 xiiii. uiłłi 7 vii. borđ hnt. vii. caŕ.

Ibi molin de. xiiii. ſoliđ. Valuit. xl. ſoł. Modo. l. ſoł.

*v.   Idē. G. ten *WAPEBERIE*. Ibi funt. v. hidæ. Tra. ē. xv.

caŕ. In dnio funt. iii. caŕ. 7 vi. ſerui. 7 xix. uiłłi 7 vi.

borđ cū. x. caŕ. Ibi molin de. vi. ſoliđ 7 viii. denaŕ.

Silua dimiđ leuŭ lḡ. 7 ii. q̃rent laŕ. Valuit 7 uał. cx. ſoł.

*vii.   Idē. G. ten *HANTONE*. Ibi funt. x. hidæ.

Tra. ē. xxii. caŕ. In dnio funt. ii. 7 ii. ſerui. 7 ii. ancillæ.

7 l. uiłłi cū pbro 7 xvi. borđ hnt. xiii. caŕ. Ibi molin

de. xl. denaŕ. 7 x. ac pti. Silua. iii. leuŭ lḡ. 7 iii. laŕ.

Valuit 7 uał. c. ſoliđ.

LAND OF GEOFFREY OF LA GUERCHE

In BRINKLOW Hundred

1 Geoffrey of la Guerche holds (MONKS) KIRBY from the King. 15 hides.   7
Land for 20 ploughs. In lordship 7; 6 male and 2 female slaves;
   41 villagers and 2 smallholders with 2 priests who have 21 ploughs.
   Meadow, 40 acres.
   In this manor the monks of St. Nicholas have 2 ploughs and
      22 villagers and 6 smallholders with 5 ploughs.
   The total value was 100s; later 40s; now £10.
   Leofwin held it freely.

Geoffrey also holds

2 NEWBOLD (-on-Avon). 8 hides. Land for 16 ploughs.   4
In lordship 3; 2 slaves;
   25 villagers and 8 smallholders with 11 ploughs.
The value was and is 100s.
   Leofwin held it freely.

3 NEWBOLD (REVEL). 8 hides. Land for 16 ploughs.   4
In lordship 4 ploughs; 8 slaves;
   26 villagers and 3 smallholders with 10 ploughs.
   Meadow, 10 acres.
The value was and is £7.
   Leofwin held it freely.

in MARTON Hundred

4 in (LONG) LAWFORD 5 hides. Land for 14 ploughs. In lordship 1.   2
   14 villagers and 7 smallholders have 7 ploughs.
   A mill at 14s.
The value was 40s; now 50s.

5 WAPPENBURY. 5 hides. Land for 15 ploughs.   5
In lordship 3 ploughs; 6 slaves;
   19 villagers and 6 smallholders with 10 ploughs.
   A mill at 6s 8d; woodland ½ league long and 2 furlongs wide.
The value was and is 110s.

[in COLESHILL Hundred]

6 HAMPTON (-in-Arden). 10 hides. Land for 22 ploughs.   7
In lordship 2; 2 male and 2 female slaves.
   50 villagers with a priest and 16 smallholders have 13 ploughs.
   A mill at 40d; meadow, 10 acres; woodland 3 leagues
      long and 3 wide.
The value was and is 100s.

⌐De eoď . G . teń Sotus *SCOTESCOTE* . Ibi ſunt . IIII . hidæ
Tŕa . ē . VIII . caŕ . In dñio . ē una caŕ . 7 III . ſerui . 7 x . uiłti
⌐cū . III . caŕ.

243 d

Ibi . XVI . aĉ p̃ti . Silua . I . leuu̇ lḡ . 7 dimiď leuu̇ laŧ.
Valuit 7 uaŧ . XL . ſoliď.

⌐De . G . teń Anſgot p̃br . I . hiď in *BENECHELIE* . in elem̄
Tŕa . ē . II . caŕ . 7 ibi ſunt cū . IIII . uiłtis . Silua dim̄ leuu̇
lḡ . 7 III . q̃reñŧ laŧ . Valuit 7 uaŧ . LXIIII . denar.

⌐De . G . teń Bruno . II . hiď in *GAVRA* . Tŕa . ē . II . caŕ . 7 ibi
ſunt cū . IIII . uiłtis 7 III . borď 7 II . ſeruis . Ibi . II . aĉ p̃ti.
Valuit 7 uaŧ . xx . ſoliď.

⌐De . G . teń Robŧ . v . hiď in *WARA* . Tŕa . ē . VIII . caŕ.
In dñio ſunt . II . cū . I . ſeruo . 7 IX . uiłti 7 II . borď cū . v.
caŕ . Ibi moliñ de . II . ſoliď . 7 x . aĉ p̃ti 7 dimiď.
Valuit 7 uaŧ . XL . ſoŧ.

⌐De . G . teń Anſegis . I . hiď in *NIWEHĀ* . Tŕa . ē . VIII . caŕ.
In dñio . ē una . 7 III . ſerui . 7 XVI . uiłti 7 v . borď cū . VI . caŕ.
Ibi . xx . aĉ p̃ti . Valuit . xx . ſoŧ . Modo . LX . ſoliď.

⌐De . G . teń Vluric . III . hiď in *APLEFORD* . Tŕa . ē . III . caŕ.
7 ibi ſunt cū . VI . uiłtis 7 II . ſeruis . Ibi . v . aĉ p̃ti.
Valuit . xx . ſoŧ . Modo . xxx . ſoliď . Idē Vluric liƀe tenuit.
Om̄s ſup̃diĉtas ᵗʳᵃˢ tenuit Leuuiń . 7 potuit ire quo uoluit.

7 Also from Geoffrey, Soti holds SHUSTOKE. 4 hides.   2
  Land for 8 ploughs. In lordship 1 plough; 3 slaves;
    10 villagers with 3 ploughs.
    Meadow, 16 acres; woodland 1 league long and ½ league wide.   243 d
  The value was and is 40s.

From Geoffrey
8 Ansgot the priest holds 1 hide in BENTLEY in alms.
  Land for 2 ploughs. They are there, with
    4 villagers.
    Woodland ½ league long and 3 furlongs wide.
  The value was and is 64d.

  [in BRINKLOW Hundred]
9 Brown holds 2 hides in (BROWNS)OVER. Land for 2 ploughs.
  They are there, with
    4 villagers, 3 smallholders and 2 slaves.
    Meadow, 2 acres.
  The value was and is 20s.

10 Robert holds 5 hides in (CESTERS?)OVER. Land for 8 ploughs.
   In lordship 2, with 1 slave;
     9 villagers and 2 smallholders with 5 ploughs.
     A mill at 2s; meadow, 10½ acres.
   The value was and is 40s.

11 Ansegis holds 1 hide in NEWNHAM (PADDOX). Land for 8 ploughs.
   In lordship 1; 3 slaves;
     16 villagers and 5 smallholders with 6 ploughs.
     Meadow, 20 acres.
   The value was 20s; now 60s.

12 Wulfric holds 3 hides in HOPSFORD. Land for 3 ploughs.
   They are there, with
     6 villagers and 2 slaves.
     Meadow, 5 acres.
   The value was 20s; now 30s.
     Wulfric also held it, freely.

Leofwin held all the above mentioned lands; he could go where he would.

.XXXII.TERRA GISLEBERTI DE GAND.

Gislebertvs de Gand teñ de rege . i . hiđ 7 unã v̄ træ
7 dim in *Vllavintone* . 7 Fulbric de eo . Tra . ē . i . cař
Ibi . ē uñ uilłs 7 ii . borđ 7 iiii . ſerui . cũ . i . cař . Ibi moliñ
de . v . ſoł . 7 xv . ac̄ p̃ti . Valuit 7 uał . xx . ſoł . Aluuard libe
tenuit.

.XXXIII.TERRA GISLEBTI FILIJ TVROLDI *IN BERRICESTON HVND*.

Gislebertvs . F . Turoldi teñ de rege . vi . hiđ in *Stratone* .
7 Walter de eo . Tra . ē . viii . cař . In dñio . ē una cař 7 dim .
7 iiii . ſerui . 7 viii . uilłi 7 iii . borđ cũ p̃bro 7 uno milite hñt
. v . cař . Ibi . xxiii . ac̄ p̃ti . 7 paſturæ . xl . ptic̃ lḡ . 7 tñtđ lač .
Valuit . lxx . ſoł . Modo . c . x . ſoł . Chenuard 7 Brictric libe
tenueř.

.XXXIIII.TERRA GERINI.

Gerinvs teñ de rege . v . hiđ in *Benitone* . Tra . ē . iiii .
cař . In dñio ſunt . ii . cũ . i . ſeruo . 7 v . uilłi 7 v . borđ cũ . i . cař .
Ibi moliñ de . iiii . ſoł . 7 xv . ac̄ p̃ti . Valuit . xl . ſoł . M̊ . lx . ſoł .
Grim libe tenuit . T.R.E.

.XXXV.TERRA VRSON DE ABETOT. *IN FERNECVBE HĐ*.

Vrso teñ de rege . i . hiđ 7 dimiđ in *Hildeborde* . Tra . ē
ii . cař . In dñio . ē una . 7 ii . ſerui . 7 iii . borđ cũ dimiđ cař .
Ibi . ix . ac̄ p̃ti . 7 ſalina in Wich redđ . iii . ſoliđ .
Valuit . xvi . ſoliđ . Modo . xx . ſolid . Ernui libe tenuit T.R.E.
Idē Vrſo teñ . ii . hiđ in *Benitone* . Tra . ē . ii . cař . In dñio
eſt una . 7 iii . uilłi 7 i . borđ cũ . i . cař . Ibi moliñ de . ii . ſoliđ .
Valuit . xvi . ſoliđ . Modo . xl . ſoł . Ernui libe tenuit.

32   LAND OF GILBERT OF GHENT

[In BARCHESTON Hundred]
1   Gilbert of Ghent holds from the King 1 hide and 1½ virgates of
land in WILLINGTON, and Fulbric from him. Land for 1 plough.
    1 villager, 2 smallholders and 4 slaves with 1 plough
    A mill at 5s; meadow, 15 acres.
The value was and is 20s.
    Alfward held it freely.

33   LAND OF GILBERT SON OF THOROLD

In BARCHESTON Hundred
1   Gilbert son of Thorold holds from the King 6 hides in
STRETTON (-on-Fosse), and Walter from him. Land for 8 ploughs.
In lordship 1½ ploughs; 4 slaves.
    8 villagers and 3 smallholders with a priest and 1
      man-at-arms have 5 ploughs.
    Meadow, 23 acres; pasture 40 perches long and as wide.
The value was 70s; now 110s.
    Kenward and Brictric held it freely.

34   LAND OF GERIN

[In FERNCOMBE Hundred]
1   Gerin holds 5 hides in BINTON from the King. Land for 4 ploughs.
In lordship 2, with 1 slave;
    5 villagers and 5 smallholders with 1 plough.
    A mill at 4s; meadow, 15 acres.
The value was 40s; now 60s.
    Grim held it freely before 1066.

35   LAND OF URSO OF ABETOT

In FERNCOMBE Hundred
1   Urso of Abetot holds 1½ hides in HILLBOROUGH from the King.
Land for 2 ploughs. In lordship 1; 2 slaves;
    3 smallholders with ½ plough.
    Meadow, 9 acres; a salt-house in Droitwich which pays 3s.
The value was 16s; now 20s.
    Ernwy held it freely before 1066.

2   Urso also holds 2 hides in BINTON. Land for 2 ploughs. In lordship 1;
    3 villagers and 1 smallholder with 1 plough.
    A mill at 2s.
The value was 16s; now 40s.
    Ernwy held it freely.

.XXXVI. TERRA STEFANI.

Stefanvs ten de rege.i.hiđ in *DORSITONE*.Tra.e.ii.car.
In dnio funt.ii.7 un liƀ hõ cũ.viii.borđ cũ.i.car.
Ibi.iiii.ac pti.Valuit xx.fot.m.xxx.Ordui liƀe tenuit.
Idẽ Stef ten.iii.hiđ in *MELECOTE*. *IN PATELAV HVND.*
Tra.e.iiii.car.In dnio funt.ii.7 vi.uitti 7 vi.borđ cũ.iii.car.
Ibi.xv.ac pti.Valuit.xl.fot.m.l.fot.Vlstan eps 7 Ælftan liƀe
tenueꝛ.

.XXXVII. TERRA OSBERNI FILIJ RICARDI.

Osbernvs fili Ricardi ten de rege *ESTONE*.
Ibi funt.v.hidæ.Tra.e.x.car.Ibi funt.ix.flandrenfes
7 xvi.uitti cũ pƀro 7 x.borđ hñtes.xii.car.Ibi molin
de.viii.foliđ 7 v.ftich anguitt.7 xl.ac pti.Silua.i.leuu
in lg 7 lat.Valuit.c.fot.Modo.vi.liƀ.Algar com tenuit.
De eođ.O.ten Vrfo.iii.hiđ in *WILMECOTE*. *IN PATELAV HĐ.*
Tra.e.iiii.car.In dnio funt.ii.7 ii.ferui.7 ii.uitti 7 ii.borđ
cũ.ii.car.Ibi.xxiiii.ac pti.Valuit xxx.fot.Modo.lx.fot.
Leuuin doda liƀe tenuit.T.R.E. *IN MERETON HĐ*
De.O.ten Witts.v.hiđ in *DONECERCE*.Tra.e.ix.car.
In dnio.e una.7 iii.ferui.7 xii.uitti cũ pƀro 7 xi.borđ
hñt.v.car.Ibi.xxx.ac pti.Valuit,7 uat.c.fot.Vlmar tenuit.

36 LAND OF STEPHEN

[In FERNCOMBE Hundred]

1 Stephen holds 1 hide in (LITTLE) DORSINGTON from the King.
Land for 2 ploughs. In lordship 2;
1 free man with 8 smallholders with 1 plough.
Meadow, 4 acres.
The value was 20s; now 30s.
Ordwy held it freely.

In PATHLOW Hundred

2 Stephen also holds 3 hides in MILCOTE. Land for 4 ploughs.
In lordship 2;
6 villagers and 6 smallholders with 3 ploughs.
Meadow, 15 acres.
The value was 40s; now 50s.
Bishop Wulfstan and Alstan held it freely.

37 LAND OF OSBERN SON OF RICHARD 244a

[In FERNCOMBE Hundred]

1 Osbern son of Richard holds ASTON (CANTLOW) from the King. 5 hides.
Land for 10 ploughs.
9 Flemings and 16 villagers with a priest and 10
smallholders who have 12 ploughs.
A mill at 8s and 5 sticks of eels; meadow, 40 acres;
woodland 1 league in length and width.
The value was 100s; now £6.
Earl Algar held it.

In PATHLOW Hundred

2 Also from Osbern, Urso holds 3 hides in WILMCOTE.
Land for 4 ploughs. In lordship 2; 2 slaves;
2 villagers and 2 smallholders with 2 ploughs.
Meadow, 24 acres.
The value was 30s; now 60s.
Leofwin Doda held it freely before 1066.

From Osbern
in MARTON Hundred

3 William holds 5 hides in DUNCHURCH. Land for 9 ploughs.
In lordship 1; 3 slaves.
12 villagers with a priest and 11 smallholders have 5 ploughs.
Meadow, 30 acres.
The value was and is 100s.
Wulfmer held it.

ꝑDe.O.ten Hugo.IIII.hiđ in *BEREFORDE*. *IN ꞂEMELAV HĐ*.
Tra.ē.XII.caꝛ.In dñio.ē una.7 II.ſerui.7 II.miliꞇ cū pᵬro
7 IIII.uitti 7 XI.borđ hñt.III.caꝛ.Ibi moliñ de.II.ſoliđ
7 XIII.ſticħ anguitt.7 LX.aꝫ ꝑti.Valuit 7 uat.XL.ſoliđ.

ꝑDe.O.ten idē Hugo.III.hiđ 7 dimiđ. *IN FERNECV̄BE HĐ*.
in *HILDEBEREVRDE* 7 in *BENINTONE*.Tra.ē.IIII.caꝛ.In dñio
ē una.7 IIII.ſerui.7 VII.uitti 7 II.borđ cū.II.caꝛ.
Ibi moliñ de.XII.denaꝛ.7 XX.aꝫ ꝑti.Valuit 7 uat.XL.ſot.
Lodric tenuit liƀe.T.R.E.

ꝑDe.O.ten idē Hugo.III.hiđ in *EPESLEI*.Tra.ē.VII.caꝛ.
In dñio.ē una.7 II.ſerui.7 VII.uitti cū pᵬro 7 XIII.borđ
cū.IIII.caꝛ.Ibi moliñ de.XVI.den.Silua.I.leuū lꞡ.7 dim̄
leuū laꞇ.Valuit.XXX.ſot.Modo.XL.ſot.Alᵍar tenuit.

ꝑDe.O.ten Giſteƀt.v.hiđ in *GRASTONE*.Tra.ē.v.caꝛ.
In dñio ſunt.II.7 IIII.ſerui.7 VI.uitti 7 cū pᵬro 7 VI.borđ
cū.v.caꝛ.Ibi.XXIIII.aꝫ ꝑti.Valuit.III.liƀ.m̄.IIII.liƀ.
Meruin 7 Scrotin 7 Toti 7 Toſti liƀe tenueꝛ.T.R.E.

ꝑDe.O.ten Walteri.II.hiđ in *STRATONE*. *IN BERICEST HĐ*
Ibi hꞇ dimiđ caꝛ in dñio.7 II.uittos cū.I.caꝛ.Valuit.XX.
ſoliđ.Modo.XXX.ſoliđ.Bꞁictric liƀe tenuiꞇ.

ꝑDe.O.ten Witts *MOLLITONE*.Ibi ſunt.v.hidæ.Tra.ē.v.
caꝛ.In dñio.ē una.7 IIII.uitti 7 v.borđ cū.I.caꝛ.Ibi.XX.
aꝫ ꝑti.Valuit.XL.ſot.Modo.LX.ſoliđ.Maꞇ Leuuini
de Niuuehā liƀe tenuit T.R.E.

in TREMLOW Hundred
4 Hugh holds 4 hides in BARFORD. Land for 12 ploughs.
In lordship 1; 2 slaves.
2 men-at-arms with a priest, 4 villagers
and 11 smallholders have 3 ploughs.
A mill at 2s and 13 sticks of eels; meadow, 60 acres.
The value was and is 40s.

in FERNCOMBE Hundred
5 Hugh also holds 3½ hides in HILLBOROUGH and in BINTON.
Land for 4 ploughs. In lordship 1; 4 slaves;
7 villagers and 2 smallholders with 2 ploughs.
A mill at 12d; meadow, 20 acres.
The value was and is 40s.
Ludric held it freely before 1066.

6 Hugh also holds 3 hides in IPSLEY. Land for 7 ploughs.
In lordship 1; 2 slaves;
7 villagers with a priest and 13 smallholders with 4 ploughs.
A mill at 16d; woodland 1 league long and ½ league wide.
The value was 30s; now 40s.
Earl Algar held it.

7 Gilbert holds 5 hides in (TEMPLE) GRAFTON. Land for 5 ploughs.
In lordship 2; 4 slaves;
6 villagers with a priest and 6 smallholders with 5 ploughs.
Meadow, 24 acres.
The value was £3; now £4.
Merwin, Scroti, Toti and Tosti held it freely before 1066.

in BARCHESTON Hundred
8 Walter holds 2 hides in STRETTON (-on-Fosse). He has ½ plough
in lordship;
2 villagers with 1 plough.
The value was 20s; now 30s.
Brictric held it freely.

[in HUNSBURY Hundred]
9 William holds MOLLINGTON. 5 hides. Land for 5 ploughs.
In lordship 1;
4 villagers and 5 smallholders with 1 plough.
Meadow, 20 acres.
The value was 40s; now 60s.
Leofwin of Newnham's mother held it freely before 1066.

TERRA HAROLDI FILIJ COMITIS. *In Coleshelle Hd*

Harold . F . Radulfi ten de rege *Celverdestoche*.   *iiii

Ibi funt . VIII . hidæ . Tra . ē . x . cař . In dňio . ē dimiđ cař.

7 IX . ſerui . 7 xv . uitti 7 VII . borđ cū . VII . cař . přū . IIII . q̃ƺ

lḡ . 7 I . lat . Silua . I . leuu 7 dim lḡ . 7 una leuu lat.

Valuit . XL . ſot . Modo . L . ſoliđ . Pater ej tenuit.   *HVND*.

Idem Harold ten . xv . hiđ in *Dercetone* . *In Onesberie*

Tra . ē . XXIII . cař . In dňio . ē una cař . 7 IIII . ſerui . 7 XLVI.

uitti cū přro 7 IX . borđ hñt . xxvi . cař . Ibi . III . milites

hñt . XII . uittos cū . III . cař . Ibi . xxvii . ac̄ při.

Valuit xvi . liƀ . Modo . xx . liƀ . Harold tenuit T.R.E.

TERRA HASCVLFI   *In Meretone Hd.*

Hascvlfvs muſard ten de rege in *Lvnintone*

XII . hiđ 7 dimiđ . 7 dimiđ virg træ . Tra . ē . xxvii . cař.

In dňio ſunt . VII . cař . 7 xv . ſerui . 7 xxxiii . uitti cū přro

7 XXIIII . borđ hñt . xviii . cař . Ibi moliñ de . II . ſoliđ.

7 xx . ac̄ při . Valuit . x . liƀ . Modo . xii . liƀ . Azor liƀe

⌐ tenuit . T.R.E.

⌐De Haſc ten Hunfrid . II . hiđ in *Witenas* . *In Stanlei Hd*.

Tra . ē . VIII . cař . In dňio ſunt . II . 7 v . ſerui . 7 xi uitti 7 VIII.

borđ cū . vi . cař . Ibi . x . ac̄ při . Valuit . LX . ſot . modo . c . ſot.

Alured liƀe tenuit T.R.E.   *In Kemtlav Hd*.

⌐De Haſc ten iđ Hunfrid . v . hiđ in *Nivebold* . Tra . ē

IX . cař . In dňio ſunt . IIII . cař . 7 v . ſerui . 7 xi . uitti 7 xi.

borđ cū . VIII . car 7 dimiđ . Ibi . x . ac̄ při . Valuit . LX . ſot.

Modo . c . ſoliđ . Alured liƀe tenuit . T.R.E. *In Fernecvbe Hd*.

⌐De Haſc ten iđe Hunfrid *Haseleia* . Ibi ſunt . III.

38   LAND OF HAROLD SON OF EARL [RALPH]

In COLESHILL Hundred
1 Harold son of Earl Ralph holds CHILVERS (COTON) from the   4
   King. 8 hides. Land for 10 ploughs. In lordship ½ plough; 9 slaves;
      15 villagers and 7 smallholders with 7 ploughs.
      Meadow, 3 furlongs long and 1 wide; woodland 1½
         leagues long and 1 league wide.
   The value was 40s; now 50s.
      His father held it.

In HUNSBURY Hundred
2 Harold also holds 15 hides in (BURTON) DASSETT. Land for 23 ploughs.
   In lordship 1 plough; 4 slaves.
      46 villagers with a priest and 9 smallholders have 26 ploughs;
         3 men-at-arms have 12 villagers with 3 ploughs.
      Meadow, 27 acres.
   The value was £16; now £20.
      Harold held it before 1066.

39   LAND OF HASCOIT [MUSARD]

In MARTON Hundred
1 Hascoit Musard holds 12½ hides and ½ virgate of land from
   the King in LEAMINGTON (HASTINGS). Land for 27 ploughs.
   In lordship 7 ploughs; 15 slaves.
      33 villagers with a priest and 24 smallholders have 18 ploughs.
      A mill at 2s; meadow, 20 acres.
   The value was £10; now £12.
      Azor held it freely before 1066.

In STONELEIGH Hundred   244 b
2 Humphrey holds 2 hides in WHITNASH from Hascoit. Land for 8 ploughs.
   In lordship 2; 5 slaves;
      11 villagers and 8 smallholders with 6 ploughs.
      Meadow, 10 acres.
   The value was 60s; now 100s.
      Alfred held it freely before 1066.

In TREMLOW Hundred
3 Humphrey also holds 5 hides in NEWBOLD (PACEY) from Hascoit.
   Land for 9 ploughs. In lordship 4 ploughs; 5 slaves;
      11 villagers and 11 smallholders with 8½ ploughs.
      Meadow, 10 acres.
   The value was 60s; now 100s.
      Alfred held it freely before 1066.

In FERNCOMBE Hundred
4 Humphrey also holds HASELEY from Hascoit. 3 hides
   and ½ virgate of land.

hidæ 7 dim virg træ. Tra.ē.ii.car. In dnio.ē una.
7 iii. uilli cū pbro 7 vii. bord hūt.ii.car. Ibi molin
de.iiii. solid.7 vi. ac pti. Silua.i. leuu lg.7 ii. q̄ʒ lat.
Valuit.xx. solid. Modo.xxx. sol. Azur libe tenuit.

.XL. TERRA NICOLAI BALISTARIJ. *IN KEMELAV HD*

NICOLAVS Balistarius ten de rege.iii. hid 7 unā v træ
in *ALNODESTONE*. Tra.ē.v. car. In dnio sunt.ii.7 iiii.
serui.7 iii. ancillæ.7 ix. uilli 7 iii. bord cū.iii. car. *J HD.*
Valuit 7 ual.lx. so id. Leuric libe tenuit *IN FERNECVBE*
Idē Nicol ten.v. hid in *HASELOVE*.7 unā v træ
Tra.ē.ix.car. In dnio sunt.ii.car.7 v. int seruos 7 ancill.
7 xvi. uilli cū.i. bord hūt.vii. car. Ibi molin de.vi.
solid 7 viii. den.7 salina redd.iiii. sol 7 ii. sūmas salis.
Ibi.ii. francig.7 un burgsis redd.vii. denar 7 obolū.
Valuit.iiii. lib. Modo. vi. lib. Vluiet 7 Aluric libe tenuer.

.XLI. TERRA NIGELLI DE ALBINGI.

NIGELLVS de Albingi ten de rege *ALDVLVESTREV.*
Ibi sunt.v. hidæ 7 dimid 7 una v træ. Tra.ē. x. car.
In dnio sunt.ii.7 xii. uilli cū pbro 7 viii. bord hūt.v. car.
Ibi pti.i. q̄ʒ lg.7 alia lat. Valuit. vi. lib. Modo. iii. lib.
Octo teini libe tenuer T.R.E.
Idē Nigel ten.ii. hid 7 dim in *ALTONE*. Tra.ē.iiii. car.
Ibi sunt.iii. uilli cū.i. bord hntes.ii. car 7 dim. Valuit 7 ual.xx.sol.
Vluuin 7 Leuric libe tenuer.

Land for 2 ploughs. In lordship 1.
   3 villagers with a priest and 7 smallholders have 2 ploughs.
   A mill at 4s; meadow, 6 acres; woodland 1 league long
     and 2 furlongs wide.
The value was 20s; now 30s.
   Azor held it freely.

40   LAND OF NICHOLAS THE GUNNER

In TREMLOW Hundred

1 Nicholas the Gunner holds 3 hides and 1 virgate of land
in AILSTONE from the King. Land for 5 ploughs.
In lordship 2; 4 male and 3 female slaves;
   9 villagers and 3 smallholders with 3 ploughs.
The value was and is 60s.
   Leofric held it freely.

In FERNCOMBE Hundred

2 Nicholas also holds 5 hides and 1 virgate of land in HASELOR.
Land for 9 ploughs. In lordship 2 ploughs; 5 slaves, male and female.
   16 villagers with 1 smallholder have 7 ploughs.
   A mill at 6s 8d; a salt-house which pays 4s and 2
     packloads of salt; 2 Frenchmen and 1 burgess who pay 7½d.
The value was £4; now £6.
   Wulfgeat and Aelfric held it freely.

41   LAND OF NIGEL OF AUBIGNY

[In COLESHILL Hundred]

1 Nigel of Aubigny holds AUSTREY from the King. 5½ hides and 1
virgate of land. Land for 10 ploughs. In lordship 2.
   12 villagers with a priest and 8 smallholders have 5 ploughs.
   Meadow, 1 furlong long and another wide.
The value was £6; now £3.
   8 thanes held it freely before 1066.

[In FERNCOMBE Hundred]

2 Nigel also holds 2½ hides in HATTON. Land for 4 ploughs.
   3 villagers with 1 smallholder who have 2½ ploughs.
The value was and is 20s.
   Wulfwin and Leofric held it freely.

.XLII. TERRA CRISTINÆ.   IN COLESHELLE HD.

CRISTINA teñ de rege. VIII. hid in VLVERLEI. Tra. e
. XX. caŕ. In dñio. e una. 7 III. ferui. 7 XXII. uilli cũ pbro
7 IIII. borđ hñt. VII. caŕ. Ibi XII. ac pti. Silua. IIII. leũ lg.
7 dim leu lat. cũ onerat ual. XII. fot. Valuit. X. lib. M. IIII. lib.
Eduin tenuit.   Cũ hac appciat 7 fequeʒs tra.

Ipfa Criftina teñ. I. hiđ in ARLEI. Ibi funt. IIII. uilli hñtes. II. caŕ.
Silua. I. leu lg 7 dim. 7 in lat. I. leuũ. I. cũ onerat uat. LX. fot.

Ipfa. C. teñ ICENTONE. Ibi funt. XXIIII. hidæ. IN MÆRETON HD.
Tra. e. XXI. caŕ. In dñio funt. V caŕ. 7 X. ferui. 7 qt XX 7 III.
uilli cũ. II. pbris 7 IIII. borđ hñt XVII. caŕ. Ibi. II. molini
de. VI. foliđ 7 VIII. denaŕ. 7 XVI. ac pti. Paftura. II. ɣrent lg.
7 una qʒ lat. Valuit. XII. lib. Modo. XX. lib. Qdo rex dedit
criftinæ. reddeb. XXXVI. lib.

.XLIII.   ELEMOSINÆ REGIS.

LEVEVE teñ de rege SALFORD in elemos. Ibi funt. III. hidæ
Tra. e. X. caŕ. In dñio funt. II. 7 VII. ferui. 7 VIII. uilli 7 VIII. borđ
cũ pbro hñtes. VIII. caŕ. Ibi moliñ de. V. foliđ. 7 XII. ac pti.
Silua. II. qʒ lg. 7 dimiđ qʒ lat. Valuit. XL. fot. modo. VI. lib.
Godeua tenuit uxor Leurici comit. IN FERNECVBE HD.

Eddiđ teñ de rege. V. hiđ in BICHEMERSE. Tra. e. IX. caŕ.
In dñio funt. III. caŕ. 7 IIII. ferui. 7 XIII. uilli 7 III. borđ cũ. VI.
caŕ. Valuit. IIII. lib. Modo. C. foliđ. Ipfa tenuit T.R.E.

244 b

LAND OF CHRISTINA

In COLESHILL Hundred
1 Christina holds 8 hides in ULVERLEY from the King.
Land for 20 ploughs. In lordship 1; 3 slaves.
    22 villagers with a priest and 4 smallholders have 7 ploughs.
    Meadow, 12 acres; woodland 4 leagues long and ½ league
      wide; when exploited, value 12s.
The value was £10; now £4.
    Earl Edwin held it.

The following land is assessed with it.

2 Christina holds 1 hide in ARLEY herself.
    4 villagers who have 2 ploughs.
    Woodland 1½ leagues long and 1 league in width;
      when exploited, value 60s.

In MARTON Hundred
3 Christina holds (LONG) ITCHINGTON herself. 24 hides.
Land for 21 ploughs. In lordship 5 ploughs; 10 slaves.
    83 villagers with 2 priests and 4 smallholders have 17 ploughs.
    2 mills at 6s 8d; meadow, 16 acres; pasture 2 furlongs
      long and 1 furlong wide.
The value was £12; now £20.
    When the King gave it to Christina it paid £36.

THE KING'S ALMS LANDS

[In FERNCOMBE Hundred]
1 The nun Leofeva holds SALFORD (PRIORS) from the King in
alms. 3 hides. Land for 10 ploughs. In lordship 2; 7 slaves;
    8 villagers and 8 smallholders with a priest who have 8 ploughs.
    A mill at 5s; meadow, 12 acres; woodland 2 furlongs
      long and ½ furlong wide.
The value was 40s; now £6.
    Godiva, Earl Leofric's wife, held it.

In FERNCOMBE Hundred
2 Edith holds 5 hides in BICKMARSH from the King. Land for 9 ploughs.
In lordship 3 ploughs; 4 slaves;
    13 villagers and 3 smallholders with 6 ploughs.
The value was £4; now 100s.
    She held it herself before 1066.

XLIIII. TERRA RICARDI FORESTARIJ. *IN BOMELAV HVND.*

RICARD Foreſtari ten de rege *HERDEBERGE*. Ibi
ſunt. IIII. hidæ 7 dimid Tra. e̅ totid car. Ibi ſunt. IIII.
uilli 7 IIII. bord cu̅. I. car. Ibi. xx. ac̅ p̅ti.   ſ nuer.

Valuit. x. ſot. Modo. xx. ſolid. Quattuor teini libe te

Ide̅. Hic ten dimid hid in *BRANCOTE*. Tra. e̅. I. car.
Ibi. e̅ un uilts cu̅ dimid car. Valet. II. ſot. Sexi libe tenuit.

R. ten de rege. II. hid in *GRENEBERGE*. *IN MERETON HD.*
Tra. e̅. IIII. car. In d̅nio ſunt. II. 7 III. ſerui. 7 VI. uilti
⊕ 7 II. bord cu̅. II. car. Ibi. xx. ac̅ p̅ti. Valuit. xx. ſot. m̅. L. ſot.

Ide̅. R. ten dimid hid in *SOCHEBERGE*. Tra. e̅. I. car.
7 ibi. e̅ cu̅. v. uiltis. Valuit. x. ſot. Modo. xx. ſolid.
Edric libe tenuit.   ⊕ Bundi libe tenuit.

Ide̅. R. ten. I. hida̅ in *MORTONE*. Tra. e̅. II. car. In d̅nio
e̅ dimid car. 7 III. uilti 7 III. bord cu̅. I. car. Ibi. x. ac̅ p̅ti.
Valuit 7 ual. xx. ſolid. Wiching libe tenuit.

ſ De eod. R. ten Ermfrid. I. hida̅ *IN HONESBERIE HD.*
ad firma̅ in *RADVVEIA*. Tra. e̅. III. car. In d̅nio ſunt. II.
cu̅. I. ſeruo. 7 un uilts 7 III. bord cu̅. I. car. Ibi. III. ac̅ p̅ti.
Valuit. xx. ſot. Modo. xxv. Comes. R. tenuit T.R.E.

In BRINKLOW Hundred

1 Richard the Forester holds HARBOROUGH from the King. 4½ hides.
Land for as many ploughs.
    4 villagers and 4 smallholders with 1 plough.
    Meadow, 20 acres.
The value was 10s; now 20s.
    4 thanes held it freely.

2 Richard also holds ½ hide in BRAMCOTE. Land for 1 plough.
    1 villager with ½ plough.
Value 2s.
    Saxi held it freely.

In MARTON Hundred

3 Richard holds 2 hides in GRANDBOROUGH from the King.
Land for 4 ploughs. In lordship 2; 3 slaves;
    6 villagers and 2 smallholders with 2 ploughs.
    Meadow, 20 acres.
The value was 20s; now 50s.
    Bondi held it freely.

4 Richard also holds ½ hide in SHUCKBURGH. Land for 1 plough.
It is there, with
    5 villagers.
The value was 10s; now 20s.
    Edric held it freely.

5 Richard also holds 1 hide in (HILL)MORTON. Land for 2 ploughs.
In lordship ½ plough;
    3 villagers and 3 smallholders with 1 plough.
    Meadow, 10 acres.
The value was and is 20s.
    Wicking held it freely.

In HUNSBURY Hundred

6 Also from Richard, Ermenfrid holds 1 hide at a revenue in RADWAY.
Land for 3 ploughs. In lordship 2, with 1 slave;
    1 villager and 3 smallholders with 1 plough.
    Meadow, 3 acres.
The value was 20s; now 25s.
    Earl Ralph held it before 1066.

R.uenator ten de rege.1.hid in *SOWA*. *IN STANLEI HD*.

Tra.ē.11.car. In dñio.ē una.7 11.uilli 7 11.bord cū dimid

car.Ibi.111.āc p̄ti. Silua ibi int ipsū 7 regē 7 abbem:

ht.111.leuu lg.7 1.leuu lat.Valuit.xx.fot. Modo.lx.

folid.Colebran libe tenuit.T.R.E. *IN KEMELAV HVND*

R.uenator ten.111.hid in *CESTRETONE*.Tra.ē.vi.

car. In dñio funt.111.car.7 vi.uilli 7 1111.bord.cū.111.

car.Ibi.xxx.āc p̄ti.Valuit.xl.fot.Modo.c.folid.

Quattuor teini libe tenuer.

T HVND.

Alvric ten de rege.|1.hid 7 dim' virg træ *IN BERRICEST*   In BERRICESTVNE

Tra.ē.11.car.In dñio.ē una.7 1111.uitti hnt.11.car.

Ibi.x.āc p̄ti.Valuit.xx.fot.Modo.xl.fot.Wichig libe tenuit.

Alsi ten de rege dimid hid *IN COLESHELLE HVND*.Tra.ē   In FELINGELEI

.1.car.7 ipfa.ē in dñio cū.1.feruo.7 vii.uitti cū.1.bord hnt

.1.car.Silua de.x.fot cū onerat.Valet.xxx.fot.Idē ipfe te

Lewin ten de rege.1.hid 7 dim *IN MERETON HD*.7 nuit.

in *FLECHENHO*.Tra.ē.11.car.In dñio.ē una.7 111.ferui.

7 111.uitti cū.1.bord hnt.1.car.Valuit.x.fot.m̄.xxx.fot.

Hic Leuuin emit ab Aluuino fre fuo.

In STONELEIGH Hundred

7 Richard Hunter holds 1 hide in (WALSGRAVE-ON-) SOWE from the King.
Land for 2 ploughs. In lordship 1;
  2 villagers and 2 smallholders with ½ plough.
  Meadow, 3 acres; woodland 3 leagues long and 1 league wide, (shared)
    between him and the King and the Abbot (of Coventry).
The value was 20s; now 60s.
  Colbran held it freely before 1066.

In TREMLOW Hundred

8 Richard Hunter holds 3 hides in CHESTERTON.
Land for 6 ploughs. In lordship 3 ploughs;
  6 villagers and 4 smallholders with 3 ploughs.
  Meadow, 30 acres.
The value was 40s; now 100s.
  4 thanes held it freely.

In BARCHESTON Hundred

9 Aelfric holds 1 hide and ½ virgate of land in BARCHESTON
from the King. Land for 2 ploughs. In lordship 1.
  4 villagers have 2 ploughs.
  Meadow, 10 acres.
The value was 20s; now 40s.
  Wicking held it freely.

In COLESHILL Hundred

10 Alfsi holds ½ hide in FILLONGLEY from the King. Land for 1 plough.
It is in lordship, with 1 slave.
  7 villagers with 1 smallholder have 1 plough.
  Woodland at 10s, when exploited.
Value 30s.
  He also held it himself.

In MARTON Hundred

11 Leofwin holds 1½ hides in FLECKNOE from the King.
Land for 2 ploughs. In lordship 1, and 3 slaves.
  3 villagers with 1 smallholder have 1 plough.
The value was 10s; now 30s.
  Leofwin bought it from his brother Alwin.

Idē Leuuin ten . II . hid 7 dim virg træ in *FLECHENHO*.
Tra . ē . II . cař . Ibi . ē una cū . II . uiłłis 7 I . borđ . 7 vI . ač p̄ti.
Valuit . x . fol . Modo . xx . folid.

Hanc trā dix̄ Leuuin fe tenere de Vlftano ep̄o . fed ep̄s
ei defecit in placito . unde ipfe . L . ē in mifc̄dia regis.

ORDRIC ten de rege . I . hid in *ETEDONE* . H uafta . ē.

GODVIN ten de rege . I . hid in *CORNELIE* . Tra . ē . II . cař.
In dñio . ē una . 7 III . ferui . 7 IIII . uiłłi 7 II . borđ cū . II . cař.
Ibi . vI . ač p̄ti . Silua hñs in lonḡ . IIII . partē leuue . 7 in lat
. IIII . partē dim leu . Valuit . x . fol . Modo . xxx . folid.

Idē Goduin liƀe tenuit T.R.E.

* .XLV TERRA VXORIS HVGON DE GRENTEmaifnil.

ADELIZ uxor Hugon ten de rege . IIII . hid in *MILDENTONE*.
Tra . ē . IIII . cař . In dñio . ē . I . cař 7 dimiđ . 7 III . ferui . 7 xII . uiłłi
7 v . borđ cū . III . cař 7 dimiđ . Valuit . IIII . liƀ . modo . vI . liƀ.

Turgot liƀe tenuit . T.R.E.

244 d

ROƀt ten de rege dim hid in *BERCESTONE* . 7 ibi hɫ . I . cař.
7 moliñ de . xx . deñ . Valet . xx . fol . Turchil liƀe tenuit.

ANSEIS ten de rege . IIII . hid in *HERDEBERGE* . Tra . IIII . cař.
Nc̄ in dñio . I . cař . 7 vIII . uiłłi cū p̄bro 7 vII: borđ hñt . II . cař.
Ibi moliñ de . xvI . deñ . Valuit . x . folid . modo . xx . folid.

Bruning liƀe tenuit . T.R.E

12 Leofwin also holds 2 hides and ½ virgate of land in FLECKNOE.
Land for 2 ploughs. 1 there, with
  2 villagers and 1 smallholder.
  Meadow, 6 acres.
The value was 10s; now 20s.
  Leofwin said that he holds this land from Bishop Wulfstan,
but the Bishop failed him in the plea, and therefore Leofwin
is in the King's mercy.

[In TREMLOW Hundred]
13 Ordric holds 1 hide in ETTINGTON from the King. Waste.

[In COLESHILL Hundred]
14 Godwin holds 1 hide in CORLEY from the King.
Land for 2 ploughs. In lordship 1; 3 slaves;
  4 villagers and 2 smallholders with 2 ploughs.
  Meadow, 6 acres; woodland which has the fourth part of a league
    in length and the fourth part of half a league in width.
The value was 10s; now 30s.
  Godwin also held it freely before 1066.

45   **LAND OF HUGH OF GRANDMESNIL'S WIFE**

[In COLESHILL Hundred]
1 Adelaide, Hugh's wife, holds 4 hides in MIDDLETON from the King.
Land for 4 ploughs. In lordship 1½ ploughs; 3 slaves;
  12 villagers and 5 smallholders with 3½ ploughs.
The value was £4; now £6.
  Thorgot held it freely before 1066.

[44] (continued)

15 Robert holds ½ hide in BARSTON from the King. He has 1 plough.   244 d
  A mill at 20d.
Value 20s.
  Thorkell held it freely.

[In BRINKLOW Hundred]
16 Ansegis holds 4 hides in HARBOROUGH from the King.
Land for 4 ploughs. Now in lordship 1 plough.
  8 villagers with a priest and 7 smallholders have 2 ploughs.
  A mill at 16d.
The value was 10s; now 20s.
  Browning held it freely before 1066.

WARWICKSHIRE HOLDINGS
ENTERED ELSEWHERE IN THE SURVEY

The Latin text of these entries is given in the county volumes concerned

Now in Birmingham

Staffordshire

	2		LAND OF THE BISHOP OF CHESTER	
		In OFFLOW Hundred ...	
EB	22	The Bishop holds LICHFIELD himself...These members belong to	247b
S1		this manor...HARBORNE, land for 1 plough; Robert holds it...	

	12		LAND OF WILLIAM SON OF ANSCULF	
		In OFFLOW Hundred ...	
EB	27	Drogo holds 3 hides from William in PERRY (BARR).	250a
S2		Land for 3 ploughs. In lordship 1 plough.	

4 villagers and 3 smallholders.
A mill at 16d; meadow, 4 acres; woodland 1 league long and ½ league wide.
The value was and is 20s.
Leofwara held it, with full jurisdiction.

EB	29	Drogo also holds 1 hide from William in HANDSWORTH.	250b
S3		Land for 2 ploughs. In lordship 1;	

6 villagers with 4 smallholders have 2 ploughs.
A mill at 2s; meadow, 2 acres; woodland ½ league long and as wide.
The value was and is 20s.
Alfward and Alwin held it, with full jurisdiction.

Worcestershire

	1		LAND OF THE KING	
		[In CAME Hundred]	
EB	1a	The King holds BROMSGROVE in lordship, with 18 outliers,	172b
W1		MOSELEY, (KING'S) NORTON, LINDSWORTH...TESSALL, REDNAL....	

Earl Edwin held this manor before 1066...

	9		LAND OF ST.MARY'S OF PERSHORE	
		[In PERSHORE Hundred]	175b
EB	6	The Church holds BEOLEY itself, with one member, YARDLEY.	
W2			

	23		LAND OF WILLIAM SON OF ANSCULF	
		In CAME Hundred	177a
EB	1	William son of Ansculf holds SELLY (OAK) from the King, and	
W3		Wibert from him. One outlier, BARTLEY (GREEN), belongs	

there. In total, 4 hides. In lordship ½ plough;
2 villagers and 9 smallholders with 4 ploughs.
A wood, 1 league long.
Value before 1066, 100s; now 60s.

Wulfwin bought this manor before 1066 from the Bishop of Chester,
for the lives of three men. But when he was ailing and had come
to the end of his life, he summoned his son, the Bishop of Li(chfield?),
his wife and many of his friends, and said

"Hear me, my friends, I desire that my wife hold this land which
I bought from the Church so long as she lives, and that after her
death the Church from which I accepted it shall receive it back.
Let whoever should take it away from the Church be excommunicated."
The greater men of the whole county testify that this was so.

EB 2
W4 William holds NORTHFIELD. Alfwold held it. 6 hides. In lordship 1 plough; 177 b
a priest, 7 villagers, 16 smallholders and 16 cottage-men
with 13 ploughs; a further 5 ploughs possible.
2 male slaves, 1 female slave; woodland ½ league long
and 3 furlongs wide.
Value before 1066 £7; now 100s.

EB 5
W5 William also holds SELLY (OAK). Tumi and Aelfeva held it   177 b
as two manors. Robert holds from William. 1 hide.
In lordship 1 plough;
3 villagers, 2 smallholders and 2 ploughmen with 2 ploughs.
Woodland, 1 league.
Value before 1066, 20s; now 15s.

Gloucestershire

1   **LAND OF THE KING**

In KIFTSGATE Hundred   163 a
EG 12 King Edward held LONGBOROUGH, with a member called MEON, 8 hides in each.
1
24 In TEWKESBURY there were 95 hides before 1066 .....   163 b
EG 39 In CLIFFORD (CHAMBERS) 7 hides belong to this manor. 3 ploughs   163 c
2 in lordship.
14 villagers with 5 ploughs.
A mill at 12s; meadow, 2 acres. 13 slaves, male and female;
a church and a priest with 1 plough.
The value was £8; now £6.
The Queen gave this land to Roger of Bully. It paid tax
for 4 hides in Tewkesbury.

[In WITLEY Hundred]   163 d
EG 44 In WINCOT a thane held 3 hides. The Queen gave this land
3 to Reginald the Chaplain.
3 villagers with ½ plough.
The value was 40s.

11   **LAND OF WINCHCOMBE CHURCH**

In CHELTHORN Hundred ....   165 d
EG 11 The Church holds ADMINGTON itself. 3½ hides. In lordship 2 ploughs;
4 13 villagers with 6 ploughs. 4 male and 2 female slaves.
The value was £4; now £3.

E

12   LAND OF ST. MARY'S OF EVESHAM

166 a

In WITLEY Hundred ...

EG
5
  8   The Church holds WESTON (-on-Avon) itself. 3 hides; 1 free.
In lordship 2 ploughs;
    5 villagers and a priest with 2 ploughs.
The value was 20s; now 40s.

EG
6
  9   The Church holds (LARK) STOKE itself. 2 hides. In lordship 1 plough;
    7 villagers and 2 smallholders with 2 ploughs. 1 slave.
The value is and was 40s.

15   LAND OF ST. MARY'S COVENTRY

166 a

In CHELTHORN Hundred

EG
7
St. Mary's Church, Coventry, holds (LONG) MARSTON. 10 hides.
In lordship 3 ploughs;
    15 villagers and 3 smallholders with 12 ploughs. 6 slaves.
    A meadow at 10s.
The value was £8; now 100s.

19   LAND OF ST. PETER'S OF WESTMINSTER

166 b

In DEERHURST Hundred

  1   St. Peter's Church of Westminster holds DEERHURST ...

EG
8
  2   These outliers belong to this manor .....SUTTON (-under-Brailes), 5 hides. .

20   LAND OF ST. DENIS OF PARIS

166 b

In DEERHURST Hundred

EG
9
  1   St. Denis' Church holds these villages...
    (LITTLE) COMPTON, 12 hides; PRESTON (-on-Stour), 10 hides;
    WELFORD (-on-Avon), 15 hides ...

33   LAND OF WILLIAM THE CHAMBERLAIN

167 a

In WITLEY Hundred

EG
10
  5   William the Chamberlain holds WINCOT. Wenric held it before 1066. 3 hides.
In lordship 3 ploughs;
    2 villagers and 2 smallholders with 1 plough. 4 slaves.
The value is and was £4. This manor pays tax.

34   LAND OF WILLIAM GOIZENBODED

167 b

In CHELTHORN Hundred ...

EG
11
  3   William also holds CLOPTON. Guard held it before 1066. 10 hides.
In lordship 3 ploughs.

12 villagers, 4 smallholders and 1 riding-man with 9 ploughs.
In Winchcombe 1 burgess.
The value was £8; now 100s.

40 **LAND OF ROGER OF BEAUMONT** *FRANCE?*

In CHELTHORN Hundred 168 a

EG 1 Roger of Beaumont holds DORSINGTON, and Robert from him. 10 hides.
12 Saxi held it. In lordship 3 ploughs.
  8 villagers with 5 ploughs; 6 slaves.
The value was £8; now 100s.

62 **LAND OF HUGH OF GRANDMESNIL** *FRANCE?*

In CHELTHORN Hundred ... 169 b
Hugh also holds

EG 3 QUINTON. 2 hides. A thane held it. In lordship 2 ploughs;
13 5 villagers and 1 smallholder with 3 ploughs.
  4 male slaves, 1 female slave.
Their value was £7; now £4.

EG 4 QUINTON, and Roger from him. 12 hides. Baldwin held it before 1066.
14 In lordship 3 ploughs;
  17 villagers and 2 smallholders with 9 ploughs. 6 slaves.
The value was £7; now £6.

EG 5 WESTON (-on-Avon), and Roger from him. 4 hides. Baldwin held it.
15 In lordship 2 ploughs.
  6 villagers with 3 ploughs. 4 male and 5 female slaves.
  A mill at 10s.
The value was £7; now £6.

EG 6 WILLICOTE, and his clerk from him. 2½ hides. In lordship 2 ploughs;
16 2 villagers and 1 smallholder with 1 plough.
  4 male slaves, 1 female slave.
The value was 40s.; now 30s.
  Leofric held it.

Northamptonshire

10 **LAND OF THORNEY CHURCH**

EN 3 In SAWBRIDGE Thorkell holds 5 hides from the Abbot. 222 c
1 Land for 5 ploughs.
  12 villagers and 5 smallholders with 4 ploughs.
  Meadow, 8 acres.
The value was 50s.; now 60s.

19 **LAND OF THE COUNT OF MEULAN** *FRANCE!*
[In COLESHILL Hundred] 224 a, b
EN 2 The Count of Meulan also holds BERKSWELL, in lordship. 4 hides.
2 He has 3 of these hides in lordship. Land for 8 ploughs.
  In lordship 1; 4 slaves.

E

       7 villagers with 3 smallholders have 1 plough.
       Meadow 5 acres; woodland 1 league long and 1 league wide.
   Value 40s.

EN 3   The Count also holds ½ hide, waste, in (OVER?) WHITACRE.
3   Value 12d.
       Leofnoth held these lands freely before 1066.

SAXON

27   **LAND OF ROBERT OF STAFFORD**

     In WARDEN Hundred   225 b
EN 1   Robert of Stafford holds 3 virgates of land in STONETON,
4   and Hugh from him. Land for 3 ploughs. In lordship 1; 3 slaves;
       6 villagers and 5 smallholders with 2 ploughs.
       Meadow, 3 acres.
     The value was 10s; now 30s.
       Aelfeva held it freely before 1066.

SAXON

[36]   **LAND OF WILLIAM SON OF ANSCULF**

EN (3   Ralph holds 3 hides from William in BROMWICH ...)   226 b
(5)
EN 4   William son of Mauger holds 1 hide from William in OVER.
6   Land for 2 ploughs. In lordship 1, with
       1 villager.
       Meadow, 4 acres; woodland 1 furlong long and ½ furlong wide.
     The value was and is 10s.
       Wulfwin, like the others, held it freely before 1066.

SAXON

46   **LAND OF GILBERT OF GHENT**

EN 7   Robert holds WHICHFORD from Gilbert. 15 hides.   227 c
7   Land for 19 ploughs. In lordship 4; 10 slaves.
       33 villagers and 21 smallholders have 15 ploughs.
       2 mills at 15s; meadow 3 furlongs in length and as much in width;
       woodland 1 furlong long and as wide.
     The value was £10; now £20.
       Ulf held it freely before 1066.

SAXON

Worcestershire

2   **LAND OF WORCESTER CHURCH**

     1   St Mary's Church, Worcester, has a Hundred called OSWALDSLOW...   172c
EW 45 In the same Hundred the Bishop also holds TREDINGTON with one 173b
1   member, TIDMINGTON. 23 hides paying tax; one of them is waste. 173c
       In lordship 5 ploughs;

42 villagers, 30 smallholders; a priest who has 1 hide;
1 rider; between them they have 29 ploughs.
10 slaves; 3 mills at 32s 6d; meadow, 36 acres.
The value was £10; now £12 10s.

EW 46   At BLACKWELL are 2 hides which belong to the supplies of the monks.
2   In lordship 3 ploughs;
10 villagers and 6 smallholders with 4 ploughs.
6 male slaves and 1 female slave; meadow, 10 acres.
The value was and is 50s.

EW 47   Gilbert son of Thorold holds 4 hides of this manor at LONGDON.
3   He has 2 ploughs;
8 villagers and 2 smallholders with 4 ploughs.
4 male and 4 female slaves; meadow, 8 acres.
The value was £4; now £3.
Leofric the reeve held it as the Bishop wished.

EW 64   The Church holds SHIPSTON (-on-Stour) itself. 2 hides paying tax.   173 d
4   In lordship 2 ploughs;
15 villagers and 5 smallholders with 6 ploughs.
4 male slaves and 1 female slave; a mill at 10s; meadow, 16 acres.
The value was and is 50s.

9   **LAND OF ST. MARY'S OF PERSHORE**

[In PERSHORE Hundred]   175 b
EW 7   (ALDERMINSTER-ON-) STOUR. 20 hides. In lordship 4 ploughs;
5   24 villagers and 8 smallholders with 11 ploughs.
5 slaves; 2 mills at 17s 6d.
1 man-at-arms holds 2 hides; 2 riders.
Meadow, 20 acres.
The value was £12; now £9.
This land pays tax.

10   **LAND OF EVESHAM CHURCH**

In FISHBOROUGH Hundred ...   175 c
EW 4   In OLDBERROW are 12 acres of land. 2 countrymen, pigmen.
6   Woodland, 1 league.
Value 5s.

In ASH Hundred....   175 d
EW 15   The Church holds BEVINGTON itself. 1 hide and 1 plough.
7   3 smallholders.
Woodland, 3 acres.
The value was 20s; later 15s; now 10s.

NOTES

ABBREVIATIONS used in the notes.　　Abingdon..Abingdon Chronicle (Rolls 2 ii,1858).†† BCS.. Birch, *Cartularium Saxonicum*. DB..Domesday Book. DG..H.C.Darby and G.R.Versey *Domesday Gazeteer* Cambridge 1975. EPNE..English Place-Name Elements (EPNS 25-26). EPNS..English Place-Name Society Survey (13, Warwicks.).* Evesham A..ed. P.H.Sawyer, Worcester Historical Society, 1960.†† Heming..*Chartularium Ecclesiae Wigorniensis*, ed. T. Hearne, 1723.†† KCD..Kemble, *Codex Diplomaticus*. MS..Manuscript. OEB..G.Tengvik, Old English Bynames.† PNDB..O. von Feilitzen, Pre-Conquest Personal Names of Domesday Book.† VCH..Victoria County History (Warwicks.,vol.1).

*unless otherwise indicated. †*Nomina Germanica,* Uppsala, vols. 3 and 4. †† Texts which transcribed documents that were contemporary with DB, or formed part of the Survey, cited only when their statements differ from DB, or add to it.

The manuscript is written on leaves, or folios, of parchment (sheep-skin), measuring about 15 inches by 11 (38 by 28 cm). There are two columns to each page, four to each folio. The folios were numbered in the 17th century, and the four columns of each are here lettered a,b,c,d.

WARWICSCIRE in red, at the top of each page, centred over the two columns; on page 244 a,b the first R was omitted, and inserted above the line.

CHAPTER numbers and titles are throughout in red ink. Hundred headings, place names, and the landholder's name in the first section of each chapter are scored through in red, but 'de', where it occurs in such names, is not scored through, except in ch. 7; on pages 238 c,d to 242 a,b (ch.21, ~~ROBERTUS~~ de ~~Oilgi~~) both halves of the name are scored, but from 242 c,d onward (ch.22, ~~ROBERTUS~~ de Stadford) only the first name is scored. Each chapter begins with an extra large capital, outlined in red. The account of the Borough begins with a huge I, entirely in red, covering three lines, and the initials T and C (sections 4 and 6) are large red-outlined capitals.

SECTIONS within chapters are throughout distinguished by a new line beginning with a capital, outlined in red except in 17,18.

MEN'S HOLDINGS in Warwickshire, in lay, but not church, chapters, are meticulously distinguished, by a small space, up to ch. 22; by section signs, resembling a gallows in shape, as shown in Farley, (ch. 12, and from col. 241 b, excepting 19,2-4; 6); and, up to ch. 22, by an extra large capital letter. Except in ch. 16, and in entries beginning 'idem', they begin with 'De'. The MS here uses two types of capital Ð, not distinguished from each other by Farley, a rounded letter resembling an inverted Q (here represented by D) and an angular letter, tapering to a blunted point at the top (here represented by d), both used sometimes to mark the beginning of the men's holdings, sometimes for decorative effect. D is found at 12,3, with d in 12,4 ff.; in ch. 17 and 18,D and d alternate regularly, except that 17,22-23 are both d, 64-65 both D; ch. 19 has D, without section sign, in sections 2-4 and 6,d with section sign in section 5; ch. 22,11 has D without sign, 22,12 ff. d with sign; and d with sign is used throughout in later chapters.

The Text

B 2	MS 'buili', with a stroke through the 'l', for 'builli'. Farley, in error, 'budi'.
3,4	MS 'totum suum regnum'. Farley omits 'suum'.
6,1	MS scraped. There is too little room for an intermediate value, too much room to fill with further figures. Probably 'x.solid' was intended, possibly 'xx.solid'.
6,2	Restore 'aeccla [ten(et) G] RANEBERGE'; 'te' seems just legible. Traces of letters, probably 'trae' or 'irg' after 'una v'.
6,9	Added at the foot of the column in the same small lettering as 3,4, at the foot of the facing column, probably at the same time, and separated from it by the vertical line, which is not a gallows-like section sign, since it lacks the short curved cross piece shown in Farley.
7-10	In smaller and closer lettering, without the spaces shown in Farley.
12-13	As 7 - 10.
16,5-6	Marginal figures, in dark ink, as also in ch. 28,16-18. 30,2. 31,1-7. 38,1, seem to be in the same hand as the body of the MS. All except 28,18 are reproduced in the facsimile.
16,8	MS 'tenuit' repeated, probably in error for 'fuit', as elsewhere.
16,9	MS 'valuit iii lib'. Farley, in error, 'vi lib'.
16,13	MS gap between 'libi' and 'fuer', equivalent to about two letters.
16,15	MS omits 'ten(et)', perhaps by accident, but see 16,43 note.
16,20	MS 'ferer', in error for 'fuer'.
16,22	Preceded by a small gap, reproduced by Farley, here concealed by the start of a new page.
16,43	MS omits 'ten(et)', as in 16,15. Both omissions are in the first entry on a page.
18,12	Read '[In W] atercote'. The last stroke of the W seems legible.

20,1	MS *ut dicit* with a flourish to the top stroke of the T; not, as Farley, *ut dicit'*, suggesting 'dicit(ur)'.
21	MS leaves a large space, of 2½ inches, between ch. 20 and ch. 21.
22,2	MS omits the figure for the number of ploughs after 'sunt'.
22,3	MS 'tenuit' clearly; the 'u' is underinked in most copies of Farley.
22,11	Preceded by a small space, not shown in Farley.
22,26	MS 'Iudichel', rather than 'Ludichel', as Farley. In DB script, L and I are easily confused. The I of Iudichel here is exactly parallelled by the I of 'Iuhell', in 28,3.
23,1	Marginal 'fr', in thinner letters, may be by the same hand, but might be later.
24,1	MS damaged. 'iii' is discernible and probable, but 'iiii' is possible.
28	No space was left between the initial capital and the preceding line; chapter number and title were added between the lines.
28, 16-18. 30,2. 31, 1-7. 38,1. Marginal figures, see note to 16, 5-6.
39,1	MS 'LVNNJTONE'. Farley, in error, 'LVNINTONE'.
45,1	Added at the foot of the column in closer lettering.

The Translation

B 1	BARONS. Not yet a title. The 'men' of the King, or of a magnate, here denoting the listed Landholders, including a nun.
B 2	MONKS OF PILLERTON. Of St. Evroul, see 18,11.
	GILBERT OF BOUILLE. See OEB 77. Since the other 25 'barons' were all listed Landholders, he was probably identical with Gilbert son of Thorold.
	GUNNER. *Balista* included all missile weapons, from crossbow to large artillery piece. The English word 'gun' was used of such weapons before the introduction of gun-powder. Nicholas was probably a master of ordnance, evidently a person of substance, since he held a dozen manors in Devon (ch. 49). The Gloucester Cartulary (Rolls 33, 1863,i,74) calls him Nicholaus de la Pole.
	STEERSMAN. The commander of a ship or of a fleet. Since he also held two houses in Southampton (Hants. S 3; col. 52 a), Stephen was presumably a senior naval officer.
	HAROLD. Listed twice, evidently by accident. Discounting repetitions, the houses listed total 114, not 112; later chapters list only two dozen.
B 4	SHERIFFDOM..COUNTY. Since each county had its Sheriff (*vicecomes*), but few had an Earl (*comes*) in 1086, the terms are interchangeable. See note to 1,6 Shire.
	DOG-CUSTOM. Payment for providing, feeding and keeping hunting hounds.
	£24 8s. DB uses the old English currency system, which endured for a thousand years until 1971. The pound contained 20 shillings, each of 12 pence, and the abbreviations £.s.d preserved the DB terms *librae, solidi and denarii*.
1,1	THE KING HOLDS. Repeated at the beginning of 1,2-7.
	EARL EDWIN. Of Mercia, c. 1063-1070. DB Oxon. 1,12 (154 d) notes that 'from Earl Edwin's land in Oxford and Warwickshire the King has £100 and 100s.'
1,6	THIRD PENNY. One third, with two thirds to the King, as normally before 1066.
	SHIRE. Used of the divisions of Wessex from at least the 8th century; but the midland Shires were first organised by Edric Streona (the Acquisitive), Alderman of Mercia 1007-1017, who 'joined provinces to provinces at will' (Heming 280 = folio 129 B). 12 of the 13 Shires are first mentioned between 1010 and 1016, see C.S.Taylor in *Bristol and Gloucester Transactions* 21,1898,32ff.; 32,1909,109ff. (condensed and edited in H.P.R.Finberg, *Gloucestershire Studies*, Leicester 1957,17ff.). Districts were attached to Boroughs during the Danish wars, a century or more earlier, see Herts B 11 note, but their boundaries are unknown, and did not always coincide with those of the later Shires.
1,7	VALUE. Includes the values of 1,8 and 1,9.
1,8	ALBERT. Of Lorraine, landholder in half a dozen counties before and after 1066.
3	BISHOP OF WORCESTER. Heming (311 = folio 140 B) lists the same holdings, giving hides and holders only, except for 3,4, given in full. *Monachi* is substituted for *episcopus* 3,3 and 3,5, and *habent monachi* for *habuit archiepiscopus* in 3,4.
3,3	THE BISHOP ALSO HOLDS. The words are repeated at the beginning of 3,5 - 3,7.
3,3	STICK. Normally 25 eels to a 'stick'.
3,6	URSO. Of Abetot, Sheriff of Worcestershire.
3,7	THE ENTRY is duplicated, with additional detail, in 44,12.
3,4	ALDRED. Bishop of Worcester 1016-1061, Archbishop of York 1061-1069; he crowned King William in 1066. He claimed jurisdiction over Worcester, which had been united with York from 972 to 1016.
	FOUR FORFEITURES. Defined as breach of the King's peace, burglary, highway robbery, and evasion of military service, in the Laws, 2 Canute 12;14-15.
	COULD TURN. From Earl Leofric's lordship.
	COUNTY. *Comitatus*. The word ultimately prevailed since the old kingdoms of the south-east, from East Anglia to Sussex, are not and never have been 'Shires'.

WULFSTAN. Bishop of Worcester 1061-1095, the only English Bishop to survive King William, revered for his simple and saintly practice and precept.

QUEEN MATILDA. King William's wife.

FOUR SHERIFFDOMS. Or Shires. The Assembly (see also DB Worcs. 10,12 (175 d); Evesham Register, folio 28 (H.W.C.Davis *Regesta Regum Anglo-Normannorum* 185 (= xxiii) and 186 (= xxiv, where 'vij' is a copyist's error for 'iiij'), of about 1080; etc.) met at the 'Guildborough' (*Gildenberg*) at the Four Shire Stone(s) (SP 231 321), where 7 parishes and the Shires of Gloucester, Oxford, Warwick and, until 1931, Worcester converge. The bounds attached to a grant (BCS 1238 = Heming 214 (folio 100 B) = KCD 1362), dated 969, fifty years before the Shires were formed, locate four stones by the *Gild Beorh*. If the bounds are contemporary with the grant, the Stones were older than the Shires, the cause rather than the consequence of the meeting of so many boundaries at this point. The site may have been an earlier assembly place for all or part of the kingdom of the Hwicce, of the Cotswolds and lower Severn. *Beorg* (EPNE 1,29) means a natural or artificial hill, here a barrow, since there is no natural hill. *Gild* EPNE 1,200) meant a place of worship, a tax or payment, or an association, especially for meeting financial and religious obligations, not yet limited to associations of merchants or craftsmen. The term (selected instances in EPNS Worcs. 125) sometimes occurs elsewhere where three or more Shires adjoin, as at Guilden Morden (Cambs., Beds., Herts.); Peterborough, where five Shires join, was termed *Gildeneburch* shortly after the establishment of the Shires, the name interpreted by later local chroniclers as meaning 'Golden', rich in endowments; and also at the junctions of several Hundreds. Further references will be noted in the appropriate county volumes.

4 BISHOP OF BAYEUX. Half-brother of King William.

4,2 THE BISHOP HOLDS. Repeated 4,2-6.

5 BISHOP OF COUTANCES. Geoffrey of Mowbray, a principal minister of King William.

6,2 THE CHURCH ITSELF HOLDS. Repeated 6,2 -8 and 6,10-20.

6,9 THE ENTRY is duplicated, with fuller detail, in 14,2.
   ALWEN. Father of Thorkell (ch.17).

7,1 HILL. Abingdon 2,8 and 2,20 reports the purchase of a gift, confirmed by Thorkell's son Siward, 'then adolescent', and by the King's writ, addressed to Robert d'Oilly, Sheriff of Warwickshire in the 1080s (ch. 21), where the donor is styled Thorkell of Arden. Chesterton (17,67) was transferred at the same time. Abingdon (2,284) says that these holdings were bought from the King.

11,2 THE CHURCH ITSELF HOLDS. Repeated 11,3-5.

11,4 RANULF. Brother of Abbot Walter of Evesham, VCH 282.

12 EARL ROGER. Of Montgomery.

12,1 WULFWIN. Written Olwin, as in Worcs. 14,1, see PNDB 428.

12,5 KETELBERN. MS Chetelbert, but probably identical with Ketelbert (Ketelbern) (17,56) probably Thorkell's brother, and Ketelbern of 16,53.

13 EARL HUGH. Of Chester.

14 EARL AUBREY. Of Northumbria, in the early 1080s, 'of little use in difficult circumstances, he went home' to Normandy (Simeon *Historia Regum* Rolls 75, 1885,ii, 199). His extensive holdings in England had not yet been granted to others in 1086.

14,1 NUNEATON. The hides are omitted.

14,2 THE EARL HIMSELF HELD. Repeated 14,3-6.
   CLIFTON. The entry is summarised in 6,9.

15 COUNTESS GODIVA. Widow of Earl Leofric, grandmother of Earl Edwin, died between 1066 and 1086. Her lands had not yet been granted to others.

15,2 THE COUNTESS HERSELF HELD. Repeated 15,3-6.

16 COUNT OF MEULAN. Robert of Beaumont, who inherited Meulan through his mother. His brother Henry, keeper of Warwick Castle since 1068, was created Earl of Warwick soon after 1086, and was granted Robert's Warwickshire lands, soon after supplemented by Thorkell's (ch. 17 note). These lands, with those of Robert of Stafford (ch. 22), comprise about three quarters of the Warwickshire lay holdings in DB.

16,1 MYTON. See 17,60. It is probable that on Edwin's death Myton was equally divided between the Count and Thorkell, whose half the Count held from him.

16,2 THE COUNT HIMSELF HOLDS. Repeated 16,2-18; 20-64. See notes to the text, 16,15; 43.

16,5-6 MARGINAL FIGURES. See 28,16 note.

16,7 COULD SELL BUT..NOT DEPART. The distinction is unusual; most such men could do neither or both.

16,8 HE WAS. The second *tenuit* is probably a MS error for *fuit*.

16,9 £3. See note to text.

16,55 COUNT'S MANOR. See 16,6.

16,58 BALDWIN. See 18,7 note.

15,61	TRANSPOSITION MARKS correct the word order.
17	THORKELL. Of Arden (7,1 note), son of Alwin, Sheriff of Warwickshire before and after 1066. He was one of the few English magnates who retained their lands in 1086, but soon afterwards his inheritance *(patrimonium)* was granted by William II 'at the beginning of his reign' to the Earl of Warwick (see 16 note) 'to supplement the Earldom' *(in comitatus supplementum)* (Abingdon 2,20). The reason is not known. It may be that his son (7,1 note) died before him, and that he left no direct heir. His family, the Ardens, held some land from the Earls of Warwick for another 200 years.
17,2	THORKELL ALSO HOLDS. Repeated 17,3-6.
17,7	FROM THORKELL. Repeated 17,7-59 and 17,61-70.
17,13	UNTAN. Also Staffs. 12,23, and 17,69 below. PNDB 402 suggests Otam, or Wulfstan, or Hunstan.
17,15	THE ENTRY is duplicated in 23,4, with a different first line, listing 10 hides under Robert the Bursar. The exact correspondence of unusual detail in the remaining four lines makes it unlikely that this is a divided holding like Myton (16,1 note) and Shuttington (16,22-23). The probable cause of duplication and dispute is that the land was sold to Thorkell's father, but had been held by Robert the Bursar's predecessor, Aelmer.
17,27	FREEMEN. *Franci homines* occur in, e.g., Worcs. 8,26 (175 b), there meaning all the free men of Westminster's two Hundreds.
17,53	WULFWY. Possibly identical with Wulfwin.
17,56	KETELBERN. MS Chetelbern. An early modern English translation of a lost charter of 1072, *Staffordshire Collections* 2,178, cited VCH 278, makes 'Ketelbearne' brother of Thorkell, probably here intended.
17,60	MYTON. See 16,1 note. The entry is inserted at the top of a column in the middle of the Hunsbury Hundred entries.
	R. HALEBOLD. Possibly for *emit R de Halebold,* 'R(obert) bought the land from Halebold'. Since 'Halebrix' and 'Alebrix' occur several times in Devon (PNDB 180), apparently for Aelfric, 'Halebold' might conceal Albold, or conceivably 'Haligbold', a man who had held from Thorkell.
17,67	CHESTERTON. Abingdon claimed that it was granted with Hill (7,1 note), but does not mention the pledged hide (17,68).
17,69	WILLIAM. Evidently Bonvallet, since he held 1 house in Warwick, see B 2.
	UNTAN. See 17,13 note.
18,2	HUGH ALSO HOLDS. Repeated 18,3-7.
18,7	BALDWIN. The Lapworth ½ hide was granted by Bishop Brictheah to Herlwin, his companion as escort to Canute's daughter Gunhild at her marriage to [Henry, son of] the emperor Conrad in 1036, Heming 267 (folio 125). Before 1066, a Baldwin son of Herlwin held manors in Gloucs. (1,22..163 b) and Bucks.(4,31..144 d). He is therefore probably the Baldwin who held Lapworth from Hugh, and perhaps also the Baldwin who was Hugh's predecessor in Gloucs., Leics., Northants. and Oxon., as well as the Warwicks. Baldwin. Heming reports that the ½ hide paid 1s a year to Worcester at the Feast of the Assumption, and the Worcester Register (79 b, cited VCH 287) claimed 8d a year as church-tax at Martinmas.
18,9	FROM HUGH. Repeated 18,10-16.
18,15	CONSTANTINE. So in Bucks. ch.33 and Essex ch.74.
19	HENRY OF FERRERS. His heirs were Earls of Derby and Nottingham, probably from 1138.
19,1	SIWARD BAIRN. He joined Hereward, Edwin and Morcar in the Ely rebellion of 1071. 'Bairn' probably had the same meaning as OE *cilt,* 'Childe', born to an inheritance, 'well born'.
19,2	FROM HENRY. Repeated 19,3-6.
21	ROBERT D'OILLY. Sheriff of Warwickshire from early to late 1080s.
22	ROBERT OF STAFFORD. Younger brother of Ralph of Tosny, Steward of Normandy. His heirs remained lords, and ultimately Earls of Stafford.
22,2	ROBERT ALSO HOLDS. Repeated 22,3-9.
	PLOUGHS. Figure omitted, see note to the text.
22,9	WAGA. Wootton Wawen preserves his name.
22,10	ARE THERE. *ii car quae ibi est* (for *sunt*); MS grammatical error.
22,12	FROM ROBERT. Repeated 22,13-27.
22,13	ALFWY. Possibly intended for Alwin, 22,14.
22,15	EWEIN. *Iuuein* is probably a form of the Welsh and Breton name Ewein, Owen. English Ewing, Iving (PNDB 249, 300) is a possible but less likely alternative.
22,26	IUDICHAEL. See note to the text. Called a priest in a charter of Robert of Stafford, cited, without reference, VCH 286.
23	ROBERT THE BURSAR. Brother of Urso of Abetot, Sheriff of Worcestershire.

23,1 MARGINAL NOTE 'fr', perhaps contemporary. Unexplained. Conceivably intended to be completed as *fr(ater) Ursonis*, 'brother of Urso'.

23,4 BARSTON. See 17,15 note.

24,1 £3. See note to the text.

25,1 EDRIC. Probably Edric the Wild, nephew or grandson of Edric Streona (1,6 note). His Herefordshire lands also passed to Ralph. He resisted the King until 1070, but accompanied him to Scotland in 1072. A confused local tradition reports a rebellion, that ended with his capture and imprisonment by Ralph.

27,2 FROM WILLIAM. Repeated 27,3-27,6.

27,4 ASKI. Perhaps identical with Askell, *Aschi* written for *Aschil.*

27,5 RICHARD. *Ricoardus*, probably for *Ricardus.*

27,6 ESSINGTON. The entry is a duplicate of Staffs. 12,22.

28 . WILLIAM SON OF CORBUCION. Appointed Sheriff of Warwickshire soon after 1086.

28,1 BATTOCK. See OEB 288.

28,2 FROM WILLIAM. Repeated 28,3-28,14.

28,14 STICKS. See 3,3 note.

28,15 WILLIAM..HIMSELF. Unusually, his men's land is entered first.

28,16 WILLIAM ALSO HOLDS. Repeated 28,17-19.
SALT-HOUSE. *Salina* comprehends all kinds of salt workings from coastal salt pans to the boilers of Worcestershire and Cheshire, with their associated sheds and buildings. 'Salthouse' is the most comprehensive term.

28,16 MARGINAL FIGURES. Probably contemporary or nearly so, see notes to the text, 16,5. 2½, probably virgates, as in 28,17-18, or hides. A majority of the figures correspond to about half the recorded hidage. Their meaning is unexplained.

29,1 EARL RALPH. Of Hereford, 1053 (or earlier) to 1057, nephew of King Edward, responsible for the first Norman castles in England. See 38 note below.

30 GEOFFREY DE MANDEVILLE. Ancestor of the Earls of Essex. He received Asgar's extensive lands throughout England.

30,2 MARGINAL FIGURE. See 28,16 note.

31,1 ST. NICHOLAS. Of Angers. La Guerche lies on the road from Angers to Rennes, just west of the border between Anjou and Brittany; Geoffrey also held Pouence, just on the Anjou side of the border. The grant (charter cited VCH 275 from Nichols' *Leicestershire* 2, Appendix,125), dated 1 July 1077, was witnessed by Geoffrey's wife, named Adlfeva. Her English name suggests that Geoffrey may have acquired his Warwickshire lands through her, by inheritance rather than by confiscation; she may have been Leofwin's heiress.
LEOFWIN. Since he held Newnham Paddox, probably Leofwin of Newnham (37,9); distinct from Leofwin of Nuneham Courtenay (Bucks. ch.57).
MARGINAL FIGURES. See 28,16 note.

31,2 GEOFFREY ALSO HOLDS. Repeated 31,2-31,6.

31,7 SOTI. A Scandinavian name (PNDB 368), not French (as EPNS 92). Soting occurs in Bucks. and Berks.

31,8 FROM GEOFFREY. Repeated 31,9-31,12.

33 GILBERT SON OF THOROLD. Of Bouille, see B 2 note.

35,1 URSO. Sheriff of Worcestershire.
SALT-HOUSE. See 28,16 note.

36 STEPHEN. See B 2 note.

36,2 BISHOP WULFSTAN. Of Worcester, see 3,4 note.

37 RICHARD. Of Richard's Castle (Hereford 24,13; 186 d). He was one of the few Normans whom Godwin permitted to remain in England after 1052.

37,3 FROM OSBERN. Repeated 37,4-37,9.

37,5 LUDRIC. See PNDB 321.

38 HAROLD. See 29,1 note. Ewias Harold (Hereford 19,1; 186 a) preserves his name.

40 NICHOLAS THE GUNNER. See B 2 note.

40,2 SALT-HOUSE. See 28,16 note.
BURGESS. Evidently the occupier of Nicholas' house in Warwick, B 2.

42 CHRISTINA. Sister of Prince Edgar, grand-daughter of King Edmund Ironside. She became a nun at Romsey in 1086.

43,2 BICKMARSH. 1 hide of Bickmarsh is entered in Gloucs. (78,7; 170 c), also held by Edith ,with 2 ploughs in lordship, 1 villager, 1 smallholder, and 4 slaves,value 20s before and after 1066.

44,1 THE FORESTER. Warden of Cannock Chase, for which he received 'tres partes de Cestreton'(where he held 3 of its 7 hides) *Testa de Nevill,*;cited VCH 291. See also Staffs. ch.13 (where 'the' is accidentally omitted). The office is rare in DB.

44,3 BONDI. Directed to its proper place by transposition signs.

44,6 EARL RALPH. See 29,1 note.

44,7	HUNTER. Holder of Chesterton, therefore identical with the Forester. *Venator* (OEB 273) is a commoner DB term, not normally used of Foresters. It need not imply an appointment; marked enthusiasm or skill in hunting inspired several bynames (Venner, Grosvenor, etc.). In 1086 hereditary bynames were a recent but growing Norman fashion (Freeman *Norman Conquest* (ed.1) 5,563; OEB 10 ff.).
44,11	ALWIN. Possibly the Sheriff.
44,12	THE ENTRY duplicates the details of 3,7.
44,12	FOURTH PART. Probably *iiii[am]parte(m)* rather than *iiii parte(s)*.
45	THE ENTRY is an insertion at the foot of the column, interrupting ch.44.
EB	PLACES within the 1970 Birmingham boundary are included, for convenience.
EB W3	WOOD. *Nemus*.
	CHESTER. An anachronism. Until 1075/6 the Bishop's seat was at Lichfield. Other transfers to larger towns were made at the same time, including the move from Dorchester-on-Thames to Lincoln. Soon after 1086 Chester was replaced by Coventry.
	LIVES OF THREE MEN. A lease, in this case for Wulfwin, his widow, and his son.
	LI(CHFIELD?). The MS leaves room for 3 or 4 letters after Li. Since the land was to revert to Chester (Lichfield), Wulfwin's son was probably Leofwin, Bishop of Lichfield 1053-1067. But since DB names the new see of Chester, 'Li' may also stand for a new contemporary see, Lincoln, in which case the son was Wulfwy, Bishop of Dorchester, also 1053-1067. Space may have been left in the MS because Winchester did not know which see was meant. The purpose of the oral will was to deter claims by lay heirs; it failed, for William succeeded to Selly Oak, as to other holdings of Wulfwin. The date of the will is after 1062, since Wulfwin was a thane of Earl Edwin (Worcs. 1,1e), but before 1067.
EB W4	COTTAGE-MEN. *Cotmanni*, a category named in DB Worcs., but there distinguished from the more numerous *cotarii* (cottagers).
EG 11	GUARD. *Huscarl*, used as a personal name.
EG 13	THEIR VALUE. *Valuer(unt)*. The plural, referring to the hides, is unusual.
EN 6	LIKE THE OTHERS. Named in the preceding entries in Northants. DB.
EW 1	RIDER . *Radman*, of higher standing than a villager, originally a man who rode with messages for the King. The term is common in north-west Mercia, up to the Ribble. In the south-western Welsh marches and in Hampshire *radchenestre*, riding-man, predominates. TREDINGTON. The 23 hides included EW 2-3, Heming 314 (folio 141). Value £15, Evesham A 123, perhaps including EW 2.
EW 5	11 PLOUGHS. Evesham A 158 prints *ix caruce*.
EW 6	COUNTRYMEN, PIGMEN. *Ibi sunt ii rustici porcarii.*

Places

The identification of places is less sure than in many counties. Many places share the same DB name, and many are entered in other counties, due to extensive modern boundary changes. Serious study begins with Dugdale's *Antiquities of Warwickshire* (1656), far in advance of its time, but written before modern philology developed. VCH (1904) often printed Dugdale's identifications, adding query marks and footnotes, by Round or the translator, doubting or rejecting them. EPNS (1936) and DG sometimes repeat them without the doubts and queries. Most are straightforward, but others require a fuller study of the evidence, which this edition cannot undertake. A few problems are discussed below, beginning with places that share the same name.

The COMPTONS. There are 6 Warwickshire Comptons and 9 DB entries. 7 entries and 4 places are clearly identified (see Index of Places); Verney and Fenny, 10 hides each, are the only Comptons in their Hundreds; Long Compton (30 hides) was held by Geoffrey de Mandeville's heirs; Little Compton, 12 hides (EG 9) was in Gloucs. (Deerhurst) until 1844. Wynyates is in Fexhole Hundred, where DB enters no Compton; there are no grounds for inserting a relevant heading. One place Compton Scorpion, and two entries, Robert of Stafford's 5 hides at *Parva Contone* and 1 hide at *Contone* (22,17-18) are less easily identified. VCH (312), followed by EPNS (279) and DG, suggested Wynyates for the 1 hide, without noticing that it was in the wrong Hundred, to which EPNS addenda drew attention. Round firmly rejected the identification (VCH 329), since Wynyates was a Warwick, not a Stafford, holding; the Stafford lordship of Wynyates adduced in VCH 5,65 is first recorded in 1386, after Earl Hugh of Stafford had married the Earl of Warwick's daughter; it may have been acquired through marriage. Whatever its location, *Parva Contone* means Little Compton, and is so translated here. The most likely explanation is that Little Compton was divided between Deerhurst and Stafford, Stafford's 5 hides later transferred to his adjoining holding of Barton, to which DB gives the disproportionately small assessment of half a hide. 22,18 should therefore be Scorpion, or possibly a lost Compton.

The MARSTONS. 6 places and 7 entries. Butler's and Jabbett are the only Marstons in their Hundreds, and Long Marston (EG 7) was in Gloucs. until 1931. In Coleshill Hundred, 17,10, listed between Mackadown and Elmdon, survives as Marston Green and Hall, on the northern edge of Birmingham Airport. Robert Dispensator's 10 hides, held by his heirs, were at Lea Marston, two adjoining places amalgamated in the 14th century (EPNS 84). Robert d'Oilly bought two Marston hides in Coleshill Hundred (21,1), and held another, whose Hundred is uncertain (see 17,48 note, below) from Thorkell, whose father had bought land in Lea Marston. He may well have bought land that adjoined his holding, more probably at Lea Marston than Marston Green. Marston-on-Avon, doubtfully suggested for 17,48 by VCH 323, was claimed as a Coventry holding (KCD 939; 916), not named in DB.

The NEWBOLDS. Comyn and Pacey are the only Newbolds in their Hundreds. In Brinklow, DB distinguishes Fenny (now Revel, EPNS 120) from Newbold-on-Avon.

The OVERS. The river Over, now Swift, runs south from Leics. to the Avon, opposite Rugby, and names the places on its banks. The 10 and 5 hide holdings are probably Churchover and Cestersover (see Index of Places). Opposite Brownsover, 2 hides, named from its 1086 holder, is Newbold-on-Avon, with 8 hides; it may be that Geoffrey of La Guerche, who inherited both places from Leofwin, detached 2 hides from a 5 or 10 hide place for his man, Bruno. The one hide of EN 5 is not identified; its name places it on the Over; a possible location is Harborough Fields (50 80), opposite Churchover, since no right bank Over name survives south of Cestersover, and DB gives 8½ hides to Harborough.

The WHITACRES. VCH 319 points out that *Witecore* (17,14; 24,2), 2½ hides, is larger than *Witacre* (18,16; EN 3), 1 hide, and that Nether is larger than Over Whitacre.

B 2   PILLERTON. Pillerton Priors, see 18,11.
1,2   WELLESBOURNE. In Tremlow Hundred, but entered as a dependency of Kineton in
        Fexhole, without mention of its own Hundred, as normally in DB.
1,5   TAMWORTH. 9 miles from Coleshill. DB omits the Borough; see Staffs. 1,9 note.
1,6   COTEN. A suburb of Warwick, located east of the Borough by the Warwick street name
        Coten End (SP 288 652), EPNS 264.
1,8   UPTON. In Haselor, EPNS 212.
3,2   STRATFORD. DB does not distinguish Stratford-on-Avon from Old Stratford.
3,5   LOXLEY. EPNS 235.
6,14   PRIORS HARDWICK. The large area probably included Priors Marston, also held by
        Coventry.
11,3   ABBOTS SALFORD. See VCH 341, note 4.
12,1   LEAMINGTON PRIORS. Renamed 'Royal Leamington Spa' in 1838, EPNS 175.
12,7   WOLSTON. In Marton Hundred, on the Avon, here the Hundred boundary. DB distinguishes
        1 virgate in Stoneleigh, evidently across the river. 12,4 and 12,7 were held by the same
        holders before and after 1066.
16,17   DONNELIE. Located as Wedgnock-Donele Wood (Dugdale 182, cited VCH 313).
16,29   MARTON HUNDRED. The missing heading might alternatively belong before 16,28.
16,35   HILLMORTON. Identified with Marton by Dugdale, queried by VCH, followed without
        query by EPNS and DG. VCH 314 note 7 properly observed that Marton is always spelt
        'Meretone' in DB, and suggests Hillmorton. VCH 342 note 2 confirmed the identification with Hillmorton, but left [?Marton] uncorrected in 16,35; 37. The conclusion is
        plainly right, since *Mortone* is not *Meretone,* and there is only one Morton in Marton
        Hundred.
16,49   THE COUNT'S MANOR. Omitted from DB. The virgate was probably in Barnacle.
16,58   TACHBROOK MALLORY. The brook that names the place (EPNS 258) separates the
        Bishop's holding (2,3) from the lay holding; it is the boundary between Hundreds, and
        also between the dioceses of Lichfield (Chester) and Worcester. The Bishop of Chester's
        holding lay in Worcester diocese.
17,3   OTHER BICKENHILL. Perhaps Middle Bickenhill, EPNS 59.
17,7   HUNDRED. In the entries of Thorkell's men's land, up to section 61, seven Hundred headings are omitted, one is misplaced, and only one (57) is rightly placed.
17,8   LONGDON. Merged with Ulverley in Solihull, EPNS 67.
17,13   DOSTHILL. EPNS 17.
17,16   BADDESLEY ENSOR. Rather than Clinton, VCH 320 note 2; EPNS 14.
17,17   MARTON HUNDRED. Since 17,17-27 are all in Marton Hundred, the Hundred heading
        at 17,28 is misplaced.
17,44   BIGGIN. Including both Biggin Farm and Biggin Mills, EPNS 117-118.

17,48 COLESHILL HUNDRED? Entered between places in Brinklow and Stoneleigh Hundreds. There is no Marston in Stoneleigh. Marston Jabbett in Brinklow is unlikely; probably Lea Marston in Coleshill, rather than Marston-on-Avon in Marton, see note to the Marstons, above.

17,70 NUNEATON. A possible, but unlikely, alternative is Water or Wood Eaton in Oxfordshire, held by Robert and his 'sworn brother' Roger of Ivry, Oxon. 28,5; 29,7...158 b; d; a lost place in Ferncombe Hundred is possible.

22,9 WOOTTON WAWEN. Named from Waga. In Pathlow Hundred, three miles north-east of Pathlow, along the line of a possible Roman road from Stratford to Metchley (in Birmingham University grounds), but surrounded by places in Ferncombe Hundred. Since Pathlow is central to the combined Hundred, but on the border between the DB Hundreds, it is likely that Ferncombe, mentioned only in DB, was a comparatively recent separation from Pathlow. Wootton may have been entirely enclosed by Ferncombe Hundred, or the narrow strip linking it with Pathlow, now followed by the Stratford Canal, may have remained in Pathlow Hundred.

22,21 RUIN CLIFFORD. Across the river from Clifford Chambers. 'Ruin' from *rygen*, rye, EPNS 239.

25,1 BUDBROOKE. Written as though it were a Hundred name.

31,12 HOPSFORD. EPNS 121.

36,1 LITTLE DORSINGTON. EPNS 201.

37,6 IPSLEY. Now in Worcs.

37,9 MOLLINGTON. Divided between Warwicks., Northants. and Oxon. in DB; now all in Oxon.

40,1 AILSTONE. Three Shire Ash (23 51) marks the county boundaries before 1931.

41,2 HATTON. So VCH 340 note 6, probably rightly. Alton (EPNS 154) is first noted in 1789.

42,1 ULVERLEY. Merged with Longdon in Solihull, EPNS 67.

42,2 ARLEY belonged *(belimpeth)* to Itchington before 1001, KCD 705, and was therefore in later record a detached part of Marton Hundred. DB emphasises that it had not yet been transferred out of its geographical Hundred in 1086. *Cum hac..terra* may have linked Arley to Itchington before the text was arranged under Hundreds.

43,2 BICKMARSH. Now in Worcs. Three Shire Elms (10 48) marks the county boundaries before 1931.

EB W1 BROMSGROVE. The outliers include Lea Green (09 75), just in Worcestershire.

EG THE PLACES were transferred to Warwicks. at different dates, EG 8 and 9 (Little Compton) in 1844, EG 2,3,5,7,9 (Preston and Welford), 10,12 16 in 1931, EG 1,4,6,11,13-15 in 1935.

EN NORTHAMPTONSHIRE DB includes an unusually large number of places in other counties. All those in Warwickshire are at the end of their chapter. One entry (EN 2-3), and probably all, were late additions, assigned to the right Landholder in the wrong county.

EN 1 SAWBRIDGE. The last of three holdings of the distant Cambridgeshire Abbey entered after Charwelton in Northants., six miles to the south, of which it may have been an outlier; or the Abbey, which held no other Warwickshire land, may have left the county heading out of its return.

EN 2-3 BERKSWELL, WHITACRE. Added after the page had been written, across the foot of both columns. Mistakenly added to the Count's Northants., instead of his Warwicks., chapter.

EN 4 STONETON. Transferred to Warwickshire in 1896.

EN 5 BROMWICH. Probably West Bromwich (Staffs. EN 3), but conceivably Castle, Wood and Little Bromwich (EPNS 40 and 32). Mistakenly added at the end of William's Northants. return, as with EN 2-3, but before the page was written.

EN 7 WHICHFORD. Mistakenly added at the end of Gilbert's Northants. entry.

EW 1 OSWALDSLOW. The Hundred, formed in 964 (BCS 1135, whose substance is probably accurate; see Worcs. 2,1 note), comprised the then holdings of the Church of Worcester, detached from their geographical Hundreds. The Abbey Hundreds of Evesham and Pershore were probably formed about the same time. Such arrangements were rare before 1066. When the Shires were organised, about 1008, many places that lay geographically in Warwicks. and Gloucs. were already in Worcester Hundreds, and were therefore included in Worcs., and remained there until the 1930s. In Warwicks., these Worcs. Abbey holdings were carved out of the Hundreds of Barcheston and Tremlow.

EW 5 ALDERMINSTER. Evesham A 158 right margin, against *In STURE*, 'scilicet Aldremanestun.' Alderminster is a 15th century corruption of Aldermanneston, EPNS Worcs. 184. For the use of the river name as the town name, compare (Walsgrave-on-) Sowe. The early documents of the Worcestershire Abbeys consistently distinguish between *Sture in Ismere*, the river of Stourport, and *Sture* without suffix, the Warwickshire river.

EW 7 BEVINGTON. Wood and Cock Bevington are in Warwickshire; Bevington Waste is partly in Warwicks., partly in Worcs.

INDEX OF PERSONS

Familiar modern spellings are given when they exist. Unfamiliar names are usually given in an approximate late 11th century form, avoiding variants that were already obsolescent or pedantic. Spellings that mislead the modern eye are avoided where possible. Two, however, cannot be avoided: they are combined in the name of 'Leofgeat', pronounced 'Leffyet,' or 'Levyet.' The definite article is omitted before bynames, except where there is reason to suppose that they described the individual. The chapter numbers of listed landholders are printed in italics.

Adelaide wife of Hugh	*45*	Azor	16,6; 55. 39,1; 4
Adolf	17,52	Baldwin	16,58. 18,2-3; 7-8;
Aelfeva	22,22. 28,13. EN 4.		10; 13-14; 16.
	EB W5		EG 14-15
Aelfled	16,14	Battock, see Thorkell	
Aelfric	4,4. 16,57; 66.	Bondi	16,31. 44,3
	17,3; 64. 21,1.	Bonvallet, see William	
	22,8; 11. 40,2.	Bosker	16,53
	44,9	Bovi	16,16; 56
Aelmer	17,8; 15; 21-22;	Brian	22,16
	57-58; 65. 23,1-2;	Brictmer	16,63
	4. 28,2	Brictnoth	3,4. 16,19; 62
Aelred	16,59	Brictric	17,16. 22,17. 33,1.
Aki	12,9		37,8
Albert the Clerk	1,8	Brictwin	3,4. 17,68
Aldith wife of Gruffydd	6,5	Brown	31,9
Aldith	17,42	Browning	17,12; 55. 44,16
Archbishop Aldred	3,4	Ceolred	16,22. 17,16
Alfgeat	16,41	Christina	*42.* B 2
Alfred	39, 2-3	Colbran	44,7
Alfsi	12,11. 16,41-42;	Constantine, see Hugh	
	59. 44,10	Corbin	4,2
Alfward	17,2; 7. 32,1. EB S3	Corbucion, see William	
Alfwold	16,17. 17,67. EB W4	Derman	16,8
Alfwy	3,4. 22,13. 27,4.	Doda	22,15
	28,5	Doda, see Leofwin	
Earl Algar	16,1. 17,48.	Drogo	22,25. 27,4. EB S2-3
	37,1; 6	Edith	43,2
Algar	17,64	Edmer	3,4
Almund	12,4; 7. 17,9	Edric	12,10. 16,13; 50.
Alnoth	17,9; 68		25,1. 28,14. 44,4
Alric son of Mergeat	24,1	Earl Edwin	1,1; 6-7. 16,44.
Alric	14,5. 16,7. 17,32.		17,60; 63. 26,1.
	22,20; 27. 24,2		27,1; 3. 42,1. EB W1
Alstan	16,61. 36,2	Edwin the Sheriff	4,3. 17,10
Alwin the Sheriff,	6,9. 14,2. 17,6;	Edwin	17,14; 18; 26; 28-
father of Thorkell	15; 32; 62. 23,4		29; 56
Alwin brother of Leofwin	44,11	Edwulf	17,25
Alwin	5,1. 16,21; 65. 17,	Ermenfrid	6,20. 17,18-19;
	39; 47; 51; 59; 66;		49; 56; 65. 44,6
	70. 22,14; 18.	Ernwin	28,17-18
	23,3. 29,2. EB S3	Ernwy	22,26. 28,3; 6. 35,1-2
Ansculf, see William		Esbern	4,2
Ansegis	31,11. 44,16	Ewein	22,15
Ansgot the Priest	31,8	Fulbric	32,1
Arkell	17,16; 51	Fulk	16,38-39; 63
Arngrim	4,5	Geoffrey of La Guerche	*31.* B 2. 14,6
Arnulf	4,5; 16,24-25.	Geoffrey de Mandeville	*30.* B 2.
	17,8	Geoffrey	28,11
Asgar the Constable	30,1	Gerald	4,3-4
Askell	17,5	Gerin	*34*
Aski	27,4	Gilbert of Ghent	*32.* B 2. EN 7.
Earl Aubrey	*14.* B 2. 6,9	Gilbert son of Thorold	*33.* EW 3
Auti	12,8	Gilbert of Bouille	B 2

Churches and Clergy. Archbishop (of York)...Aldred. **Bishop** of Bayeux 4. 20,1. Chester 2. B 2. 28,19. EB S1. EB W3. Coutances 5. B 2. Worcester 3. B 2. EW 1. See alsoWulfstan. **Abbeys** Abingdon 7. 17,67-68. Angers 31,1. Burton 8. Coventry 6. B 2. 14,2. 44,7. EG 7. Evesham 11. EG 5-6. EW 6-7. Malmesbury 9. B 2. Paris EG 9. Pershore EB W2. Preaux 16,56. Thorney EN 1. Warwick 17,63. Westminster EG 8. Winchcombe 10. EG 4. **Saints** Chad...Lichfield. Denis...Paris. Evroul 18,11. Mary... Coventry, Evesham, Pershore, Warwick, Worcester. Nicholas...Angers. Peter...Preaux, Westminster. **Monks** B 2, 31,1. Wulfwin. **Nun**...Leofeva. **Priest**...Ansgot. **Chaplain**...Reginald.

Secular Titles. Bursar *(dispensator)*...Robert. Chamberlain *(camerarius)*...Hugh, William. Clerk *(clericus)*...Albert. Constable *(stalrus)*...Asgar. Count *(comes)*...of Meulan. Countess *(comitissa)*... Godiva. Earl *(comes)* Algar, Aubrey, Edwin, Hugh, Leofric, Ralph, Roger. Forester *(forestarius)*... Richard. Gunner *(balistarius)*...Nicholas. Hunter *(venator)*...Richard, Robert. Queen *(regina)*..Matilda. Reeve *(prepositus)*...Leofric. Sheriff *(vicecomes)*...Alwin, Edwin. Steersman *(stirman)*...Stephen

INDEX OF PLACES

The name of each place is followed by (i) the initial of its Hundred and its location on the Map in this volume; (ii) its National Grid reference; (iii) chapter and section references in DB. Bracketed figures denote mention in sections dealing with a different place. The National Grid reference system is explained on all Ordnance Survey maps, and in the Automobile Association Handbooks; the figures reading from left to right are given before those reading from bottom to top of the map. Places marked with a (*) are in the 100 kilometre grid square lettered SK; others are in square SP. The Warwickshire DB Hundreds are Barcheston (Ba); Brinklow (Br); Coleshill (C); Ferncombe (Fc); Fexhole (Fh); Hunsbury (H); Marton (M); Pathlow (P); Stoneleigh (S); Tremlow (T). Entered elsewhere in DB are, in Birmingham, Staffs. and Worcs. (BS; BW); Gloucs. (G); Northants. (N); Worcs. (W) .

Snitterfield	Fc	19 21 60	16,15
'Sole'	Br	3 32 87	16,43
Solihull, see Longdon, Ulverley			
Southam	M	25 41 61	6,8
Spernall	Fc	27 08 62	29,4
Stoneleigh	S	9 33 72	1,4; (9). (16,49)
Stoneton	N	1 46 54	EN 4
Stratford	P	6 20 55	3,2
Stretton Baskerville	Br	1 42 91	25,1
Stretton-on-Dunsmore	M	10 40 72	12,3
Stretton-on-Fosse	Ba	11 22 38	33,1. 37,8
Studley	Fc	26 07 63	28,16. 29,5
Surland	M	- - -	6,3
Sutton Coldfield	C	11 12 96	1,7
Sutton-under-Brailes	G	14 30 36	EG 8
Bishop's Tachbrook	T	4 31 61	2,3
Tachbrook Mallory	S	24 31 62	16,58
Tessall	BW	6 01 78	EB W1
Three Shire Ash	T	0 23 51	40,1 note
Three Shire Elms	Fc	0 10 48	43,2 note
Thurlaston	M	13 46 71	16,33. 18,8
Tidmington	W	7 26 38	EW 1
Tredington	W	4 25 43	EW 1
Tysoe	Fh	5 33 44	22,4
Ufton	S	25 37 62	6,11
Ullenhall	Fc	2 12 67	22,6
Ulverley	C	45 13 81	42,1
Upton	Fc	35 12 57	1,8. 29,3
'Walcote'	M	22 50 68	17,37
Walsgrave	S	3 37 81	6,10. 44,7
Walton	T	12 28 53	16,9-10
Wappenbury	M	15 37 69	31,5
Warmington	H	9 41 47	16,6; 55
Warwick see Thorkell	T	1 28 64	B (1,6. 3,1;3. 17,69. 18,2; 3; 14. 22, 4; 8. 26,1. 28,17-18)
Wasperton	T	5 26 58	6,18
Weddington	C	20 36 93	16,26
Wedgnock, see *Donnelie*			
Weethley	Fc	38 05 55	11,5
Welford-on-Avon	G	1 14 52	EG 9
Wellesbourne	T	7 27 55	1,2
Werlavescote	C?	- - -	16,28
Weston-in-Arden	Br	5 38 87	16,38
Weston-on-Avon	G	2 15 51	EG 5; 15
Weston-under-Wetherley	S	16 36 69	16,52. 17,53. 28,8
Whatcote	Fh	3 29 44	18,12
Whichford	Ba	7 31 34	EN 7
Nether Whitacre	C	17 23 92	17,14. 24,2
Over Whitacre	C	26 24 91	18,16. EN 3
Whitchurch	Ba	8 22 47	16,21; 65
Whitley	Fc	9 14 65	22,25
Whitnash	S	23 32 63	39,2
Wibtoft	Br	9 47 87	16,39-40
Wiggins Hill	C	14 16 93	17,12
Willey	Br	20 49 84	16,39-40
Willicote	G	6 17 49	EG 16
Willington	Ba	2 26 39	22,15. 32,1
Willoughby	M	23 51 67	17,34; 37; 40. 18,1
Wilmcote	P	2 16 58	37,2
Wilnecote	C	6 *22 01	16,24
Wincot	G	7 18,49	EG 3; 10
Wishaw	C	15 17 94	28,4
Witton	C	21 08 91	27,2
Wixford	Fc	40 09 54	11,1
Wolfhampcote	M	30 52 65	17,5; 17
Wolford	Ba	4 24 34	4,4. 16,66. 22,2; 13-14
Wolston	M	1 41 75	12,4; 7
Wolverton	Fc	15 20 62	22,24. 28,17
Wolvey	Br	8 42 88	24,1
Woodcote	S	12 28 69	16,3; 51
Wootton Wawen	P	1 15 63	22,9
Wormleighton	H	4 44 53	16,54. 17,61. 30,2
Yardley	BW	4 12 85	EB W2

Place not named

In STONELEIGH Hundred   17,64

Places not in Warwickshire

Elsewhere in Britain. Places starred are indexed above.

GLOUCESTERSHIRE Deerhurst EG 8. Longborough EG 1. Tewkesbury EG 2. Winchcombe EG 11. OXFORDSHIRE Mollington*. Spelsbury 3,6. STAFFORDSHIRE Bushbury 27,6. Chillington 28,19. Essington 27,6. Lichfield 2,3. EB S1. Stafford, see Robert. Tamworth 1,5. (Now in SHROPSHIRE Quatt, Romsley, Rudge, Shipley, 12,8-11). WORCESTERSHIRE Beoley EB W2. Bickmarsh*. Bromsgrove EB W1. Droitwich 28,14. 35,1. Ipsley*. See also Index of Churches.

Places outside Britain (see Index of Persons)

Abetot...Urso. Angers...Abbey. Aubigny...Nigel. Bayeux...Bishop. Bouille...Gilbert. Coutances...Bishop. Ferr(i)er(e)s...Henry. Ghent...Gilbert. Grandmesnil...Hugh. La Guerche...Geoffrey. Ivry...Roger. Limesy...Ralph. Mandeville...Geoffrey. Meulan...Count. Mortimer...Ralph. Oilly...Robert. Paris, Preaux, St. Evroul...Abbeys. Vessey...Robert.

Barcheston. 1 Barcheston. 2 Willington. 3 Burmington. 4 Wolford. 5 Barton. 6 Long Compton. 7 Whichford. 8 Whitchurch. 9 Ilmington. 10 Compton Scorpion. 11 Stretton-on-Fosse. 12 Ditchford.

Brinklow. 1 Stretton Baskerville. 2 Astley. 3 'Sole'. 4 Martson Jabbett. 5 Weston. 6 Burton Hastings. 7 Bramcote. 8 Wolvey. 9 Wibtoft. 10 Smercote. 11 Bedworth. 12 Bulkington. 13 Foleshill. 14 Barnacle. 15 Anstey. 16 Shilton. 17 Hopsford. 18 Monks Kirby. 19 Newnham Paddox. 20 Willey. 21 Smeeton. 22 Newbold Revel. 23 Harborough. 24 Cestersover. 25 Churchover. 26 Little Lawford. 27 Newbold-on-Avon. 28 Brownsover. 29 Newton. 30 Biggin.

Coleshill. 1 Seckington. 2 Austrey. 3 Amington. 4 Shuttington. 5 Dosthill. 6 Wilnecote. 7 Grendon. 8 Middleton. 9 Baddesley Ensor. 10 Atherstone. 11 Sutton Coldfield. 12 Kingsbury. 13 Bentley. 14 Wiggins Hill. 15 Wishaw. 16 Lea Marston. 17 Nether Whitacre. 18 Hartshill. 19 Caldecote. 20 Weddington. 21 Witton. 22 Erdington. 23 Minworth. 24 Curdworth. 25 Shustoke. 26 Over Whitacre. 27 Arley. 28 Ansley. 29 Chilvers Coton. 30 Nuneaton. 31 Aston. 32 Birmingham. 33 Edgbaston. 34 Castle Bromwich. 35 Coleshill. 36 Mackadown. 37 Marston Green. 38 Fillongley. 39 Corley. 40 Elmdon. 41 Bickenhill. 42 Middle Bickenhill. 43 Packington. 44 Kineton Green. 45 Ulverley. 46 Hampton-in-Arden. 47 Alspath. 48 Longdon. 49 Barston. 50 Berkswell.

Ferncombe. 1 Lapworth. 2 Ullenhall. 3 Rowington. 4 Beausale. 5 Shrewley. 6 Haseley. 7 Hatton. 8 *Donnelie*. 9 Whitley. 10 Preston Bagot. 11 Claverdon. 12 Budbrooke. 13 Kington. 14 Langley. 15 Wolverton. 16 Norton Lindsey. 17 Edstone. 18 Bearley. 19 Snitterfield. 20 Fulbrooke. 21 Sherbourne. 22 Ipsley. 23 Mappleborough. 24 Morton Bagot. 25 Sambourne. 26 Studley. 27 Spernall. 28 'Offord'. 29 Coughton. 30 Kinwarton. 31 Great Alne. 32 Aston Cantlow. 33 Newnham. 34 Oversley. 35 Upton. 36 Haselor. 37 Billesley. 38 Weethley. 39 Arrow. 40 Wixford. 41 Exhall. 42 Ardens Grafton. 43 Temple Grafton. 44 Bevington. 45 Broom. 46 Binton. 47 Abbot's Salford. 48 Salford Priors. 49 Bidford-on-Avon. 50 Hillborough. 51 Bickmarsh and Little Dorsington.

Fexhole. 1 Kineton. 2 Idlicote. 3 Whatcote. 4 Oxhill. 5 Tysoe. 6 Honington. 7 Brailes.

Hunsbury. 1 Priors Hardwick. 2 Burton Dassett. 3 Fenny Compton. 4 Wormleighton. 5 Avon Dassett. 6 Radway. 7 Ratley. 8 Arlescote. 9 Warmington. 10 Farnborough. 11 Mollington.

Marton. 1 Wolston. 2 Marston. 3 Church Lawford. 4 Long Lawford. 5 Rugby. 6 Clifton-upon-Dunsmore. 7 Cawston. 8 Bilton. 9 Hillmorton. 10 Stretton-on-Dunsmore. 11 Frankton. 12 Bourton. 13 Thurlaston. 14 Dunchurch. 15 Wappenbury. 16 Hunningham. 17 Marton. 18 Birdingbury. 19 Leamington Hastings. 20 Hill. 21 Grandborough. 22 Walcote. 23 Willoughby. 24 Long Itchington. 25 Southam. 26 Calcutt. 27 Shuckburgh. 28 Sawbridge. 29 Flecknoe. 30 Wolfhampcote. 31 Napton. 32 Ladbroke. 33 Hodnell. 34 Radbourn.

Pathlow. 1 Wootton Wawen. 2 Wilmcote. 3 Clopton. 4 Alveston. 5 Hampton Lucy. 6 Stratford. 7 Luddington. 8 Milcote. 9 Ruin Clifford. 10 Loxley.

Stoneleigh. 1 Coundon. 2 Coventry. 3 Walsgrave. 4 Binley. 5 Baginton. 6 Ryton-on-Dunsmore. 7 Brandon. 8 Kenilworth. 9 Stoneleigh. 10 Bubbenhall. 11 Roundshill. 12 Woodcote. 13 Ashow. 14 Bericote. 15 Cubbington. 16 Weston-under-Wetherley. 17 Milverton. 18 Lillington. 19 Myton. 20 Leamington Priors (Spa). 21 Newbold Comyn. 22 Radford Semele. 23 Whitnash. 24 Tachbrook Mallory. 25 Ufton. 26 Harbury. 27 Bishop's Itchington.

Tremlow. 1 Warwick. 2 Coten. 3 Barford. 4 Bishop's Tachbrook. 5 Wasperton. 6 Charlecote. 7 Wellesbourne. 8 Newbold Pacey. 9 Moreton Morrell. 10 Lighthorne. 11 Chesterton. 12 Walton. 13 Compton Verney. 14 Chadshunt. 15 Ettington. 16 Pillerton Hersey. 17 Butlers Marston. 18 Fullready. 19 Pillerton Priors. 20 Atherstone. 21 Ailstone.

Birmingham (Staffordshire). 1 Handsworth. 2 Perry Barr. 3 Harborne. (Worcestershire). 1 Bartley Green. 2 Selly Oak. 3 Moseley. 4 Yardley. 5 Rednal. 6 Tessall. 7 Northfield. 8 King's Norton. 9 Lindsworth.

Gloucestershire. 1 Welford-on-Avon. 2 Weston-on-Avon. 3 Clifford Chambers. 4 Dorsington. 5 Long Marston. 6 Willicote. 7 Wincot. 8 Preston-on-Stour. 9 Quinton. 10 Meon. 11 Clopton. 12 Admington. 13 Lark Stoke. 14 Sutton-under-Brailes. 15 Little Compton.

Northamptonshire. 1 Stoneton.

Worcestershire. 1 Oldberrow. 2 Alderminster. 3 Blackwell. 4 Tredington. 5 Longdon. 6 Shipston-on-Stour. 7 Tidmington.

Not Mapped. *Surland* (Marton). *Werlavescote* (Coleshill ?).

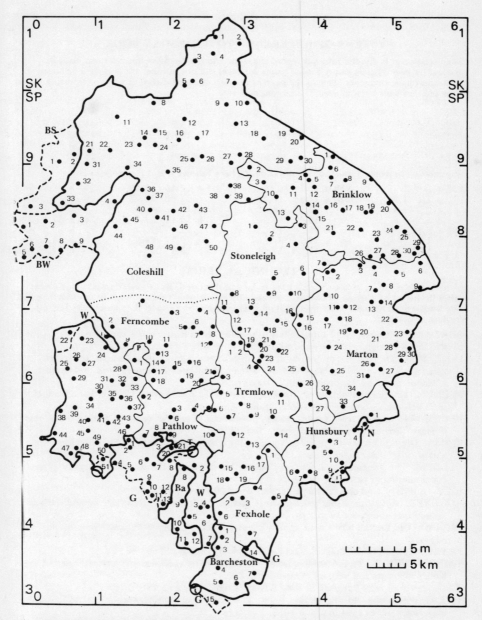

The County Boundary is marked by thick lines, continuous for 1086, broken for modern boundaries; Hundred boundaries (1086) by thin lines, dotted where uncertain.

Four Shire Stone and Three Shire Ash and Elms are marked by open circles.

National Grid 10-kilometre squares are shown on the map border.
Each four-figure grid square covers one square kilometre, or 247 acres, approximately 2 hides, at 120 acres to the hide.

SYSTEMS OF REFERENCE TO DOMESDAY BOOK

The manuscript is divided into numbered chapters, and the chapters into sections, usually marked by large initials and red ink. Farley however did not number the sections. References in the past have therefore been to the page or column. Several different ways of referring to the same column have been in use. The commonest are:

(i)	(ii)	(iii)	(iv)	(v)
152a	152	152a	152	152ai
152b	152	152a	152.2	152a2
152c	152b	152b	152b	152bi
152d	152b	152b	152b.2	152b2

The relation between Vinogradoff's notation (i), here followed, and the sections is:

238 a B - L	239 d 16,1 - 16,14	241 c 17,45 - 17,59	243 b 28,6 - 29,1
b 1,1 - 1,9	240 a 16,15 - 16,26	d 17,60 - 17,70	c 29,2 - 31,7
c 2,1 - 3,4	b 16,27 - 16,42	242 a 18,1 - 18,14	d 31,7 - 36,2
d 4,1 - 6,9	c 16,42 - 16,57	b 18,14 - 21,1	244 a 37,1 - 39,1
239 a 6,10 - 10,1	d 16,58 - 17,6	c 22,1 - 22,17	b 39,2 - 43,2
b 11,1 - 13,1	241 a 17,7 - 17,22	d 22,17 - 24,2	c 44,1 - 45,1
c 14,1 - 15,6	b 17,23 - 17,44	243 a 25,1 - 28,5	d 44,15 - 44,16

TECHNICAL TERMS

Many words meaning measurements have to be transliterated. But translation may not dodge other problems by the use of obsolete or made-up words which do not exist in modern English. The translations here used are given in italics. They cannot be exact; they aim at the nearest modern equivalent.

BORDARIUS. Cultivator of inferior status, usually with a little land. *smallholder*

CARUCA. A plough, with the oxen who pulled it, usually reckoned as 8. *plough*

DOMINIUM. The mastery or dominion of a lord *(dominus)*; including ploughs, land, men, villages, etc., reserved for the lord's use; often concentrated in a *home farm* or *demesne*, a 'Manor Farm' or 'Lordship Farm'. *lordship*

FEUDUM. Continental variant of *feuum*, not used in England before 1066; either a landholder's total holding, or land held by special grant. *Holding*

FEUUM. Old English *feoh*, cattle, money, possessions in general, compare Latin *pecunia* and German *Vieh*; in later centuries, *feoff*, 'fief' or 'fee'. *holding*

FIRMA. Old English *feorm*, provisions due to the King or lord; a sum paid in place of these and of other miscellaneous dues. *revenue*

GELDUM. The principal royal tax, originally levied during the Danish wars, normally at an equal number of pence on each *hide* of land. *tax*

HIDE. A unit of land measurement, reckoned at 120 acres. *hide*

HUNDRED. A district within a shire, whose assembly of notables and village representatives usually met about once a month. *Hundred*

INLAND. Old English lord's land, usually exempt from tax, comparable with *dominium*. *inland*

PRAEPOSITUS, PRAEFECTUS. Old English *gerefa*, a royal officer. *reeve*

TAINUS, TEGNUS. Person holding land from the King by special grant; formerly used of the King's ministers and military companions. *thane*

T.R.E. *tempore regis Edwardi*, in King Edward's time. *before 1066*

VILLA. Translating Old English *tun*, town. The later distinction between a small *village* and a large *town* was not yet in use in 1086. *village*

VILLANUS. Member of a *villa*, usually with more land than a *bordarius*. *villager*

VIRGATA. A quarter of a *hide*, reckoned at 30 acres. *virgate*